Readings in Greek Tragedy
vol. II

Edited by
Stephen Russell

Dept. of Classics
McMaster University

Copyright © 2014 by Stephen Russell
All rights reserved. This book or any portion thereof may not be reproduced or used in any manner whatsoever without the express written permission of the publisher.

Printed in Canada.

First Printing, 2014

Dept. of Classics
McMaster University
L8S 4M2

Contents

Euripides
The Cyclops *1*

Euripides
Medea *19*

Sophocles
The Women of Trachis *41*

Sophocles
Ajax *67*

Euripides
Helen *89*

Sophocles
Electra *126*

Euripides
Electra *153*

Euripides
The Bacchae *177*

Chapter 10
Euripides
The Cyclops

THE STORY: *The Cyclops* is known as a "satyr play." After a day in which one tragic poet presented his trilogy of plays, usually all of which were based on the same theme or narrative, there would then be a short satyr play at the end of the day that would take a scene from that trilogy and poke fun at it. Satyrs are half-goat, half-human creatures who like to drink and fornicate – and who are closely associated with the god of wine, Dionysus. Their leader is Silenus, and the characters in these plays often wore large phallic-like appendages to emphasize that it was a farce. Euripides' play *The Cyclops*, a reworking of the scene from *The Odyssey* in which Odysseus meets the Cyclops Polyphemus, is the only surviving satyr play that we have, so most of our ideas on how these plays functioned stem from this play.

NOTE: This play is not a tragedy. Rather, it's a coarse and often vulgar comedy. So do feel free to laugh while you read. I hope that I have translated this play in a way that does justice to its comic intent.

CHARACTERS

SILENUS, THE FATHER OF THE SATYRS
CHORUS, OF SATYRS (WHO HAVE BEEN CAPTURED BY THE CYCLOPS)

ODYSSEUS
POLYPHEMUS, THE CYCLOPS
ODYSSEUS' CREW (SILENT)

SCENE: in front of the cave that belongs to the Cyclops Polyphemus

Enter Silenus from the cave

SILENUS: O Dionysius, the labours and agonies that I have had because of you have been numberless – the one that I have now as well as the ones I had when I was young and had a stronger body. The first labour that comes to mind is the one when you were a child and Hera drove you mad and you went off and left behind your mountain nymphs and your nurses – and I had to go after you to find you.

[5] The second time was the battle with the earth-born Giants and I took my position and made my stand at your right side, protecting you with my shield, and I struck Enceladus with my spear right in the centre of his breastplate, and I killed him dead!

[9] Hmmm... let me think... did I really do this, or did I dream it all up? Am I telling another lie

right now? No, by Zeus, I'm not, Dionysus, for I even shared the spoils with you later.

[10] But now I am suffering from a labour that is so much greater than those other ones. This third one is a doozy, for when Hera stirred up those Tuscan pirates against you so that she could have you sold as a slave to some far off country, I heard all about it and so I got into my ship with my sons and then set out to find you.

[14] I stood there, right at the front of the ship, and I myself steered the boat while my sons rowed along and made the grey sea turn white when they moved their oars – all the while we kept our eyes on the look-out for you, my lord.

[18] But when we were going around Cape Malea, a wind from the east suddenly hit the ship and we were pushed toward this crag of land next to Mt. Aetna. It's here that the one-eyed sons of Poseidon, those man-eating Cyclopes, live in their caves that are so far off from the rest of the world.

[23] One of these Cyclopes – his name is Polyphemus – has caught us and we are kept here as slaves in his house. So instead of drinking wine and eating, doing the kinds of things you world approve of, O Dionysus, we now have to take care of the flocks in this for this godless one-eyed Cyclops.

[27] And so my sons, since they are young, are taking care of the sheep out on the hillsides, while I have been told to stay here and do the housework. I sweep, fetch the water, and cook the thankless meals for this damn Cyclops. And now, my lord Dionysus, please excuse me for a moment, because I have to give the house a quick sweep right now with this rake so that my master, that one-eye, and his sheep can come home to find a clean cave….uhh…I mean, a clean house.

Enter the Chorus (of satyrs), driving sheep in ahead of them

[36] But now I can see my sons coming this way with the flocks. My boys, what's this? You look like you now have the same rhythm and beat to your step as you did when you went partying with Dionysus to Althea's house, dancing all the while to the music from the lyre.

CHORUS (TO A WANDERING RAM):
[41] *And where do you think you're going,*
O you son of a noble family of goats –
Don't you realize that this road leads
To the crags and cliffs?
Isn't it rather this way that's the best path
To reach the gentle breezes and the meadows?
There at the mouth of the cave there's some food
And the wave of a river to drink,
And all of your bleating children
Are sheltered there in their bed.

[49] *C'mon now, shoo shoo! This way here!*
Come on now over here to feed
On the slopes of your pleasant and dewy home.
Do I have to throw a rock at you?
On with you, this way here,
You horny old head of the household!
You're supposed to be the protector and guardian
Of the Cyclops' sheepfold, for all the while
That he is out wandering in the wilderness.
(to a ewe)
[55] *And that goes for you as well,*
Time to get those mammaries of yours home!
It's about time for you to get in that cave
And nurse your young'uns!
Those little bleaters of yours
Have slept all day and really miss their mommy.
Come on! Get on in – time to give up
The crags of Aetna and get on inside
This nice big pen of yours.

[63] *O, but there's no Dionysus here,*
No wine, no dancing, no waving the wand
In our Bacchic worship, no mighty beating of drums,
No fresh drops of wine.

⁶⁸ *And I can't join the nymphs on Mt. Nysa*
And sing drinking songs to Aphrodite,
Like when we chased after the goddess of love so swiftly
In the old days, me and my girlfriends,
Those Bacchants who were so fast
On their white feet.
⁷⁴ *O dear lord Dionysus,*
Where are you right now
Without us, your companions,
Where are you shaking your golden hair?
I was once your happy servant,
But I now am a slave to this one-eyed Cyclops;
I'm a slave in exile,
And I have to wear these crappy rags for clothes,
This damn goatskin,
And I miss your friendship and company,
O dear lord Dionysus.

SILENUS: ⁸² Shhh! Be quiet, boys! Take the animals and get inside the cave quickly!

CHORUS LEADER: You heard him! Let's do what he says. But first, father, what's the rush? What's wrong?

SILENUS: ⁸⁵ I can see a ship down there on the beach. And it's Greek! And the sailors are headed right now toward our cave with the person who must be their leader. On top of their heads and around their necks they're carrying empty containers and sacks, so they must be after food – and some of them are carrying pails for water.

⁸⁹ O strangers – whoever you are – what shitty luck you have!

⁹⁰ But who on earth can they be? They surely have no idea what our master Polyphemus is like, or that this ground here is unfriendly to visitors and guests, or that their rotten luck has taken them to the land of the Cyclopes, who make meals out of human flesh.

⁹⁴ Now all of you just be quiet while I try to find out why they have come to this rocky area around Sicily and Mt. Aetna.

Enter Odysseus and members of his crew

ODYSSEUS: ⁹⁶ Hey there! Hello! Strangers, do you think you might be able to show me where I can find a stream with freshwater? Our thirst is killing us. And do you know of anyone who might sell some supplies to some needy sailors?

⁹⁹ But what's this? It looks like I've just marched into a festival for Dionysus – or his city even! For I didn't realize that you were a group of satyrs gathered at the front of the cave here. I should pay my respects to the oldest first, since he's no doubt the man in charge. Hello there, my dear man!

SILENUS: ¹⁰² And a big hello to you in return, stranger. But please tell me your name and country, if you don't mind.

ODYSSEUS: I am Odysseus, from Ithaca – the lord of Cephallene.

SILENUS: Oh, I've heard of you – you're that famous liar, the bastard son of Sisyphus.

ODYSSEUS: ¹⁰⁵ Yeah, that's right – but you might want to keep the abuse to yourself.

SILENUS: And from what port did you set out so that you'd come here to Sicily?

ODYSSEUS: My crew and I came from Troy and the war that happened there.

SILENUS: What? You couldn't figure out a way to get home?

ODYSSEUS: Well, the winds and the storm blew us here.

SILENUS: ¹¹⁰ Damn – that's the same thing that happened to me.

ODYSSEUS: You were also forced to come here against your will?

SILENUS: Oh yes – we were in the midst of chasing the pirates who had carried off Dionysus.

ODYSSEUS: Then what is this place here? And who lives here?

SILENUS: This is Mount Aetna – the highest peak in all of Sicily.

ODYSSEUS: But where are the walls, and the streets, and the towers, and all the other marks of civilization?

SILENUS: [115] This isn't a city, dude – no people live in these rocks.

ODYSSEUS: But what is it that lives in this land – wild animals?

SILENUS: That's easy – the Cyclopes live here, and they have these caves here, not houses.

ODYSSEUS: But who is in charge of them here? Who is their ruler? Or is there some form of democracy here?

SILENUS: [120] They have no use for that kind of stuff. They're savages and live alone – there's nobody in charge.

ODYSSEUS: But how do they survive? Do they plow the field and sow the grain of Demeter?

SILENUS: They live entirely on milk, cheese, and the flesh of sheep.

ODYSSEUS: Do they have any of the drink of Dionysus – the wine that comes from the vine?

SILENUS: Hell no! That's why this land that they inhabit never has any dances or any fun at all.

ODYSSEUS: [125] Are they friendly toward strangers here?

SILENUS: Oh, they say that the meat from the flesh of strangers makes a lovely dinner.

ODYSSEUS: What? Are you telling me that they eat human flesh here?

SILENUS: Yup – everyone who comes here has been eaten up so far.

ODYSSEUS: And this Cyclops of yours, where is he right now? In his house over there?

SILENUS: [130] Nope – he's taken his dogs and gone off to hunt wild game on the side of Mount Aetna.

ODYSSEUS: So what do we have to do if we want to get out of here?

SILENUS: I have no idea, Odysseus – but I'll do anything that I can to help you.

ODYSSEUS: Ok, maybe you can sell us some bread – we don't have any left.

SILENUS: I already told you – there's nothing to eat here except for meat.

ODYSSEUS: [135] Well, meat is ok – that's a good way to get rid of hunger.

SILENUS: Oh – and we also have cheese and milk, of course.

ODYSSEUS: So bring it all out then – the customer should get a chance to see what he is buying.

SILENUS: But how much money or gold are you going to give me in return?

ODYSSEUS: I don't really have a lot of money or gold… but I do carry the drink of Dionysus – wine.

SILENUS: [140] No fucking way! Thank the gods – that's what we've been dreaming about for so long now.

ODYSSEUS: Yes, the son of the god, Maron, gave this wine to me.

SILENUS: You mean the boy that I once raised in my very arms?

ODYSSEUS: Absolutely – the son of Dionysus.

SILENUS: And….is the wine still on your ship…or do you happen to have it with you right now?

ODYSSEUS: [145] I have some in this wineskin here, old man – take a look.

Silenus: That thing there? Psh! That wouldn't even amount to one mouthful for me.

Odysseus: I promise you – you won't be able to drink this wineskin dry.

Silenus: What is this? Does this wineskin produce its own wine?

Odysseus: Yep – for every gulp you take the wineskin gives two.

Silenus: Wow! What a lovely fountain you have there. I am in love!

Odysseus: Would you like to have a little taste of it first without water?

Silenus: [150] That seems fair – the buyer should get a chance to sample the merchandise, after all.

Odysseus: Check this out – I even have a cup to go with the wineskin.

Silenus: Quick, pour some of it in there. I want to remember what it feels like to drink.

Odysseus: There you go!

Silenus: Oh god, what a beautiful wine!

Odysseus: How can you already know that? But I haven't even given it to you yet…

Silenus: My dear boy, I can smell it!

Odysseus: [155] Fair enough – then it's time for you to take it and drink it. Now your praises won't be just words.

Silenus: Ahhhh…ohhhh…damn - Dionysus is asking me to dance…boom bam..la la la… sh'mone motherfucker!

Odysseus: Doesn't it go down your throat nicely?

Silenus: Oh yeah – all the waaaay down to the – burp – I mean, to the tips of my toes.

Odysseus: [160] But we'll also give you some money in addition to this wine.

Silenus: Screw the money, friend – just keep pouring the wine!

Odysseus: Ok – then you bring out some of that cheese, or a lamb or two.

Silenus: [163] No problems – right away. I don't give a fig for my master. I'd do anything to drink down a full cup of that heavenly wine. I'd give you the entire flock of all the Cyclopes for it, and then when I am good and drunk, I'd go take a run from the highest cliffs and leap into the sea. Wheee! Any man who doesn't like to drink is a fool and has no dick. Hmmm….yeah, that's right, in fact when you're drunk that's the best way to make our peckers stand on end, and it helps us when we are trying to grab a handful of titties, and browse our hands over the soft and wet areas while we stroke her pussy. And of course it also leads us to dance and forget our cares.

[172] And so why shouldn't I want to drink this down all the way so that I can forget about this stupid Cyclops here and his one-eye? To hell with him…

Exit Silenus into the cave

Chorus Leader: [175] Hey, look here, Odysseus – we need to have a little chat with you.

Odysseus: Sure, of course – you're all my friends and I am your friend.

Chorus Leader: Did you really capture Troy and then take Helen as your prisoner?

Odysseus: Yup, and then we sacked and looted the whole house that belonged to Priam and his sons.

Chorus Leader: [179] Well…and after you caught and took Helen as your captive…did all of you then take turns fucking her? I mean, she likes to bang a lot of men – right? That hot little traitor! She saw the tight pants on Paris' legs, and the golden necklaces that he wore, and she went all horny for him. And she left behind that poor little man, that Menelaus.

[187] Oh I wish that the female race ceased to exist – except when it's sucking on my cock, that is!

Enter Silenus from the cave

SILENUS: [188] Ok look right here, my lord and master Odysseus – here are all the flocks of lambs that now belong to you – and all the children of those lambs thrown in for good measure. And here's a shitload of cheeses – all the kinds that I could dig up, all made from the best curdled milk we have here.

[191] Go ahead – take them. Take them quickly, please, and get away from the cave as soon as you can, but not before you give me my part of the bargain – that sweet drunk that is the vine of Dionysus…

[193] Oh crap – here comes the Cyclops now… what are we going to do?

ODYSSEUS: It looks like the jig is up for us, then. Is there anywhere we can flee or hide?

SILENUS: [195] Hmmm…you could go inside the cave – nobody would see you there.

ODYSSEUS: That sounds like it could be a dangerous plan – just like walking straight into the spider's web.

SILENUS: It'll be fine – there's all kinds of places to hide in that cave.

ODYSSEUS: [198] I can't bring myself to do that. The whole of Troy would groan so loudly if it were to hear that I, Odysseus, ran away and fled from just one man when I stood my ground there so often, holding my shield in my hand, fighting off that endless number of Trojans.

[201] No – if I am going to die, I'm going to die nobly. Or, more preferably, if I live on, I'll do so with self-respect and my reputation still intact.

Enter the Cyclops

CYCLOPS: [203] Hey, what the hell is going on here? Why are you all acting so lazy? And what's up with all of this uproar? Do you think that it's some kind of Bacchic holiday? But, I hate to tell you, you're Dionysus ain't here – none his bronze clingers nor any of his rattling clangers are here either.

[206] More to the point – how are my newborn lambs doing in the cave? Have they rushed back to their mothers to get a suck at the tits? And what about the milk? Have you turned it into cheese yet and filled the baskets with this freshly made cheese?

[210] Well, what do you have to say in response? Answer me, damn it, or I'm going to have to hit someone in the head with my club and beat the crap out of all of you until you beg me to stop through your tears. Look at me, not down there, when I am talking to you.

CHORUS LEADER: [212] There – we're looking up at you as if you were Zeus himself. In fact I can even see a bit of your brother Orion in you.

CYCLOPS: Is my dinner ready for me to eat, or what?

CHORUS LEADER: [215] It is – ready and waiting for you. You only have to gobble it up.

CYCLOPS: And are the mixing bowls all filled with milk?

CHORUS LEADER: There's enough there that you could drink a whole vat of it, if you want.

CYCLOPS: Is it cow's milk or sheep's milk – or is it some mixture of both?

CHORUS LEADER: It's whatever you want – just as long as you don't swallow me.

Cyclops: ²²⁰ No, you'd be the last person I'd swallow. You'd be the death of me – dancing around inside of my belly with those dance steps of yours.

²²² Hey, what's all that going on over there at the entrance to my cave? Have some pirates or thieves come here? Who are all those people? I see lambs and sheep from my cave that are tied up and bound, and my buckets of cheese are all over the place – and the old man there looks as if someone beat him around the head, look at all those red marks that cover his face. His face is all red!

Silenus: ²²⁸ Oh…oh…poor me. I've got such a horrible fever from having been beaten up!

Cyclops: By whom? Who's the one that's been beating you about the head, old man?

Silenus: ²³⁰ Oh, it was these men right here, because I wouldn't let them take your property to give to their crew.

Cyclops: Don't they know that I am a god and that my ancestors are gods?

Silenus: ²³² Well, I told their leader here, but they just went on stealing your stuff anyway, and what's even worse, they started in on the cheese, even though I tried to stop him, and then they began to take your sheep off to their ship.

²³⁴ And then – get this – he said that they were going to chain you down with a three-foot collar, and then squeeze you so tightly that the shit would come streaming out of your one eye, and then they'd cover your back with lashes from the whip. Then they are going to tie you up in chains and throw you on their boat, so that they can sail away with you and sell you to be a slave to someone who needs help moving rocks and shit like that.

Cyclops: ²⁴¹ Hmmm…is that right? Ok – you over there, you little satyr, go and sharpen my knife – and make it snappy. And then set a big bunch of sticks in the pit and light a fire.

²⁴³ I'm going to kill this leader fellow at once – him and the rest of his crew – and I'll stuff myself from the boiled, or maybe fried, meat of their flesh. It will be so tender that I won't even need to carve it.

²⁴⁸ Sweet – I'm completely fed up with mountain food anyway. I've had enough lions and deer lately, and it's been way too long since I've had a real good taste of human flesh. Mmmm…

Silenus: ²⁵⁰ Well said, master – it's good to have a change in diet. And it has been quite some time since we've had visitors here at the cave.

Odysseus: ²⁵³ But Cyclops, please let your visitors speak. We came here from our ship hoping that we could buy some food. And this guy over here, once he had something to drink, sold us all these sheep and all this cheese in return for a cup of wine. He was just as willing to sell it as we were willing to buy it.

I mean, everything he just told you was a lie. You can see that he is trying to sell all your stuff behind your back.

Silenus: ²⁶¹ Me, steal? Lie? Why, how dare you, sir! Damn you to hell!

Odysseus: Sure – you can damn me all you like if I am lying, which I'm not.

Silenus: ²⁶² I swear, O Cyclops, I swear in the name of your father Poseidon, in the name of great Triton and Nereus, in the name of Calypso and the daughters of Nereus, in the name of the holy waves in the sea and every type of fish that swims in them…I swear, dear master, dear Cyclops, O sweet little Cyclops, that I wasn't trying to sell your stuff to these strangers. And if I am telling a lie, then you can kill my children for it, as dear as they are to me!

Chorus Leader: [270] What the fuck? And may you die as well then! I even saw you selling all of this stuff here to the stranger. And if I am lying, then you can kill my father, as dear as he is to me! But you shouldn't blame these strangers here.

Cyclops: [273] Hmm…I think that you, child, you're the one who's lying, and that your father is the honest one here. I'd put more trust in him and his honesty than I would in king Minos himself, the judge in Hades.

[275] But I do want to ask you strangers a question. Where have you come from? What's your country? And tell me what city you grew up in.

Odysseus: [278] We're from Ithaca. After we finished sacking Troy, we set sail to go home and we ended up here on your island, Cyclops. The winds blew us here off course.

Cyclops: [280] So are you the people who went to destroy Troy because that slut Helen was stolen from Greece?

Odysseus: Yes, we are those people, and that's what we did. And that terrible deed is now done – thankfully.

Cyclops: The lot of you should be ashamed of yourselves. I mean, really – going to war against the Trojans for the sake of one woman?

Odysseus: [285] But a god was the real reason for it! You really shouldn't blame any mortals for this.

[286] All the same, O noble son of the sea god Poseidon, we beg of you and ask you as free men – please, don't kill me who have come to your cave, your home, as friends. Any meal that you make out of us would be a sin against the gods.

[290] For, my lord, it is we Greeks who protected your father Poseidon and kept him safe within the walls of his temples throughout every part of Greece. We're the ones who kept his sacred harbour in Taenarus safe and unharmed, and we did the same for Cape Malea. The rocky peak of Sunium, which is filled with silver and sacred to the goddess Athena, and the sanctuaries of Geraestus – all of them are safe thanks to us.

[295] We didn't allow the great disgrace of allowing Greek possessions to fall into the hands of the Trojans. And now you too even play a role in all of these events – for where we are right now, here in Sicily under this volcano Aetna, you are living in a part of Greece in this very spot.

[299] Well, anyway, even if you don't agree with what I just said, we have this law in the human world that says that shipwrecked sailors are supposed to receive food and protection. They're supposed to receive hospitality… and clothing… and that you're supposed to treat us nicely. And, above all, this rule says that you are not – and I repeat NOT – supposed to chop us up into little bits and then roast us over the fire on sticks before you put us in your belly.

[304] The land of Priam – that Troy from which we came – has brought enough tragedy and sadness to Greece, since its plains and rivers have soaked up the blood of all those thousands who were killed in the war. Wives have been made widows, mothers have lost their sons, and old men have had their hair turn grey, going to the grave childless. If you are thinking of cooking up and eating some of the few Greek who remain from that war, in that

unholy meal of yours, then where will anyone in Greece turn for help and safety?

[309] Listen to me, Cyclops – change your plan, give it up. Forget this hunger and this horrible plan and choose to do what is right instead. For many people end up suffering in the end when they try to achieve profit by doing evil deeds.

SILENUS: [313] I want to give you a little piece of advice here, Cyclops – eat every bit of this man's flesh and don't leave anything untouched. What's more, if you have a good chew on his tongue, then you'll become very clever and eloquent, just like he is.

CYCLOPS: [316] O little man, little Greek man, it's money that is the god to wise and clever men – the rest is just bullshit and fine-sounding words. I don't care in the slightest about my father's caves along the coast. Why did you think that I would? Why did you even mention them? And I'm not afraid of Zeus' thunder either, stranger – for I don't really think that he is more powerful than I am.

[322] I've never given a thought to Zeus before, and I won't care about him in the future – and I'll tell you why. When Zeus sends down his rain from above, I get my shelter from the rain in this here cave and I have a feast on lamb or some wild animal. I fill my belly till I'm stuffed, then I stretch and wash down the meal with a vat full of milk. And then I turn the vat over and drum on it and make a noise in here that's loud enough to rival Zeus' thunder. And if that noise isn't enough, I add farts to increase the volume.

[329] And when the wind from Thrace comes down here and brings us snow, I cover and wrap my body in the skins of beasts, then I build and light a huge fire – and so I don't have to pay any attention to the snow.

[332] The earth itself brings forth the grass that feeds my flock, and it does so whether it wants to or not. And I sacrifice these animals to no god other than me. I certainly don't sacrifice them to the other gods – no, they are dedicated to my belly alone, the greatest of all the gods. To eat and drink your fill, and to do this each and every day – this is Zeus in the eyes of intelligent men. As for all those little men who pass laws and make everyone's life complicated – fuck 'em. I'm going to go right on doing what I've always been doing – pleasing myself. And that means that I am going to eat you all up.

[340] But, to be fair, I will give you some presents that people typically offer their guests. I'll give you fire to warm you up, salt to put all over your body, and water from my father, along with a bronze pot he once gave me. Of course, when the water in that bronze pot reaches the boiling point, it will cook you up really nicely.

[345] So now, I want all of you little Greek men to go inside and stand around the altar of the god who rules that cave in there – and you are going to provide some nice entertainment for me in addition to a fine meal.

ODYSSEUS: [347] Good god – I've gotten out of so many tight spots in Troy, and so many on the high seas as well, only to wind up washed ashore on the coast of this heartless and godless thing!

[350] O Pallas Athena, divine daughter of Zeus – please now, now is the time to help me, if ever there was a time! For right now I've encountered greater trouble than any I ever met when I was at Troy – this is the type of danger from which there is no escape.

[353] And you, O Zeus, protector of guests and strangers, you who live and rule among the

bright stars in the heavens – please look down on my problems and help me! For if you don't look after me now, then you can't be Zeus – but you must rather be some worthless god instead.

The Cyclops pushes Odysseus and his crew forward into the cave

Chorus:
³⁵⁶ *O Cyclops, open your huge jaws and vast mouth!*
Your dinner is ready –
The limbs of your guests,
Whether they are boiled, roasted, or even broiled,
Are ready for you to chew and devour
As you sit back and relax
Dressed in your old goatskin.
³⁶¹ *Just don't ask me to dine with you!*
You can have that feast all to yourself –
I'll just keep my distance from this cave,
As far away as I can be
From the Cyclops on Aetna;
This disgusting glutton
Who stuffs himself on the flesh
Of his guests.
³⁷⁰ *So savage, such a stranger to mercy,*
This one who cooks on his fire
The stranger who have asked for his help,
And who boils them all up
And then scoffs them down,
While his evil mouth chomps on human meat
Plucked from the burning coals of the fire.

Enter Odysseus from the cave

Odysseus: ³⁷⁵ O Zeus, how can I even begin to say what I just saw in that cave? It was all so terrible, so incredible – the kind of stuff you only hear about in stories. It's the stuff of myths – do real men act this way?

Chorus Leader: What happened, Odysseus? Did that godless Cyclops really eat up all of your crew?

Odysseus: ³⁷⁹ Not all, but he picked up two of them, the ones who had the fattest bodies – and he weighed them in his hands.

Chorus Leader: That's so horrible – how could you stand to watch it all?

Odysseus: ³⁸² As soon as we went inside this rocky cavern, he first spent his time with the fire, making sure that it blazed up to a great height, and so he tossed huge logs from a mighty oak tree on top of the fire. It was enough oak to load three wagons. And after the fire was going strong, he then put his bronze kettle on top of the fire to get the water up to boil.

³⁹² Right next to the fire he spread out a bed of pine and fir branches on the ground. After he finished milking the cows and the sheep, he filled this huge mixing bowl right to the brim with milk – it probably contained maybe five hundred litres. And then he set right next to it this huge wooden cup that must have been four feet wide and six feet deep. Then he got all the cookware ready that he needed to make a feast, and when that sick and disgusting cook had everything that he needed, he then snatched up two of my men.

³⁹⁹ When he took hold of the first one he quickly cut his throat over the bowl, then he grabbed the second one by his foot and smashed his head against a rock until his gory brains were all over the place. Next, he cut them up with a sharp blade and he roasted them on top of the fire while he put their arms and legs in the pot to boil. I was standing right next to the Cyclops while he did this – oh, why me? – and tears were pouring down my cheeks while I watched him do these horrible things. The other members of my crew were off hiding, huddled up just like birds in the corners of the caves, all of their faces were white as ghosts.

⁴⁰⁹ But then he leaned back, feeling a bit bloated after that awful meal he had just made of my two crewmembers, and so he let out the

most god-awful belch that I have ever heard. It smelled something terrible, let me tell you. At that very moment, some god sent an amazing idea to me. I filled a cup with this wine that Maron gave me and then I set the wine before while I said these words to him – "O Cyclops, son of the sea-god Poseidon, come, take a swig of this divine drink that the grapes of Greece offer you here – this joyful drink, this wine from Dionysus!"

[416] He was completely stuffed with that repulsive meal, but he took the drink into his hand and then drained it all in one quick gulp. He was overwhelmed by this, then he raised his hands in appreciation and said – "Wowza! Dear friend, you're the best – my bestest friend…my pal all right. You've given me this awesome drink and it, uh, it puts, uh, it's just great to drink this after such a good meal!"

[420] I saw that this drink was giving him pleasure, and that he was quickly becoming drunk, so I gave him another drink right-away, since I knew that the wine would soon make him completely shit-faced and that this would be his ruin, for I would be able to pay him back.

[423] Then – what an amazing sight! – he started to sing…he was becoming sooo drunk…and I was giving him one drink after the other and this started to make his belly all warm. So he's sitting in there right now, drunkenly singing away while my crew is in there crying in fear – you can hear the echo of his singing even out here.

[426] So I've just taken the chance to sneak out here because I wanted to ask you whether you want to help me out and finally be free of this monster so you can go and live again in the halls of Dionysus along with his nymphs and Naiads. Your father already agreed to this when I asked him in the cave, but he's really a weakling and, just like the Cyclops there, I can also see that he's already a bit gone on the sauce. I mean, he's holding that cup so tightly in his hand you'd think he were glued to it. But all of you are still young, and so I think I can trust you with this. So come on, follow me and you can save yourselves. This way you'll be able to get back to your old friend Dionysus – who is sooo very different from this Cyclops here.

CHORUS LEADER: [437] O my dear friend – if only we can finally see the day when we can escape from this godless Cyclops. It's been so long now that this cock of mine has been a bachelor, with no place to rest its head.

ODYSSEUS: [441] Listen to what I have in mind that will set you free. I'm planning quite the punishment for this disgusting beast.

CHORUS LEADER: Go ahead – tell me. I'd rather hear this plan of yours than all the harps in Asia.

ODYSSEUS: [445] He is so happy with this drink from Dionysus that he wants to go visit his brothers and party with them.

CHORUS LEADER: I think I catch your meaning. You're going to lay an ambush on him in the woods and then you'll cut his throat or push him off some cliff or something like that.

ODYSSEUS: What? No, nothing like that at all. I had something that involves a bit more trickery.

CHORUS LEADER: [450] What's your plan then? We've already heard a great deal about your cleverness.

ODYSSEUS: [451] Well, to start I'm going to stop him in his attempt to go out and party with his friends by telling him that he should be careful not to give any of the other Cyclopes this wine, but that he should instead keep it all for himself and enjoy all the pleasures that it brings all by himself.

⁴⁵⁴ But he'll eventually fall asleep, as happens soon after any drinking binge, and then I'll take my sword and use it to sharpen up the trunk of an olive tree that is sitting in there. I'll make it all pointy on one end and then I'll stick it in the coals of the fire to make it really really hot. Then, when it's almost to the point of burning, I'll lift it up on high and then drive the thing right through that one eye of the Cyclops. It will melt his eye and he'll be turned blind.

⁴⁶⁰ So just like a carpenter plays so comfortably with his tools, with his hammer and nails, that's how easily I'll force this burning log into that monster's eye – and I'll blind him once and for all time.

Chorus Leader: ⁴⁶⁵ That's fucking amazing! This plan of yours leaves me so excited that I want to jizz.

Odysseus: And after I stab him in the eye, then I'll take your father and all of you, set the lot of you on my ship, and we'll high-tail it out of here, sailing away from this land as fast as we can.

Chorus Leader: ⁴⁶⁹ Do you think that there might be a way for me to help out in blinding this Cyclops? I mean, it's just like pouring a libation to the gods – everyone gets to help out in some way. Perhaps I can help drive the stake through his eye? Dude, I really want to take part in this.

Odysseus: Yeah, of course – you are all going to have to take a part in this – the log is huge and we'll all need to lift the thing together.

Chorus Leader: ⁴⁷³ I could happily try to lift the weight of a hundred wagons if it would mean that we're giving that Cyclops a horrible death! Let's just burn the ugly bugger's eye as if we're burning a wasps' nest!

Odysseus: ⁴⁷⁶ Then just shush now! You all know the plan, and so when I say the word, you have to do what your master here tells you to do. That's me. There's no chance that I am going to save myself and leave my men in there alone and trapped inside. It would be easy for me to escape alone, of course, since I have just managed to come out of the cave now. But it just isn't right to save myself alone and completely abandon my crew.

Exit Odysseus back into the cave

Chorus: ⁴⁸³ Come on, everyone, who is going to stand first here, and who will stand second in line? Let's all get ready to put our hands on that burning log, the one we're going to shove right into the eye of the Cyclops and destroy his sight.

Wait! Shhh…be quiet!

⁴⁸⁷ I think I can see the Cyclops. Yes, here he comes, all liquored up and singing some drunken song. He's staggering his way out of his rocky cave, that home of his. Good grief – what a horrible voice he has!

C'mon then, let's teach him a little bit about how a good party song should sound, then after we give him this lesson in culture, we'll poke his damn eye out!

Enter the Cyclops from the cave, propped up by Silenus; Odysseus follows behind them

⁴⁹⁵ *Happy is the man who can shout*
The Bacchic song – whoo-hoo!
Off to the party,
For him the wine keeps flowing,
His arms are wrapped around
His bestest of friends!
And waiting for him, that lucky stud,
On his bed at home
Is the hot young body
Of his slutty mistress

*With her shining hair
And oiled-up body —
The man shouts,
"Who can get this door for me?"*

CYCLOPS: ⁵⁰³ I said goddamn! I am so freaking ripped right now — I love all this messing around that comes with drinking too much wine. I'm like a boat, and stuffed all the way up to the top deck — but the top deck is my belly, and I'm filled with wine — and I'm drunk — real real drunk! Bwa-ha-ha-ha!

⁵⁰⁷ But all of this good booze has….it has… what? Wait…it has made me remember… it has remembered me. Hmmm…where was I? Oh, yes, I need to share this wine with my bothers…no, my brothers. I need to go find the other Cyclo…Cyclo…Cylcodobolops… you know, all the other one-eyes like me, and then we can party all together.

Come here, my little friend, hand me the wineskin.

CHORUS:
⁵¹¹ *With the beautiful glance
From his lovely eye
The dapper Cyclops comes out
Comes out from his house,
As handsome as a groom,
As handsome as a lover-boy,
A tender young nymph waits for this groom,
She waits there in the cave;
She's burning, she's in heat,
And soon will give him the crown,
To celebrate you,
As the king of fuck-town!*

ODYSSEUS: ⁵¹⁹ Hey Cyclops, listen here for a second. I'm really good friends with this Dionysus — you know this Dionysus that you are and have been drinking.

CYCLOPS: Who is this…this Dionysus? Is he worshipped as a god?

ODYSSEUS: Oh yes — he is the greatest joy that mortal men have in their lives.

CYCLOPS (BURPS): Well, he makes a damn good burp, I tell you that!

ODYSSEUS: That's exactly the way he is — he doesn't do any harm to anyone.

CYCLOPS: ⁵²⁵ Wait — but how can a god live in this eensie-weensie little wineskin?

ODYSSEUS: Oh, he's just fine wherever you put him.

CYCLOPS: But it's not right for a god to cover himself in skins.

ODYSSEUS: What's the problem, if you're getting pleasure from him? Do you have some problem with the wine-skin?

CYCLOPS: The wineskin is shit — but I really love this wine.

ODYSSEUS: ⁵³⁰ So why don't you just stay here and get drunk, Cyclops. Just relax and enjoy yourself.

CYCLOPS: You mean I shouldn't go and give some of this to my brothers?

ODYSSEUS: Yes — just keep it to yourself. You'll bring more honour to yourself that way.

CYCLOPS: But…if I gave it to my friends I'd be more useful…I'd be more liked…

ODYSSEUS: Yes, but booze and parties always end in fights and fisticuffs.

CYCLOPS: ⁵³⁵ Yes, I may be drunk…but…no one's going to lay a hand on me, mister!

ODYSSEUS: That's right, my friend — it's best to stay at home when you've had too much to drink.

CYCLOPS: But whoever drinks and doesn't party is a dolt, a fool.

ODYSSEUS: On the contrary — whoever stays at home when he is drunk is smart and wise.

Cyclops: Silenus? What do you think we should do? Should we stay here at home?

Silenus: 540 Yes, I'd stay – what do we need with more drinkers, Cyclops?

Odysseus: And, anyway, the ground here is so soft, so perfect for resting, with all of the flowers, so good for sleeping…

Silenus: There there….isn't it nice to have a nice drink when the sun is so hot outside? Why don't you just lie down…yes, set yourself down and stretch out on the grass.

The Cyclops lies down and Silenus sneakily puts the mixing bowl behind him

Cyclops: 545 There – all down now. Wait – why did you put the bowl behind my head?

Silenus: I just don't want anyone to tip it over.

Cyclops: You little bugger! You were planning to filch my booze! Put it back here, in the middle between us, where I can keep my eye on it.

Hey stranger, I never did get your name.

Odysseus: My name – it's No-body. But how are you going to thank me for this wine that I gave you?

Cyclops: 550 Thank you?…oh…I know, I'll eat you last of all your crew…yes, eat you last.

Silenus: Excellent idea, Cyclops – that's a well-deserved present for your guest!

Silenus quickly sneaks some wine

Cyclops: What? What's that? You're drinking my wine when I'm not looking!

Silenus: No…not at all – the wine just kissed me, that's all. It said I have beautiful eyes.

Cyclops: You just had better be careful – you may love the wine, but it doesn't mean that she loves you…

Silenus: 555 That's not true at all. In the name of Zeus, this wine here has fallen head-over-heels for my good looks.

Cyclops: Hmmph…pour me a cup of it, but just pour it – and give it to me when you are done.

Silenus: But is this the right mixture? Let me have a little taste to check…

Silenus takes a quick drink

Cyclops: You little bugger – give me the damn drink? I want my booze!

Silenus: Just a second – by the gods, I won't give it to you before I see you wearing this crown of flowers here…and I have another taste.

Silenus offers the Cyclops a wreathe of flowers while he drains his cup dry

Cyclops: 560 This wine-pourer of mine is a little thief!

Silenus: That may be true, but this wine is sooo sweet. Ooh here comes another drinkie for you, Mr. Cyclops! Now, you just wipe your mouth before I give you another.

Cyclops: There – I've wiped it all up. My mouth and my beard are clean now. More wine! More!

Silenus: Just settle yourself down on your elbow there – that's it, gently – and take a good long drink…just as you see me drinking – and now you don't see me.

Silenus drains the cup, his face hidden as he empties it out

Cyclops: 565 Hey – what are you doing there?

Silenus: Just having a good guzzle of wine.

Cyclops: Stranger, I want you to be my wine-pourer. You take the flask there.

Odysseus: Well, the wine will feel at home in my hand, that's for sure.

Cyclops: Come on then – gimme gimme!

ODYSSEUS: I'm pouring it out right now – just you take it easy, friend. Relax.

CYCLOPS: Relax? That's not easy to do when you're drunk, you know.

ODYSSEUS: ⁵⁷⁰ Here – here's a cup for you. Take it and drink it all down – every last drop of it. The drunk and his bottle must reach their end together.

CYCLOPS: Oh sweetness – the vine that produced this must be a wizard, a genius even!

ODYSSEUS: And if you keep drinking after such a big meal, and keep at it with the sauce till you fill up your belly, then you'll soon sleep as sweetly as a baby. But if you don't drink it all, then Dionysus will get you! He'll make your throat all dry and make you feel icky all over.

CYCLOPS: ⁵⁷⁶ Whoa – hey-o… I feel like my head is swimming. I've never felt so much pleasure before. Ooh… ahh… the earth and the sky – they are all twirling around my head, mixed up together like a… what'dyacallit?

⁵⁷⁹ Hey – I can see – where? – oh, there it is again… it's the throne of Zeus… and there's the whole group of the holy gods. Heellooo there gods!

Do you… do you think I should try to give the gods some little kissies?

The Chorus dance around him, pretending to be ghosts or gods

⁵⁸¹ Ooh… the Graces there… they have the hots for me – I think they're making the moves on me. No – I can't fuck you tonight. With my Ganymede here… well, he'll be plenty good enough for me if I take him off to the sack. He'll bring me a great sleep – a magnificent honour to fuck him. Sorry about this, my Graces – but I like boys more than girls, for some reason…

The Cyclops grabs Silenus, mistaking him for Ganymede

SILENUS: ⁵⁸⁵ What is this, Cyclops? Am I supposed to be Zeus' little boy Ganymede?

CYCLOPS: Damn right you are! And I'm Zeus – you're the boy I stole from Dardanus!

SILENUS: Oh crap – I'm done for, my children. Horrible. Unspeakable things are going to happen to me.

CYCLOPS: What's this? Are you going to be so snooty to your lover just because he's drunk?

SILENUS: Fuck me – the wine that I have to drink now is going to be pretty bitter.

Exit the Cyclops into the cave, dragging his lover Ganymede/Silenus

ODYSSEUS: ⁵⁹⁰ Come here, quick, you children of Dionysus, you sons of nobility. Our mark is inside the cave right now. In a few minutes he'll puke out his disgusting meal of human flesh – that's what drinking does. And in the cave, just inside the long hallway, our poking-stick, that log of oak, is all ready on the flame and it's started to give out smoke.

⁵⁹⁴ There's nothing really left to do other than poke out this Cyclops' eye. But all of you will have to prove that you are men.

CHORUS LEADER: ⁵⁹⁶ Oh, but our wills are like rocks or stones inside! But let's go into the cave before my father gets raped… or eaten. Everything is ready to rock and roll on our side.

ODYSSEUS: ⁵⁹⁹ O lord Hephaestus, ruler of the land of Aetna here, please help us burn out the eye of this neighbour of yours. Let's all be rid of him for once and all.

⁶⁰¹ And you, O Sleep, the child of dark Night, please come here with all your might and

help us attack this beast that is so hated by the gods!

⁶⁰³ After all of our amazing and glorious deeds that we performed at Troy, please don't let Odysseus – me – and his crew be killed by a thing who has no respect for gods or men. If he does kill us, then we'll all just have to make Chance into a goddess, and to rank her even higher than all other ones.

Exit Odysseus into the cave

CHORUS:
⁶⁰³ A bitter wrench is about to grab
The neck of this beast
Who likes to eat his own visitors;
Fire is about to destroy that one shining eye of his;
Our poking-stick, so large and daunting,
Already is waiting, its tip burning hot
And sitting and resting in the coals.
Oh come on you wine! Do your thing!
Help us rip out the eye of this lunatic Cyclops;
Make sure that he'll forever
Regret the day that he drank you down!
⁶²⁰ For myself, all I want to do is to see Dionysus
Wearing his ivy,
And to leave far behind this cave of the Cyclops –
Will I ever see such pleasure and joy again?

Enter Odysseus from the cave

ODYSSEUS: ⁶²⁵ Be quiet, will you, shhh! Be quiet you little animals, for heaven's sake – just keep it down. I don't want to hear any one of you even breathe, or clear his throat, or even blink for that matter. He's asleep now and we can't let this monster wake up, for then we won't be able to burn out his eye with our fire-stick.

CHORUS: Ok – we're keeping quiet. No sound will escape these lips.

ODYSSEUS: ⁶³⁰ Good – then let's all get to work. You're all going to go inside and grab hold of the end of our fire-log. Its pointy end is now red-hot.

CHORUS LEADER: You should tell us what roles you'd like each of us to play in this. Who's going to be the first one to lift this burning piece of wood? Let us know how we all can take part in this adventure, so we can all burn out his eye together and share in whatever fate has in store for us.

ONE MEMBER OF THE CHORUS: ⁶³⁵ But here where we're standing, over here by the cave's door…it's a bit too far away for us to lift the log and reach his eye.

ANOTHER MEMBER OF THE CHORUS: And all of a sudden I'm finding it hard to walk.

ONE MEMBER OF THE CHORUS: The same for us too! We can't walk either. Just while we were standing here we suddenly sprained our ankles and legs. Oww!

ODYSSEUS: ⁶⁴⁰ So you sprained your ankles just by standing there, doing nothing?

ANOTHER MEMBER OF THE CHORUS: And my eyes are all full of dust and ash, and I can hardly see straight.

ODYSSEUS: It looks like these helpers of mine are worthless cowards.

CHORUS LEADER: ⁶⁴³ Hey now, just because I'm worried about my back and my spine, and I really don't want to see my teeth lying on the ground – is that supposed to mean that I'm a coward?

⁶⁴⁶ But I know a spell and song from Orpheus that's so amazing it will make our weapon stand up all on its own and then fly into the skull of old one-eye there and set him on fire.

ODYSSEUS: ⁶⁴⁹ I knew from the very start that this is the type of people you were, and now it even becomes clearer. It's necessary for me to make use of my friends in this caper. So if you don't have the strength and daring to help me, at least you can cheer on my men so that your words of support will give them courage.

Exit Odysseus into the cave

CHORUS LEADER: [654] I'll do this, and he can let his soldiers take all of the risks for us. We'll be the cheerleaders from the sidelines. Let the Cyclops burn!

CHORUS:

[656] *Hey hey, ho ho*
That one-eyed Cyclops has got to go!
Do it, boys, go to it!
Push it in hard,
Burn out the eye of that monster
Who eats his guests!
Burn him down, light him on fire –
That shepherd of Mt. Aetna.
Twist it in, turn it then, but watch out,
For in pain he might do some harm to you!

Enter the Cyclops from the cave, with blood streaming from his eye

CYCLOPS: [663] Ahhhhh! Ohhhh! My eye! My eye! It's been burned – there's nothing left.

CHORUS LEADER: What a lovely tune – please keep singing that for us, Cyclops.

CYCLOPS: [665] What? Ohhhh! Fuck….ohhhh! I've been assaulted – they've destroyed me! But you'll never be able to get away from me, you dirty pile of scum that did this to me. I'm just going to stand here in the doorway to the cave and block the entrance with my hands and arms.

CHORUS LEADER: Why are you shouting like that, Cyclops?

CYCLOPS: I'm ruined.

CHORUS LEADER: [670] Well you do look rather shitty, that's for sure.

CYCLOPS: I feel like shit.

CHORUS LEADER: Did you get so drunk that you ended up falling into the hot coals?

CYCLOPS: No-body destroyed me.

CHORUS LEADER: Good, then nobody's hurt you at all.

CYCLOPS: No – No-body blinded me… No-body stabbed me in the eye!

CHORUS LEADER: So then you're not blind at all.

CYCLOPS: I'm as blind as you, it seems!

CHORUS LEADER: And how is it that nobody could make you blind?

CYCLOPS: [675] You are making fun of me. But where is this No-body? Where's No-body?

CHORUS LEADER: That's easy – nobody is no-where, Cyclops.

CYCLOPS: I'm talking about the damn stranger – you know what I mean. He's the one who did this to me. He got me so drunk and then did this to me. What a horrible guest!

CHORUS LEADER: Well, wine is very dangerous and tricky – it creates all kinds of problems when you try to wrestle with it.

CYCLOPS: Just tell me this, please – have they already escaped or are they still inside the cave?

CHORUS LEADER: [680] They're actually over there, keeping quite quiet – under the cover of that cliff.

CYCLOPS: Where? To which side of me? To my left or to my right?

CHORUS LEADER: Uhhh… to your right. Yes, to your right side.

The Cyclops moves away from the entrance and heads to the right; Odysseus, his crew, and Silenus, sneak silently out of the cave

CYCLOPS: Where?

Chorus Leader: Right there – a little bit more...do you have them?

Cyclops: Ahhh...crap! No – I don't have them, but I think I've done some more damage to my head!

Chorus Leader: [685] And it looks like they've just given you the slip as well.

Cyclops: What? But didn't you say they were this way here?

Chorus Leader: No I mean this way here?

Cyclops: Dammit – what way are you pointing?

Chorus Leader: Just turn to your left, now turn to your right, now left again – there they are on your right!

Cyclops: Assholes – you're making fun of me, tricking me while I am in misery.

Chorus Leader: Ok – I won't trick you anymore. He's right there in front of you now.

Cyclops: Where are you then, you little bastard who did this to me?

Odysseus: [690] Oh, I'm at a safe distance from you – where I can keep the body of Odysseus safe from any harm.

Cyclops: What? Odysseus? This is a new name that you are using.

Odysseus: [692] But this name is the very one that my father gave me – Odysseus. And it looks like it was your destiny to be punished for that ungodly meal you made out of my crew. It would have been wrong of me to raze Troy to the ground and not get my revenge on you for what you just did to two of my men.

Cyclops: [696] Oh my – the ancient prophecy has been fulfilled! It said that one day a man named Odysseus would come from Troy and blind me. But the prophecy also said that you, in turn, would be punished for doing this to me – that you would have to wander over the seas for many years.

Odysseus: [701] Whatever, buddy. I really don't care what you have to say – this thing is over here. As for me, I'm going to head down to my boat on the shore. Then we'll take the ship and sail for home over this Sicilian Sea.

Exit Odysseus and his crew

Cyclops: [704] Oh no you don't! I'm going to break off a piece of this here rock and crush you and your crew beneath it. I may be blind, but I'll be able to reach the top of the mountain quickly through the tunnel in my cave.

Exit the Cyclops into the cave

Chorus: [708] And as for us, we'll join with Odysseus and his crew. And we'll always take our orders from sweet delicious Dionysus!

Exit the Chorus and Silenus

Translated from the Greek by Stephen Russell, PhD

Chapter 11
Euripides
Medea

THE STORY: Jason led his ship the Argo to Medea's homeland of Colchis to obtain the Golden Fleece. When he was there, Medea, the daughter of the king and a witch, fell in love with Jason and helped him steal the Fleece. She also killed her young brother in an effort to convince her father to stop chasing them as they fled.

On the return voyage to Greece, Medea assisted the Argonauts greatly, and Jason and Medea married and had two young boys. When they arrived back in Greece she helped Jason's aged father become young again as well as tricked the daughters of Jason's enemy Pelias into killing their father.

They eventually settle in Corinth as guests of King Creon. But Jason has grown tired of Medea and is planning to leave her so that he can marry Creon's daughter.

This play is the story of what Medea does when she finds out that Jason has betrayed her – this is the story of Medea's revenge.

CHARACTERS

NURSE (OF MEDEA AND THE CHILDREN)
TUTOR (OF THE CHILDREN)
MEDEA
CHORUS (WOMEN OF CORINTH)
CREON, KING OF CORINTH

JASON
AEGEUS, KING OF ATHENS
MESSENGER
CHILDREN (OF MEDEA AND JASON)

SCENE: Corinth. Medea's house is in the background.

Enter the Nurse

NURSE: If only the Argo had never sailed between the clashing rocks into the harbour of Colchis, or the pines of Mt. Pelion never been felled, nor fit to the hands of the heroes that Pelias sent to fetch the Golden Fleece. For then my mistress, mad from love, would not have sailed for Iolcus, nor persuaded the daughters of Pelias to murder their father, and having assisted Jason in every way possible to please the citizens of this Corinthian land, come to exile with him and the children.

¹² To my mind, the greatest good is when a wife doesn't contend with her husband. But now she hates everything and sickens even toward those most dear to her. For Jason has betrayed his children and my mistress, and now shares the royal marriage bed with the daughter of Creon, ruler of this land. Dishonored, Medea cries, "What of the oaths? The right hand given

as a sign of the greatest trust?" She calls on the gods to witness her mistreatment, will not eat, but gives her wracked body over to pain and constant tears. Neither lifting her head nor her eyes from the ground, she ignores the advice of friends, who are unintelligible as stones or the sea to her. She is so quiet, only turning her snow-white neck at times to wail for her father, for her home, which she betrayed for the man who now dishonors her. Now the poor woman learns how important it is not to be cut off from your homeland.

[36] Now she despises even her own children, takes no pleasure in seeing them, and I fear she plots some fresh evil, for hers is a dangerous spirit and will not allow mistreatment. I know her, and dread that she might twist a sharpened blade through her chest, or kill the king, his daughter, as well as he who married her, before contriving some even greater calamity. She terrifies me, for I know that no one who trifles with her long sings a song of victory.

Enter the Children with the Tutor

[46] But look, here come the boys, back from play. They know nothing of their mother's troubles. Young minds cannot conceive of such pain.

TUTOR: [49] Hail, fellow toiler, why are you standing here all alone, muttering to yourself? Isn't your mistress missing you?

NURSE: [53] Well, Tutor, when things go wrong for their master, a good servant suffers in equal measure, and my suffering is so great I had to leave that oppressive house awhile to cry my mistress' troubles to the earth and sky.

TUTOR: What, has the poor woman not ceased wailing yet?

NURSE: [60] It must be nice to be so situated as to be able to ignore it. No, her pains are just in the beginning stages: they haven't even reached middle-age.

TUTOR: Poor fool – if I can speak thus about my mistress – for she can know nothing of the latest!

NURSE: What now, old man? Now is hardly the time to grow a tight lip.

TUTOR: I shouldn't have spoken…

NURSE: [65] For pity's sake, don't leave a fellow subject in the dark. I can keep a secret.

TUTOR: [67] Well, we just now passed by the place where the old men play dice – you know, near the spring – and, pretending not to listen, I overheard someone say that Creon, the king, is about to order these children and their mother exiled from this land. I don't know how good his information is, but it's bad news for you and me if it is so.

NURSE: [74] But would Jason allow this to happen to his children, even if he is fighting with their mother?

TUTOR: Old marriage ties are forsaken for new: that man is not a friend of this house.

NURSE: Great. A fresh disaster, and we're still reeling from the last one.

TUTOR: [80] Keep it to yourself: now is not the time for her to hear it.

NURSE: There children, do you see what kind of father you have? Far be it from me to pass judgment on my master, but the way he treats his loved ones…

TUTOR: [85] And what man is blameless in that regard? So a father prefers his new bride to his children: are you only just now figuring out that every man loves himself above all others?

And that some love truly, while others truly love only gain...

NURSE: [89] Go inside, children: everything will be fine. And you, keep them as far as possible from their mother. Such a look she gave them just now, like a bull preparing to charge. She won't let go of this anger – I am sure of it – until she spends it on someone. I only hope it's an enemy rather than her friends.

MEDEA (FROM INSIDE THE HOUSE): [96] My life has turned to shit! It hurts.... It hurts... so much. I can't live through it...

NURSE: [98] There! Mind your nurse, little ones. Your mother is hurt and angry. Hurry inside now, and steer clear: beware her fierce temper and the savage hate in her tortured mind. Inside now, quick as you can!

The Children and the Tutor enter the house

[106] It's clear that her groans are just the distant rumblings of a grief that will presently darken into a storm of fury. What will that terrible pride not do when stung with such injury?

MEDEA (STILL INSIDE): [111] I've done and suffered such terrible things, things worth cursing. Oh cursed children of a hated mother – you should die along with your father! Curse this house! Curse our home!

NURSE: [115] Oh, this is agony! Why tar the children with their father's sin? O my lovely boys, I am sick with the fear of what you may suffer! The moods of royalty are fierce – they are so used to ruling over everyone and everything, except their own ungovernable tempers.

[122] Far better, I think, to live down among equals. I, at any rate, hope to grow old safely, on modest means, moderation and modesty being by far the best way for mortals to live. Excess is no boon to mortals and a god's anger is drawn like lightning to an over-proud house.

Enter the Chorus (of Corinthian women)

CHORUS: [131] We're here because we keep hearing the cries of that poor woman from Colchis. Is she still so overwrought? Speak, old woman! For her wailing is plainly audible even over the double-gated walls of the city, and the sufferings of her house disturb us now because she is a friend of ours.

NURSE: [139] This house is no more. All is in ruin. He is now held in his royal marriage while she wastes her life away alone in her room and cannot be soothed by the words of her friends.

MEDEA (STILL INSIDE): [144] Oh, bastard, Jason! Oh Zeus, oh land, oh heaven, take pity and strike me dead! What's the point in living? Let me take my ease in death and leave this hateful existence behind.

CHORUS: [148] Do you hear oh Zeus and land and heaven? Do you hear the miserable song the poor woman sings? Why is your desire for Death's bed, foolish woman? Would you hurry to his arms? Don't pray for that! Though your husband occupies another marriage bed, do not eat out your heart. Zeus will seek justice on your behalf. Don't waste away grieving for your bed-mate.

MEDEA (STILL INSIDE): [160] Oh mighty goddess Justice and lady Artemis, do you see what I suffer, who bound my husband with great oaths? I long to see him and his bride – their whole house along with them – crushed to smithereens, for the wrong they inflict on me! O father, o city of my birth, from which I was shamefully spirited away! I killed my own brother for you and you do this to me?

NURSE: [168] Do you hear her? How she prays to Justice and to Zeus, protector of oaths? My mistress's anger will never die away without leaving some mark.

Chorus: [172] If only she would meet with us and listen! If only she'd let go of her rage. I hope my heart will never exclude my friends. (TO THE NURSE) Go and bring her out here quickly! Say her friends have come to visit. Hurry before she harms those inside, for this grief is explosive.

Nurse: [184] Fine, but I doubt she will be persuaded. I'll do as you ask, though she glares like a lioness with new cubs whenever one of us approaches her. But people are perennially foolish: though men invented songs, poetry, and music to please the ears at festivals, feasts, and dinners, no mortal ever yet found a way to alleviate with mere talk the sort of human misery that brings death and disaster and overthrows houses. It would be worth your breath if woes were curable with clever words. What profit is there in singing loud and long even when the banquet is plentiful? Surely the feast is pleasure enough.

Chorus: [205] We come because we heard her calling. We heard her mournful prayers to Justice, protector of oaths, the very goddess who drove her across the sea, and we have come even if the goddess will not.

Enter Medea

Medea: [214] Women of Corinth, I have come outside lest you get the wrong idea of me. Some earn a bad reputation simply by never leaving the house. And though it is unjust when, though they have never been harmed by her, new neighbors hate the stranger before they know anything of her character, by the same token, a foreigner must also try to fit into his new city, and I wouldn't praise the man who is stand-offish and by his own churlishness deservedly brings upon himself the scorn of the citizenry.

[225] A sudden blow has fallen upon me and destroyed my life. I am ruined and, having let go all my joy of life, my friends, I want to die. For I now know well that he who was my world has been revealed the worst of men.

[230] Of all creatures who live and breathe, women are the most pathetic. First we spend ourselves to buy a husband, and then we make him master of our bodies. The second part is by far the worst. Our whole fate lies in whether we take a good husband or an evil one, for divorce brings bad reputation, yet not so bad a one as not marrying at all. Every woman, therefore, must strive to be a wife, and try to be a prophet. It is worse still for a foreign wife transported among the unfamiliar customs of a faithless husband. How can she win? If by luck we manage to make all of this work out well for us, and our husband stays, and refrains from laying on too hard with the whip hand, then we'll have a "good life." And if not, it's better we were dead.

[243] A man, irritated at the people in his home, is free to go outside, and in that way put an end to the misery that he's feeling. He goes to see a friend. But women, we stay here – we stay home. They say that women live free from danger, safe at home while they go into battle with swords. They are idiots – I would sooner go into battle three times than give birth once!

[252] Even so, our situations are not the same, wives of Corinth. This is your city – your fathers are here, your friends are here. I am abandoned. I have no city; my husband insults me; I was carried off as plunder from a foreign land, and I have no mother, no brother, nor any relatives I can turn to in my misery.

[259] And so I will ask you now for one small favour – if I tell you how I fix to punish my husband for what he is doing to me – along with his new bride and father-in-law – I ask

you to keep silent! In many things a woman is often a fearful coward – in battle perhaps, handling swords – but once wronged in her bed, in her marriage, no heart is more deadly.

CHORUS: [267] Yes: punish your husband, Medea, as you should – little wonder you are in pain. But Creon approaches, with some new message....

Enter Creon

CREON: [271] You! The one so dour and dead-set against her husband – I order you to flee this land and take your brats with you! Do not dally, for I have come to see you off myself and will not return home again until you have been escorted beyond the borders of the land I rule.

MEDEA: [276] Alas, I am destroyed, for my enemies cast me out, and there is no harbor left to me. Nevertheless I will ask: Creon, why do this to me?

CREON: [282] Because I am afraid of you. There's no need to keep it secret: I fear you will do some incredible evil to my daughter. It's hardly unreasonable, is it? You are clever and notoriously well-versed in doing evil, and you are in pain. I have heard that you boast of planning something terrible for the bride-groom, the bride, and me. So I will protect against disaster before it happens. I would rather feel your hatred now, woman, than be soft-hearted and regret it later.

MEDEA: [292] This isn't the first time, Creon, that my reputation has done me harm. No one with sense should ever allow their child to become more than acceptably clever, for thoughtfulness is often mistaken for indolence, or worse yet, feared as unnatural, inspiring hatred and jealousy. For if you bring some new wisdom to fools, they either can't see it, or consider you something special, a danger to those who were previously thought wise, and a threat to the city.

[302] And that is just what has happened to me. But I am not so terribly wise, Creon. You, afraid of me? What can I, a mere woman, do? Don't turn away from me, I beg you, for I don't have it in me to harm a king. After all, what wrong have you done me? You gave your daughter in marriage to the one whom your heart pointed to you, and if I hate my husband, you, I know, have acted wisely. Let the marriage happen – and good luck to you all. But, please, let me remain in this land, and though I have been treated badly, I will remain silent, since I am wise enough, at least, to know when I am beaten.

CREON: [316] Well, these are calm and soothing words, and I now trust you less than I did before. For a woman who is quick to anger, just like a man, is easier to ward off than one who is clever and can hold her tongue.

[321] So you have to go, immediately – not another word! The matter is settled, and there is no scheme you could devise that will allow you to remain here with us, for you are my enemy.

MEDEA: Please, I beg you, on my knees and in the name of your newly-married daughter!

CREON: [325] You waste your breath – you won't persuade me to change my mind.

MEDEA: You'll drive me out, and not even hear my entreaties?

CREON: I will not love you more than I love my own family!

MEDEA: O my dear home, my dear Colchis, how dearly I remember you now!

Creon: You might have thought of it before: after my children my homeland is by far the dearest thing in life to me.

Medea: 330 Oh you bastards, the desires of men are such a terrible evil!

Creon: Now, be fair: try to see it from my point of view.

Medea: O Zeus, do not let the man who's done these things get away with them!

Creon: Just begone from here, madwoman, and cease to be a trouble to me.

Medea: But I have troubles, too! Will no one help?

Creon: 335 You'll soon be helped outside the city gates by my attendants!

Medea (grabbing Creon by the knees): Creon, I beg you, don't do this!

Creon: You are making a spectacle of yourself to no purpose, woman.

Medea: I will go into exile! I do not ask you for a pardon.

Creon: Then why won't you let go of my hand?

Medea: 340 One day – please allow me to stay just one more day to plan where I might go find refuge for my children, since their father won't be bothered to plan for their future. Have pity on them at least! You are a father yourself! My worry isn't for me, but for my children, innocent victims of cruel misfortune!

Creon: 348 I am not tyrannical by nature, woman, yet I fear I make a mistake when I say to you: you have your day. But I warn you: if the rising sun finds you or your children within my kingdom tomorrow, then you must die. This is my final decree – it will not be changed. So stay, if you must, but one day only. You won't be given the opportunity to do the terrible things I fear.

Exit Creon

Chorus (to Medea): 357 Poor woman, with all your pains and sorrows: where will you go? What protector of refugees, what house or what land will you find? What god has made things so horrible for you, Medea, leading you into this sea of troubles?

Medea: 364 All is lost, who could deny that, but don't imagine it so for me alone. There are still pains awaiting the newlyweds, and no small ones, either, for the father of the bride.

368 Come, do you really think that I would have crawled for that man a moment ago if I were not up to something? That I'd debase myself in such a way or touched him with my hands? The fool might have thwarted me neatly, but instead he has allowed me one day to make three deaths.

376 I have so many methods at my disposal, dear friends, that I don't know which to choose. Perhaps I brighten the bridal chamber with fire, silently sneaking in to burn them in their beds. But, then, if I were caught, my death would bring pleasure to my enemies. No. A more direct approach is better, where I can use talent and kill them with poison.

386 So then, let's suppose them dead. What city will then take me in? What foreign land will have me? There's no one. Still, patience, think on it, see if some place of refuge opens to me and, if it should, I'll commit my murders slyly. But if subtlety should prove impossible, I will grab a sword and, even if I die in the act, kill them myself with sheer force and daring. For never – and I swear by the goddess I worship most of all and whom I have chosen as my accomplice, Hecate, who

lives in the dark and secret places of my home – no one breaks my heart and laughs about it afterward.

[401] I'll make the newlyweds wish they'd never met, and Corinth will rue the day it exiled Medea.

[403] Come then, woman, bring all your skill for plotting to bear and move into the shadows. You know what you must do – now is the test of your mettle, so focus on what they do to you, the daughter of a noble father and the granddaughter of the sun-god Helios.....

(TO THE CHORUS) [408] And are we not women, reputed altogether useless when there's good to be done, but none more clever when crafting evil?

CHORUS: [410] The waters of sacred rivers flow backward, Justice, and thus the world, upended. The plans of men are deceitful, pledges made in the name of the gods proved lies, but now the story will change and second-class lives be afforded honour! Respect will come at last to the female race! No longer will we be slandered.

[421] Songs of of our faithlessness by singers born long ago will cease being sung. Apollo, god of music, does not allow us the gift of song or we'd long since have sung our retort, a song against the world of men, for a true history would say as much against men as it would say in favour of women.

[431] Medea, you sailed from your father's home, passed through those clapping rocks in the sea to dwell in a foreign land, but lost to you now is the harbour of your husband, poor thing – and now this country drives you out, an exile, dishonoured.

[439] The honour of promises, the grace of oaths, is dead; respect and reverence no longer reside in great Greece – it has misted up into the sky – for Medea has no father's home in which to shelter from her troubles, and another queen rules her bed.

Enter Jason

JASON: [446] This is not the first time I've seen rage lead to irremediable evil. You could have remained in this city and in this house, if only you had accepted the decisions of your masters with some humility, but by virtue of your vitriolic tongue you've lost this city forever.

[451] It is a matter of complete indifference to me if you go around trying to convince anyone who will listen that Jason is the most evil man alive. But as to what you've been saying about the rulers – well, consider yourself lucky that you're merely exiled! I have repeatedly mediated with them on your behalf – I wanted you to stay. But you will persist in your slander of the royal family. And so you must go.

[459] Through it all, I have never forgotten my loved ones, and I am here now, woman, so you and the children do not leave without money or means. For exile brings its own troubles. And even if you hate me, I could never think badly toward you.

MEDEA: [465] You crawling maggot! You lying, worthless bastard! So you've come at last, you, the enemy of the gods, and of me, and of the whole human race? It's no mere arrogance that you have the temerity to come to me whom you have destroyed and find it in yourself to look me in the eye. No, it is illness, the worst of all diseases in men: an inability to feel shame.

[472] But it is good that you are here; it gives me the opportunity to lance the boil in my soul by speaking my piece.

[475] Let's begin at the beginning, when I saved

you, just as every man who sailed with you on the Argo knows that I saved you. I saved you when you were sent to tame the fire-breathing bulls with a harness and had to sow the deadly seeds. And that serpent, the one who never slept and guarded the Golden Fleece with its twisting coils – I killed it and lit your way to safety.

483 I betrayed my father and my house, and came with you to Iolcus, filled more with passion than wisdom. I killed Pelias, gave him the most painful of deaths – at the hands of his own daughters. I destroyed his entire house, and in return, asshole, you betray me and take a new bride, despite your children, without whom your desire for this new marriage would perhaps be forgivable.

492 But henceforth the trust that people place in vows and oaths is dead. I don't know if you think the old gods no longer rule, or you've convinced yourself that new laws have been established for mankind, but you know full well that you have broken your oath to me. To hell with this right hand of mine, which you so often held; to hell with these knees of mine – tickled by you, serpent – my faith in you has been my downfall.

499 But, let's chat like old friends – what good your friendship has ever done me I don't know, but still, by all means, let us shoot the fucking breeze. For nothing you can possibly say will lighten the blackening of your name. But do advise me, husband – tell me where I should go. Perhaps I should return to my father's home and my own country? Oh, except I betrayed it for you. Or perhaps I should go to the poor daughters of Pelias? They'll be so pleased to welcome his murderer into their home.

506 That's how things stand for me now – I'm hated by those dearest to me, and even the strangers who might have succored me have become my enemies – all my bridges have been burnt, on your account. Still, as thanks, you've made me appear the luckiest of women in the eyes of these Greek ladies you see before you, for what a paragon you have turned out to be. What does it matter, therefore, if I am made an exile, driven out, friendless, alone but for your children? That will make a fine advertisement for the new bridegroom, that his children and the wife who saved him should be reduced to wandering the world as beggars!

516 O Zeus, you made it so simple to distinguish real gold from fake – why can't a woman as easily bite a man to tell a good one from a bad?

Chorus: 520 Rage wounds deep when love becomes hate.

Jason: 522 It seems I must not be a poor speaker, but like a skilled sailor use the upmost edges of the sail that I might weather your stormy tongue, woman. But as you build up the great service you've done me, I say that it was Aphrodite alone of all the gods and men who made my voyage successful and saw me here safe. You do have a clever mind, but simply cannot wrap it around the fact that it was Eros who forced you to save me with his sure arrows. But why split hairs – you did help me, it's true. However, in saving me you gained much more than you gave me: listen.

536 First of all, instead of a barbarian land you now live in Greece and you know justice and the use of laws that do now come with force. All the Greeks could see that you are wise so you have become famous – but if you lived far away at the ends of the earth, nobody would have heard of you. As for me, I wouldn't want

to have gold in my house or to be able to sing more sweetly than Orpheus if I couldn't develop some level of fame.

⁵⁴⁵ But enough about me – you're the one who started this debate. As for the infamy you shower on me for my upcoming nuptials, allow me to demonstrate how clever I've been in the matter, and how longsighted, and then you'll see what a friend I've been both to you and my children. Wait – hear me out! When I came to Corinth from the country of Iolcus, I dragged with me many seemingly insoluble difficulties: what more miraculous cure for all this could I, an exile, find than to marry the daughter of the king? It isn't – as you complain – that I was somehow overcome with lust for this new bride of mine, or that I had some great desire to sire more children with her. The children I had were just fine.

⁵⁵⁹ No, the real reason was – listen – so that we might live decently and without privation, because I know too well that a friend in need is a friend to avoid. I wanted to raise our children in a manner befitting my background and family, and by producing brothers for your sons I planned to put them all on an equal footing and bind the family together, that we would prosper.

⁵⁶⁵ Think – what need do I have of more children? But the ones I have now will profit by the existence of the ones soon to come. Am I wrong? You would see it my way, if you weren't blinded by rage at having to vacate the marriage bed.

⁵⁶⁹ Women always think life is perfect if everything goes well in the bedroom, and when your romantic life is suffering you become enemies even to those nearest and dearest to you. By Zeus, there should be some other way for mortals to reproduce – if there were no female race there wouldn't be such misery for men.

Chorus: ⁵⁷⁶ A very pretty justification you have made for yourself, Jason, but it seems to us – though you may not wish to hear it – that it does not change the fact of your betrayal.

Medea: ⁵⁷⁹ Perhaps it's just me, but I think a smooth talker merits even greater punishment for his dangerous belief that rhetoric somehow justifies any evil he might choose to commit. He talks so sweetly he even convinces himself, and then what injustice will he not stoop to? But he is not so clever, really.

⁵⁸⁴ You can end your little show now, for the final word is this – if you owed me nothing you would have talked to me first and persuaded me your new marriage was the thing to do, and not kept it secret from your loved ones.

Jason: ⁵⁸⁸ Oh, I can see it all now. And I suppose you'd be happy with such a speech, when even now you can't hold back your acid tongue?

Medea: ⁵⁹¹ That's not what stopped you: your status was suffering because you were set to grow old tied to a barbarian wife.

Jason: ⁵⁹³ I have told you, it was never about the woman: I wanted to sire royal brothers for my children and thereby keep everyone safe.

Medea: I have no desire for a "happy" life that blasts my heart.

Jason: ⁶⁰⁰ Then change your desire and be wise as your reputation, Medea. Hope and pray that you never have to do a good thing that looks like evil, and stop feeling sorry for yourself when you're actually quite lucky.

Medea: ⁶⁰³ Go on, then, hero – keep speaking to me as if I were feeble-minded – since you have somewhere to go afterward and someone waiting for you there; as for me, I am alone and about to be a wanderer.

Jason: ⁶⁰⁵ You brought it upon yourself – don't blame anyone else!

Medea: Am I set to marry someone else, then?

Jason: No, you merely threatened the royal family.

Medea: And I intend to be a curse on your house as well!

Jason: ⁶⁰⁹ Stop – I'm not going to waste any more breath on this. If you want money, tell me now. I'm prepared to be generous, and also to write letters to foreigners who might aid you. Woman, you'd be a fool not to accept these things. Let go your anger.

Medea: ⁶¹⁶ I desire neither your magnanimity nor your friends. I want nothing from you. The gifts of an evil man have no value.

Jason: ⁶¹⁹ Fine. I call upon the gods to witness that I was ready and eager to help both you and the children, but you belligerently pushed me away so as to suffer all the more.

Medea: ⁶²³ Go! Run back to your new bride! You must be overwhelmed with desire, having been away from her for so long now! Go and have your marriage! But – with the help of the gods – you may yet find that you've taken sorrow into your bed.

Exit Jason

Chorus: ⁶²⁹ When desire comes on men untempered it does them no credit, but when Aphrodite comes softly, there is no goddess so fair. Please, o goddess, never fire at us your golden arrows, unerringly aimed and tipped with your desire, but let Wisdom, most noble of gods, befriend us, and prevent those troubling shafts ever deranging us with lust for adultery, and preserve us from anger, or strife. Grant us cool contemplation in choosing our mates so that we might build marriage beds rather than battlefields. For battlefields are the proper place for arrows.

⁶⁴⁴ O fatherland, our home, grant we may never go into exile, adrift in a life of helpless suffering. Before that let us be laid low, for in death there is nothing worse than the loss of one's native land. We have seen it and have no need to be told twice – no city, no friend, will pity you nor share your burden. Let the man die without laurels who does not honour his friends or open his heart. He will never be a friend of mine!

Enter Aegeus

Aegeus: ⁶⁶³ Medea, how good to see you!

Medea: ⁶⁶⁵ Why, it's lovely to see you as well, wise Aegeus, son of Pandion. How do you come to be passing through Corinth?

Aegeus: Just passing through, on my way back from the oracle at Delphi.

Medea: Why should you have traveled to the center of the world where Apollo gives his prophecies?

Aegeus: I wanted to know how I might become a father.

Medea: ⁶⁷⁰ Heavens, no children yet?

Aegeus: No, still childless, by some cruel twist of fate.

Medea: Are you married?

Aegeus: Yes, I have a wife.

Medea: What did Apollo tell you?

Aegeus: ⁶⁷⁵ Words too clever for a man like me to understand.

Medea: Is it permissible for me to know the answer the god gave you?

Aegeus: Of course: I could use a clever mind like yours.

Medea: What did he say, then?

Aegeus: He said "not to uncork the wine-skin's spout…."

Medea: ⁶⁸⁰ Until you do what, or come to what place?

Aegeus: "Until I come to the home of my father once again."

Medea: Then why come to Corinth?

Aegeus: Pittheus lives here. You know, the king of Troezen.

Medea: Yes, the son of Pelops, and he is most wise, or so they say.

Aegeus: ⁶⁸⁵ I thought to discuss the oracle with him.

Medea: Good idea – by all accounts he sounds the ideal man for the job.

Aegeus: And the dearest to me of all my friends in arms.

Medea: Well, I hope you find what you're looking for.

Aegeus: But…your eyes – have you been crying, my dear?

Medea: ⁶⁹⁰ Aegeus, my husband is the worst man living.

Aegeus: What's this now? Please, tell me what's troubling you.

Medea: Jason has wronged me without cause.

Aegeus: What on earth has he done?

Medea: He has taken another woman as his wife.

Aegeus: ⁶⁹⁵ Surely he wouldn't do so shameful a thing?

Medea: Oh, he's done it. His old loves are now dishonored.

Aegeus: Did he fall in love, or did you start to hate your marriage-bed?

Medea: Oh, he's very much in love – traitor to his family –

Aegeus: So then let him go if he's so great an ass.

Medea: ⁷⁰⁰ He's very much in love with the idea of marrying into a royal family.

Aegeus: But who has given them his daughter? Please finish your story.

Medea: Creon, who rules the land of Corinth.

Aegeus: Then it's understandable that you should be upset, woman.

Medea: Yes. I'm ruined. I'm even being kicked out of this city.

Aegeus: ⁷⁰⁵ Who by? Here is an all new disaster!

Medea: Creon exiled me from Corinth himself.

Aegeus: And Jason let it happen? I don't approve of that at all!

Medea: ⁷⁰⁸ He says he doesn't approve, either, yet he does nothing to oppose it. I beg you, Aegeus, holding you by your knees – I am your servant and suppliant – for pity's sake don't watch me forced into lonely exile, but let me come into your country and take me into your home!

⁷¹⁴ If you do this for me, then with the help of the gods your desire for children may come true, and you will die a happy man. You don't know how great a treasure you've uncovered this day, for I can arrange it that you'll be able to have children. I know the drugs that can make it happen.

Aegeus: ⁷¹⁹ Of the many reasons I am happy to do you this favour, first among them is that it would be the will of the gods. And, then, the children whose birth you've predicted for me – for in that matter I am completely at a loss.

⁷²⁵ So this is how I see it – I cannot smuggle you out of this land, but if you can make it as far as my country, I will take you in and never give you over to anyone. But you'll have to get there on your own, for I would be blameless in the eyes of my friends and neighbours.

Medea: ⁷³¹ That seems reasonable, and if you just offer some pledge or oath to me I'll be well pleased.

Aegeus: You don't trust me? Is my word not enough?

Medea: ⁷³⁴ Oh, I trust you, I do. But both the houses of Pelias and Creon are my enemies, and if you are bound by an oath I am guaranteed you will not give me up if they try to drag me out of your land. You might be tempted to listen to their entreaties, for they have both riches and royal power, and you thus might back out of a mere promise that is not sealed with an oath to the gods.

Aegeus: ⁷⁴¹ There's a great deal of foresight in your words. Yes, if you wish, I'd be happy to give you an oath. In fact, it will be a safety net for me, since I can hold it out to your enemies as a pretext for protecting you. So, there it is: name your gods!

Medea: ⁷⁴⁶ I ask you to swear by the Earth, by Helios – the Sun – the father of my father, and every other god in addition to those ones.

Aegeus: But to what, exactly, am I contracting? Name it.

Medea: ⁷⁴⁹ Never to drive me out of your land, nor as long as you live to let someone else drag me.

Aegeus: I swear by the Earth, by the bright light of Helios, and by all the gods, to do exactly as you demand.

Medea: That's enough – and what do you agree to suffer if you don't abide by your oath?

Aegeus: ⁷⁵⁵ The kinds of things that happen to evil men.

Medea: Good then, it's settled. Have a safe journey and I will see you soon – after I have done what I need to do and got what I want.

Chorus (to Aegeus): ⁷⁵⁹ May Hermes, lord and guide, son of Maia, bring you home, and may you quickly accomplish your purpose, since in our judgment you are a noble man, Aegeus.

Exit Aegeus

Medea: ⁷⁶⁴ O Zeus and the Justice of Zeus and light of the sun! Now, my friends, sweet victory over my enemies will be mine. Now I have hope. This man has provided an answer to my greatest problem – safe harbour – and after my plot has been carried out I shall turn sail directly to him and the town and city of Pallas Athena.

⁷⁷² Now let me tell you all that I have in mind. But you won't find it pleasant.

⁷⁷⁴ I'll send one of my servants to Jason to beg him back to see me face-to-face. When he comes I'll mollify him, tell him I see everything now and understand why he has done what he has done, that he thought it through carefully to the end and did only what was best for us all when he betrayed me.

⁷⁸¹ Then I'll ask him to let my children stay here, not because I wish to leave them to be mocked by my enemies in an enemy land, but rather so that I may kill their step-mother by guile.

⁷⁸⁴ I'll send them off with gifts for the bride in

their little hands – a finely-woven dress and a golden crown – begging that they not be sent into exile. And when she wears the dress and touches it to her skin, she will die horribly, as will anyone who tries to comfort her, for I will have treated dress and crown with deadly poison.

[790] But let's not speak of this any further, for it leads inevitably to the deed that must be done next – I will have to kill my children. No-one will stop me from doing this and no-one will take them from me.

[793] Then, when I have destroyed the entire house of Jason, I will leave this land, in flight from the charge of murdering my children and having dared to do the most unspeakable deeds. For, my friends, I will not allow my enemies to laugh at me. No, that will never happen.

[797] There it is, then – what reason is there anymore for me to live? I have neither a country nor a home, nor a refuge from my own troubles. I erred fatally in leaving behind the house of my father and trusting the word of a Greek man. But he will receive his just reward very soon now, with the help of the gods.

[803] He'll never see the children he had of me again after today, nor will he have new ones with his new bride. And I will not be remembered as a weak woman, but a terrible woman, who was as good a friend as she was hateful an enemy. The lives of such people have the greatest fame.

Chorus: [811] Now that you have told us what you have in mind, and though we sincerely wish to help you, we also want to keep the laws of men, and so we beg you now: put an end to your scheme.

Medea: [814] No, this is as it must be. I understand your horror, but you would understand me better if all that has happened to me had been done to you.

Chorus: But, woman, how can you kill your own children?

Medea: Because it is the thing that will hurt my husband most.

Chorus: But you'll live to regret it, and be the sorriest of women.

Medea: [819] But I will live with it. Such talk is a waste of time: now the deed. (To the Nurse) Go now and bring Jason to me, for you are the one I trust the most, but tell him nothing of what I have in store, since you are a woman and care for me.

Chorus: [824] The Athenians have long been happy children of the blessed gods who sprung from a sacred, never conquered land, fed on the most glorious wisdom, gracefully stepping through the brightest of skies where it is said that the nine Muses Gave birth to golden-haired Harmony.

[835] A song is sung of how Aphrodite took water from the clear streams of Cephisus and breathed upon the land the gentle sweet breezes, and how, as she always wears a fragrant garland of roses in her hair, the Desires accompany her as the companions of Wisdom, inspiring all forms of virtue.

[846] How then will this city of sacred rivers and streams, the city that gives safe protection to friends, welcome you, the killer of children, the unholy one? Think of what it means to stab your children, think of what manner of murder you intend to commit! We beg at your knees, by all that is holy – don't kill your children!

[856] Where will you find the resolve, either of heart or of hand, to inflict horror, pain and destruction on your own babies? How will you look on their faces and see there their coming deaths without sobbing? And when they fall down begging before you, surely you will be unable to wash your hands in their blood.

Enter Jason

JASON: [866] I've come as you've asked, though you abuse me. So tell me, woman, what can I do for you now?

MEDEA: [869] Jason, please forgive me for all of the things I said before. Surely you can't have forgotten my moods; we have shared so many loving memories together. I have been thinking about everything I said to you and finally I realize that I'm such a stupid woman! Why do I allow my temper to make me curse those who only have my best interests at heart? Why cast myself as an enemy to the rulers of this land and to my husband, who is only doing what is best for us all by marrying the daughter of the king and producing royal brothers for our children? Should I not just let go of my anger? What's wrong with me? Haven't the gods given enough gifts to me already? Don't I already have children? Don't I know that we've been exiled and that we need friends right now?

[882] I see now that I have been very foolish, that my anger was foolish, and that I should listen to good advice. Now I am on your side – I agree that you have made a wise decision and marry for the benefit of us all. I should have been helping you all along with your plans, bringing all my considerable will to bear to make these plans happen. I should have been standing by the bed and counseling you how best to make love to your new bride. But we women are what we are – I won't say bad.

Still, what's the sense in you avenging my stupidity with evil? Forgive me – I was foolish, but now I have had a change of heart.

[894] Children, come out of the house, embrace your father and talk to him for me!

Enter the Children

[895] Put aside your hurt feelings, as your mother has, and let us all be friends again. We've made peace; all anger is gone. Take our hands – there.

[899] Oh, but the future looms large! Will our children have the opportunity to stretch out their own arms like this after a long life? I fear I'm about to start crying again, children – at last I have ended this long fight with your father. Comes, let me wet your tender cheeks with my tears.

CHORUS: [906] Tears are welling up in our eyes, too – dare we hope that things go for the better now and not for the worse?

JASON: [908] What you have just said cheers me, woman, and if I am honest I can't really blame you for what you said before. It's normal for a woman to get angry when her husband brings a new wife into the home. But now your heart has seen the wisdom in what I have done, as any sensible woman would have, in time.

[914] As for you, my boys, your father hasn't been asleep, but I have come up with a plan that will make you safe, if the gods are kind, and I think that, with your future brothers, you'll live to be the leading citizens of Corinth. You two just worry about growing up strong, and your father and whichever of the gods is on our side will take care of the rest, and one day you'll triumph your father's enemies.

[922] But you, Medea, why do you turn away?

Are you crying? Aren't you happy with what I just said?

Medea: ⁹²⁵ Oh, it's nothing, really – I'm just thinking about the children.

Jason: But why? I'm going to see that they are well provided for.

Medea: I know you will. Women are women: we cry a lot.

Jason: Of course – but so many tears?

Medea: ⁹²⁵ It's just that I gave birth to these children, and when you expressed the hope that they would live long and healthy lives I was filled with sadness, wondering if it could happen…

⁹³² But as to the reasons I asked you to come to me. I realize now that my exile is the best solution for all concerned. I won't be in your way or a worry to those who rule this country, for I have made myself an enemy to them. I go willingly. But so that your children can be raised by the hand of their father, you should ask Creon that they be allowed to stay here with you.

Jason: ⁹⁴¹ I don't know if I can convince him, but I will try.

Medea: Push your wife to ask her father.

Jason: That is a good idea – she's a woman, after all, so I should be able to persuade her.

Medea: ⁹⁴⁵ Yes, if she's a woman like the rest of us, she'll be easy to sway. In fact, I'll help you in this. I'll send the children to her carrying the most beautiful gifts the world has ever seen, a finely-woven dress and a golden crown – I'll get a servant to bring them here quickly – and she'll be doubly happy, having won you – the best of all men – as a bed-mate, and because she'll wear the garments that Helios, the Sun-god, father of my father, once gave to his children.

⁹⁵⁷ Boys, take these wedding gifts into your hands and convey them to the lucky bride – how could she resist them?

Jason: ⁹⁵⁹ But why give away your lovely things? You need them more than she does. Do you think a royal princess has any need of either gold or dresses? Don't throw them away, for if this woman sees me at all, surely she'll value me much more than money.

Medea: ⁹⁶⁴ I won't hear a word of it. They do say that gifts can persuade even the gods, and gold is certainly worth more to mortals than words. She has good fortune, the gods look on her and make her even better off, she is young, is a princess – and to save my children from exile I'd give my own life, let alone gold.

⁹⁶⁹ Go, children, to that wealthy house, and bow down before your new mother, the woman who now rules me. Ask her to spare you exile, give her these gifts, and be sure that she takes them from you with her own hands – this part is important.

⁹⁷⁴ Go now, quick as you can – do a good job for mother and bring back the good news she has been longing to hear!

Exit Jason, the Tutor, and the Children

Chorus: ⁹⁷⁶ No longer is there any hope for the children's lives – they are gone, already murdered. The bride will accept the golden crown, her own destruction, and on her golden hair she will settle the gift of Death with her very own hands. The unholy beauty of the dress will persuade her to wear it, but she will be dressed as bride for the dead below.

⁹⁹⁰ And you, poor man, are both a new husband and curse to the royal family. You have no idea that you are bringing about the

destruction of your sons and new wife. Foolish man! Prepare to learn just how far you've wandered from the life you planned!

⁹⁹⁶ We also mourn your grief, poor mother of children you will murder because their father broke the marriage law and took another woman into your bed.

Enter the Tutor with the Children

Tutor: ¹⁰⁰² Ma'am, your sons have been spared exile. The royal bride was happy to take the gifts from them, and now there's peace between her and your children.

¹⁰⁰⁵ But what's this? Why the long face when everything is going to plan? Why do you turn your face away? Aren't you happy to hear my news?

Medea: O gods!.....

Tutor: Your reaction doesn't match what I just told you.

Medea: Gods!....

Tutor: ¹⁰⁰⁹ Surely I have not brought you bad news without realizing? Was I wrong to think this what you wanted?

Medea: You've brought the message I wanted to hear – I can't blame you.

Tutor: But then why is your gaze fixed upon the ground and why are you crying?

Medea: I have to weep like this, old man, for after much planning the gods and I have brought about this wicked thing.

Tutor: ¹⁰¹⁵ Don't worry, mistress: one day you'll return here, with the children's help.

Medea: There can be no coming back for me, old man, or for certain others.

Tutor: You know, you're not the only woman ever to have been separated from her children. Neither divine wrath nor divine suffering are for you. As you are human, you should bear your troubles lightly.

Medea: ¹⁰¹⁹ Yes, yes – that's exactly what I'll do. But you go inside now and give the children whatever they need to get them through the day.

Exit Tutor

¹⁰²¹ Oh my lovely boys, you have a city and a home now, and you can always live here, deprived of your mother, left behind in her misery.

¹⁰²⁴ I'll go away into another land where I will miss seeing you prosper, and will not be there to make the plans for your weddings, or prepare your brides, or raise your wedding torches.

¹⁰²⁸ O gods, my willfulness has made me so miserable! My dears, raising you was a waste of time – a waste to wear myself down with the effort. And so too were wasted the harsh labour pains that I endured in your births. Silly me – once I put such great hopes in you, that you would care for me when I am old and bury me when I die, the envy of everyone.

¹⁰³⁶ Now that sweet future is gone from me. Ripped apart from the two of you I'll lead a life of hardship and pain, and you, you will never see your dear mother again, after you leave for your new life.

¹⁰⁴⁰ Why are you looking at me like that, my children? Why are you smiling this final smile?

¹⁰⁴² Oh gods, what will I do? O women, looking into the bright eyes of my children my courage leaves.

¹⁰⁴⁴ I cannot do this thing – I can't. I need to forget my old plan – I'll take them with me

from this place. Why on earth would I harm them to harm their father when it would make me suffer twice as much as him? No, I can't…

[1048] I can't let my enemies laugh at me. I must do this thing. I can't be a weak woman, and allow loving thoughts to creep into my head.

[1053] Go into the house now, my loves – mother will be with you in a moment. But he for whom it is not right to attend my sacrifice – Jason – let him remain outside our home until it is done. My hand does not shake, and I will not weaken.

[1056] Gods help me… Don't let yourself do this, Medea – listen to what your heart is telling you and let them be, poor girl. Spare your children! If you take them with you to Athens, to live there with you, they will make you happy.

[1059] What is this drivel? I swear by the avenging demons in Hades below that sooner than see my babes mocked by my enemies I will see them die – and since they must die, it by my hand, because I am the one who gave birth to them.

[1065] In any case, the deed is done – the princess is doomed. Already the crown is on her head and the dress upon her body, which is dying – this I know for fact – and since I am about to set out on the cruelest of roads, and send my children out another, more painful still, I must speak to them one more time.

[1071] Boys, each of you give your right hand to mother so that she may kiss it. Oh your dear hands, your lips and mouths so dear to me, both of you born looking so noble and beautiful, may you forever be happy, though it must happen over there. For your father destroyed your chances of happiness here.

[1074] Oh the sweet touch of my children, your soft skin and sweet breath! You must go in – go, inside the house! I can't look at you anymore! So overwhelmed am I by the darkness that surrounds me.

Exit the Children

[1078] I am aware that what I am about to do is evil, but my anger toward Jason is so intense that it informs my every plan, and it is just this species of anger that will always cause the greatest harm to those who live and die.

Chorus: [1081] Often we, too, have embraced dark thoughts, and seen greater troubles than woman should endure – but we always found a way through it. For women also have a Muse who travels with us and makes us wise. Though perhaps she does not speak to all of us, and perhaps only one in a great many heeds all that the Muse says. That lucky women is barren, and much happier than parents, for the childless know neither the pleasure nor the pains children bring, miss not the former nor suffer the latter.

[1098] But those in whose homes sweet children are born and raised are worn down by constant worry. First they fret about how to feed and raise them well, and then how to leave them some savings, never knowing for sure if the recipients of all their toil will turn out to have been worthy.

[1105] But the very worst possibility, and the one from which none of us can be secure, is the danger that even if we raise them well and our children come of age – no matter how good they are – some god will snap his fingers and Death will hurry them off to Hades before you go yourself. How can it be right that, on top of all that we endure for our children's sake, the gods could add this most intolerable pain?

MEDEA: [1116] Well, ladies, it seems forever that I have been watching and waiting to find out what has happened at the palace. And finally I see one of Jason's servants coming in this direction. His angry breathing suggests he has bad news.

Enter the Messenger

MESSENGER: [1121] O Medea, you've done something horrible. You've broken the law, and now you must flee. Run for your life, in whatever way you can, ship or chariot!

MEDEA: And why, pray tell, would I need to flee?

MESSENGER: [1125] The princess has died, along with her father, thanks to your skill with poison.

MEDEA: O that is excellent news! Thank you, my friend: from this point forward you are always welcome in my home!

MESSENGER: [1129] What are you saying? Are you mad, woman? You've destroyed the royal family and you rejoice?

MEDEA: [1132] I'll be happy to answer any questions you wish to put to me, but first things first: how did they die? And hold nothing back, for you'll give me double the amount of pleasure if they went screaming.

MESSENGER: [1136] When your two children arrived with their father at the rooms of the new bride, those of us servants who pitied your troubles were delighted by the news going around that you and your husband had stopped fighting and were friends again.

[1141] One of us kissed the children's hands, another their blonde hair, and I myself, out of joy, followed them in to their meeting with the new bride. My mistress, whom we now pity instead of you, at first saw only Jason, but when she noticed the children she was upset and turned away in anger. Your husband, however, tried to calm her by saying to her – "Please don't despise my dear ones. Please, don't be angry: turn your head this way again. Consider the loved ones of your husband as if they are your own, and take these gifts and ask your father not to send my children into exile. Do it for me, please."

[1156] Well, when she saw the dress, she couldn't resist – she capitulated completely to her husband's wishes, and before the boys and their father had gone too far away from the palace she had slipped the garment on, placed the golden crown atop her head, and skipped lightly about the house, thrilled with the gifts, checking herself in the mirror again and again to be sure they were properly on.

[1167] What happened next was horrible to see. Suddenly she paled and trembled and stumbled sideways, her limbs and body shaking, and just managed to fall into her chair rather than the ground.

[1171] One of the old maidservants, thinking the girl had had the good fortune to be struck by a frenzy sent from Eros, hooted joyfully, but as soon as she saw the white foam on the girl's lips – eyes rolling in her head, blood fleeing her face – then the cry was changed to a shriek. Directly another servant ran to her father and another ran to the bridegroom to tell him what was happening. The whole house was filled with the sound of people running.

[1181] A good racer might have had time to complete the final sprint to the finish line before the poor girl broke her silence, opened her eyes wide, and let forth a terrible groan. For she was doubly assaulted, the golden crown sitting on her head emitting a torrent of devouring fire, and that beautiful dress, the gift of your children, eating away at her delicate flesh.

1190 She sprang from her chair all on fire, shaking her head this way and that, trying to throw the crown, but its gold binding held fast and when she shook her hair the flames rose up twice as powerful as before.

1195 She fell to the floor consumed, unrecognizable to anyone but a parent. From the top of her head the blood was flowing down mixed together with fire, and the flesh fell away from her bones just as the pitch flows down the pine – she was ripped apart by the invisible power of your poison. It was so horrible, I tell you, we were all too afraid to touch her body, when her father, poor man, unaware of the the miseries she had just endured, burst into the room and immediately gathered her corpse to him. As he kissed her he said, "My poor child, what god has murdered and taken you from me, I wish that I could die along with you, my daughter!"

1211 But when he wanted to lift his old body from hers, he found himself attached to her fine dress as surely as the ivy clings to walls. It was a terrible struggle. He tried to get to his knees, but her body held him fast, and when he violently recoiled his old flesh ripped away from his bones. And finally the poor old man died – how could he survive?

1220 They are there still, father and daughter, side by side, dead corpses, a disaster that would make anyone cry.

1222 As to how this affects you, why speculate – you are certain to find out in a moment. I have long thought that our lives are but shadows, and I'm afraid that those who appear clever – those crafters of words – will bring upon themselves greater punishments along with their greater rewards. For one mortal can never truly be happier than another: one may appear luckier or be richer, but these things have a way of evening out.

Chorus: 1231 It certainly seems that some just god has decided to fasten many disasters to Jason today. O poor daughter of Creon, how we feel for you, gone into the halls of Hades a new bride, who made the mistake of marrying Jason.

Medea: 1236 Ladies, my mind is set for the deed – to slay the children with speed and then flee this land. I cannot delay, it would only give my enemies a chance to harm them with less gentle hands. So there it is: they have to die to be protected, and I must be the one to kill them, since I am their loving mother.

1242 Come my heart, arm yourself! Why hesitate when evil is inevitable? Come on! O my bloody hand, take the sword, take it and hurry toward the miserable final consequence of all life!

1246 Don't you dare falter! Don't you dare remember that they are your own flesh, or how dear they are to you, or how you bore them! For this short period forget that they are yours. You can weep forever, afterward.

Chorus: 1251 O bright light of Helios, look down on this cursed woman before she lays murderous hands on her children. They are born of your golden race! They are your grandchildren! Is the blood of your blood to be spilled on account of something a mortal has done? It will happen unless you, o divinely-inspired light, drive this maddened Fury from her house!

1261 The pains you suffered in giving birth will be wasted, Medea! The time spent raising them till now will have been wasted time! You who threaded the unfriendly strait and the clashing rocks! O poor woman, why is your mind so filled with anger that one murder follows so quick upon another? Murder within a family is a stain on us all, and vengeance pursues the perpetrator – sorrows delivered to your door by the gods themselves!

The Children (from inside): Help us! Help!

Chorus: ¹²⁷³ Do you hear the babes shouting? O terrible and cursed woman!

First Child (from inside): What should we do? Where can any flee to evade the blades of home?

Second Child (from inside): Brother, we are done for!

Chorus: Should we enter? Surely we should intervene…

First Child (from inside): In the name of the gods, help us, someone!

Second Child (from inside): She is killing us!

Chorus: ¹²⁸⁰ O you evil woman, she must be made of stone or iron who would wield the scythe that harvests the children she raised.

¹²⁸² We've only heard of one woman before this who raised her hand against her own – Ino, driven mad by the gods when the wife of Zeus banished her to wander. The poor woman flung herself into the sea and died along with her two children. What, I ask you, could be more horrible than that? Only her survival. O the many pains of love that women feel. They've brought so much evil to mankind!

Enter Jason

Jason: ¹²⁹² Hey you women who are standing in front of this house! Is the bitch inside, or already gone? She would have to go beneath the earth or sprout wings and fly to Heaven to escape what she has done in this place! Did she suppose that she could murder the rulers of the land and fly the palace without punishment? But it is the children I fear for. She will die badly at the hands of those she has injured still among the living, but I will save my sons despite them.

Chorus: ¹³⁰⁶ O you poor man, you don't know how wrong you are, or you'd never have come here.

Jason: What? Does she mean to kill me, too, then?

Chorus: Your children are dead: their mother has murdered them.

Jason: ¹³¹⁰ O my gods – what are you saying? Then she has killed me, after all.

Chorus: There is nothing you can do now.

Jason: But where? Are they in the house?

Chorus: If you open the doors, you'll see the bodies.

Jason: ¹³¹⁴ Servants, I order you to unlock these doors! Open them so that I can see my boys, and pay her in kind!

Enter Medea from above on a chariot drawn by winged dragons; in the chariot with Medea are the bodies of the Children

Medea: ¹³¹⁷ Why break down the doors, searching for bodies and the one who killed them? Here I am: if you want something, just say it – if you dare – but you will never lay a hand on me, for just look at the chariot that my grandfather Helios loaned me to protect me from my enemies.

Jason: ¹³²³ Hateful cunt, in one fell swoop you have become the enemy of me, the gods, and the whole human race. What evil is in you that you would thrust a sword into your own children simply to make me childless – and still dare show your face to the day? I would see you dead!

¹³²⁹ Finally I understand you. I didn't when I brought you out of your barbarian land and led you to civilisation, a bitch who betrayed her father and the land that produced and raised you. The gods have cursed me when by rights they should be cursing you, who killed your own brother before stepping lightly aboard the beautiful Argo.

¹³³⁶ That was when you learned to kill – with the death of your brother. And then you had my children, and killed them, too, when our marriage was over. No Greek woman would ever have dared do something like this, and yet I chose you over any of them to be my wife, in return for which you've taken back everything you ever gave me, leaving nothing but bitter ruin and hate. You're no woman but a lioness, an animal, more monstrous than Scylla with her many heads. But I won't dent you with ten thousand insults – your inhumanity makes you invulnerable!

¹³⁴⁶ Away with you, then, child killer – murderess! It's my fate now to mourn. I'll never enjoy my new bride nor ever look upon my children again – I have lost them all.

Medea: ¹³⁵¹ I would answer your charges point for point if father Zeus didn't already know all that I sacrificed for you, and how you treated me in return. You were never going to mock our bed and then lead a pleasant life laughing at me. Nor were the princess and her father, the one who made this marriage for you, going to send me into exile unanswered.

¹³⁵⁸ So call me a lioness, or a monster who lives in the caves and eats passers-by. I did what I had to – returned pain for pain.

Jason: ¹³⁶¹ But you feel it, too: you share in this grief!

Medea: Understand this: my pain is less knowing you will never smile again at the thought of me.

Jason: O children, what an evil mother you had!

Medea: O children, you died of your father's sickness.

Jason: ¹³⁶⁵ But it wasn't my hand that killed them!

Medea: That's right, it was your arrogance!

Jason: Do you really think it right to kill them because of a marriage?

Medea: Do you really think there is anything more important to a woman?

Jason: Well, it would be fine for a sane woman – but you find everything to be a disaster.

Medea: ¹³⁷⁰ Whatever. Your children are dead: you didn't feel for me, but this you can hardly help but feel.

Jason: But they will live, I hope, as spirits that haunt you.

Medea: The gods know which of us struck the first blow.

Jason: Yes, and they know that your soul is evil!

Medea: Vomit your bile, your piteous, canine whining!

Jason: ¹³⁷⁵ I loathe the sound of you! It will be good for us to finally be finished with each other!

Medea: Will it? Then tell me how, because I want that, too!

Jason: Just let me bury the bodies of my children so I can mourn them!

Medea: [1378] No, that will never happen, since I am going to bury them myself in Hera's shrine up on the cliff. That way none of my enemies will dare insult them by tearing up their graves – you see, I'm always thinking – and up there I'll establish a holy festival and feast, and bring in rituals as an eternal memorial to unholy murder.

[1384] Myself, I am going to the land of Athens, where I will live with king Aegeus, the son of Pandion. As for you, since you are so loathsome and small, it is fitting that your death will be bitter and pathetic as well, struck on the head by a piece of the Argo – a fitting conclusion to our marriage.

Jason: [1389] I only pray that the Fury that punishes child-murderers, and the goddess Justice as well, join forces to destroy you!

Medea: And what god will heed your prayer – oath-breaker – betrayer?

Jason: And you think they will answer you, polluted with child murder?

Medea: Go bury your whore!

Jason: [1395] I'll go to her now – alone and childless.

Medea: Your sadness is only beginning – it will ripen as you age!

Jason: O my dear children!

Medea: Dear to their mother, not to you!

Jason: She who killed them!

Medea: To cause you pain!

Jason: [1399] All that I have lost, if I could just once more hold and kiss the faces of my sons!

Medea: Now you want to talk to them, now you want to hold them, when before you tossed them away.

Jason: In the name of the gods, please let me touch them!

Medea: No, there's no chance of that - save your breath.

Jason: [1405] Zeus, do you hear how I am rejected and how I am treated by this hateful, polluted, child-killing bitch?

[1408] But though you allowed it to happen I will weep and call on all the gods to witness – it would have been better for me if they had never been born than to live to see them murdered.

Medea flies away in her chariot, taking the bodies of the Children with her

Chorus: [1415] Zeus and the court of Olympians sometimes rule in ways that may surprise us. Often we don't get the verdict we anticipate. But whatever happens is their will, so that must be what happened here...

Translated from the Greek by Stephen Russell, PhD

English by Jonathan Allen

Chapter 12
Sophocles
The Women of Trachis
("The Trachiniae")

The Story: This play focuses on the death of Heracles.

Characters

Deianira
Nurse
Hyllus
Chorus (Women of Trachis)

Messenger
Lichas, the Herald of Heracles
Doctor
Heracles

Scene: This play takes place in Trachis, in front of the house of Heracles and Deianira

Enter Deianira and her Nurse

Deianira: There is an old saying that is well known among men, which states that you can't judge whether a man's life is happy until he has reached his death – before that time you can only speak of good and bad fortune. However, even though this is true, I know that my life is going to be judged as sorrowful long before I have to go to the realm of Hades.

⁵ While I was still living with my father Oeneus in Pleuron, I developed a terrible fear of marriage. No other woman in Aetolia has even felt as much fear as I felt, for as a suitor I had Achelous, not a man but a river, and he came in three different shapes to ask my father for my hand in marriage. At one time he showed up in the form of a bull, at another time he appeared as a serpent with its shiny and slippery coils, and at still another time he came with the body of a man but the face of a bull – and from his shaggy beard long streams of water poured forth, just as if he were a fountain.

¹⁵ I was always expecting that a man like that one would one day be my husband, I constantly found myself praying – poor fool that I was – that I would die before I would ever be forced to marry someone like him.

¹⁸ But at the last moment, much to my surprise and relief, the famous son of Zeus and Alcmene showed up, and this newcomer fought against Achelous in a battle, and he won the contest, so he set me free. I can't say very much about what happened in their battle, for I don't really know what happened there. Perhaps somebody who was there and watching the events, and who wasn't completely terrified by all of it, could tell you more. As for me, I sank down as low as I

could, afraid that my looks would cause even more trouble and pain for me in the end.

[26] But it turned out that Zeus, the god who controls all contests, made the ending turn out fine, if indeed it has turned out well. For I clung to the bed of Heracles, since I was the bride that he had won, and every day since then I've had to deal with one fear after another, always worrying about him. One night will bring a new worry, and the next night will push the old worry away, only to supplant it with another one. And he and I now have children, but he only sees them from time to time – he treats them like a farmer treats a far off piece of farmland, only noticing that he happens to grow something and what he might happen to reap. That was the life that was always sending my husband quickly away from home, living a life in servitude to that damn man.

[36] But now that he has finally completed those labours of his, I am struck by an even greater fear. Ever since he has killed the mighty Iphitus, we've been been forced to move off and live here in Trachis, where we stay as the foreign guest of a friend of his. But now nobody knows where Heracles can possibly be – the only thing that I know is that when he went away I was afflicted with a great amount of pain.

[43] And I'm absolutely sure that he's in some trouble right now. He's been gone now for quite a period of time – we're had no news of him for almost fifteen months. And it has to be some serious trouble – the note that he left behind for me makes me believe it strongly. Often times I pray to the gods, wishing that I never saw this note, for all the stress that it brought me.

Nurse: [49] Deianira, my mistress, many times already I have seen you complain and mourn the fact that Heracles is not here. I've watched you cry and wail – and each time I've said nothing. But now, if in some way it's permissible for slaves to give advice to their masters, I think that I should tell you what to do.

[54] I mean, how is it that you have so many sons and you still haven't sent any of them off to search for their father, your husband? Look – you even have Hyllus there, and it would be natural to send him out, if he's concerned at all about what is happening to his father. Look, here comes the boy right now, running quickly on his agile feet toward the house. So if you think that what I had to say has any value, then you should make use of your boy here and follow my advice.

Enter Hyllus

Deianira: [61] O my child, my son, even those people who aren't born to noble parents can say wise things. This woman here is my slave, but she has just given me some solid advice.

Hyllus: What did she say? Please, mother, tell me if you can.

Deianira: [65] She says that when your father has been away from here for so long then it's shameful that you aren't out looking for him and asking about his whereabouts.

Hyllus: But I do know where he is, if I can believe what I hear from people.

Deianira: And where in the world have you heard that he is, my son?

Hyllus: [69] They say that for the past year he's been acting as the slave to a Lydian woman.

Deianira: If he had to endure that, then I suppose that anything is believable.

Hyllus: But he's been released from that servitude, or so I hear.

DEIANIRA: Then where is he now? Is he alive or dead?

HYLLUS: ⁷⁵ They say that he's in Euboea, and he is preparing to make an attack against the city of Eurytus.

DEIANIRA: Did you know, my boy, that he left me some prophecies before he left, and that these were supposed to help us when we need them the most?

HYLLUS: What prophecies do you mean, mother? I don't know this thing that you're talking about.

DEIANIRA: ⁷⁹ It said that he would either come to the end of his life by now, or he'd bring all his labours to an end and for the rest of his days he'd live a happy and pleasant life. My boy, his life clearly stands at a crossroads – so won't you go and look for him, since the only way that we can be safe is if he himself is safe. For we are also destroyed if he is.

HYLLUS: ⁸⁶ Of course I will go, mother! If I had known what the details of these prophecies were, then I would have left a long time ago. But my father's usual good luck kept me from feeling afraid and worrying about him. But now that I've heard what you had to say, I won't leave any stone unturned until I can find out what's happened to him.

DEIANIRA: ⁹¹ Please, my son – do go! There's always a reason to search for good news, even we don't learn it as early as we might like.

Exit Hyllus and the Nurse; Enter the Chorus (Women of Trachis)

CHORUS: ⁹⁴ O Sun, Sun, you whom the starry Night brings forth when she is taken away and you whom she lulls to sleep while you burn with your blazing fires – I beg you, please proclaim a search for Heracles, that son of Alcmene! Where, O you who are shining with your brilliant light, where is he living now? Is he in the narrows of the Black Sea, the Bosporus? Or is he resting at the place where those two continents meet, at Gibraltar, that place we call the "pillars of Heracles"? Please tell me, O sun, you who reign supreme and who have the keenest sight of all!

¹⁰³ I learn that Deianira, with longing in her heart, that woman whom so many men fought to have as their own, is like some miserable and sad bird, never able to fall asleep without shedding tears. The longing in her eyes reveals how strongly she holds the absence of her husband in her mind. She spends her time on her empty bed, alone and missing her mate and fearing, the poor woman, that some horrible fate has taken hold of him.

DEIANIRA: ¹⁴¹ I suppose that you've all come here because you've heard about my suffering and misery. I hope that you may never have to learn how badly I am feeling by suffering any agonies that are comparable to mine – of these things you have no experience.

¹⁴⁴ Young women tend to grow in their own places and live in their own worlds. They are affected neither by the heat of the sun, nor by the rain, nor by the wind. But they enjoy the pleasures of their life without any troubles until the time when they're no longer young women but instead fully-grown women, and then they have to take their share of worry and fear into the night, stressing about the fate of their husband and children. Only then, by looking at their own life and experience, can they finally begin to understand the troubles that are weighing me down.

¹⁵³ There are many pains that have been causing my tears. But there is one in particular that I have never known before, and I'll tell you about it now. When my lord Heracles was just setting out from home to embark on his last

journey, he left behind an old writing tablet inside the house, and there were some things marked on it. Before this he could never bring himself to speak to me of such things, even though he had to endure so many trials. He used to head off as if he were about to accomplish some great deed, and not as if he were about to die.

¹⁶¹ But now this time, it was as if he knew he wouldn't survive it, and so he told me what property I should take from the marriage after he died, and he mentioned how he was dividing his share of his ancestral land among his children. He fixed a length of a year plus three months, saying that when he had been gone for those fifteen months, then it would be his fate either to die or to survive that deadline and from that time forward he would live a life free from pain.

¹⁶⁹ He said that this was the time that was marked off by the gods to be the final end of the labours and troubles of Heracles, since this is what he heard the ancient oak at Dodona declare through its two doves, those priestesses. And the exact time when all of this is supposed to happen, after those fifteen months, is right now – this is the time when it all must come true. So that's why I'm getting so startled and frightened, leaping up from my sleep, fearing that it will be my fate to live the rest of my life robbed of my husband, the noblest of all men.

CHORUS: ¹⁷⁸ But wait – please be silent for a moment, for I can see a man who is wearing a garland coming this way to bring us some news.

Enter the Messenger

MESSENGER: ¹⁷⁸ O queen Deianira, I am the first messenger who can set you free from fear. You should know that the son of Alcmene is alive and that he is victorious – and right now he is bringing the best fruits of the battle to offer to the gods of this land.

DEIANIRA: What is this message that you've told me, old man?

MESSENGER: ¹⁸⁵ I'm telling you that soon that most enviable man, your husband, will be returning to your halls, arriving with his victorious might.

DEIANIRA: How did you hear this news? Did you hear it from a citizen or from some stranger?

MESSENGER: ¹⁸⁸ This is what the herald Lichas is telling a crowd of people who are gathered over there in the meadow where the cows graze. I heard him say it and then immediately rushed here so that I could be the first person t tell you the news ... and so that I might perhaps gain some reward for this service and perhaps gain your favour.

DEIANIRA: But if all is good with him, then why isn't Heracles here?

MESSENGER: ¹⁹³ I can't answer that, my lady. But as for Lichas, things are not so easy for him, my queen. A whole crowd of people from Malis are standing around him and asking him questions. He can't move a step forward, since everyone is curious and wants to know everything, so they won't let him go until they've heard him to their satisfaction.

¹⁹⁸ So even though he doesn't want to be there, he is staying with those who are questioning him. But you'll soon see him in person.

DEIANIRA: ²⁰⁰ O Zeus, ruler of the unharvested meadow in Oeta – even though it has taken such a long time, you have brought us such joy!

²⁰² Shout out, you women who are both inside the house and in the court outside. Now we

can enjoy the dawn, the rising sun that this news brings us – it's so wonderful!

CHORUS: ²⁰⁵ Let there be shouts of joy in the house, and let there be celebration in the streets by all the girls whose wedding is about to take place. And let shouts of men raise a song to honour Apollo, who holds the bow and quiver, defending us all.

²¹⁰ And girls everywhere raise the song, raise the song and shout out loud the name of Apollo's sister, great Artemis, the goddess who shoots deer, the girl who holds the torches, and the one who rules the nymphs in these parts.

²¹⁶ And I will rise up as well, nor will I push the flute aside, since you are the master of my heart, my soul. See how the music and the garlands excite me – hooray! hooray! – and they whirl me around as if I am in a Bacchic frenzy.

²²¹ Oh oh, let's sing, let's sing! See, look, my dear lady – now you are finally faced with the joy, it is at hand, and it is clear and safe to recognize it. Here comes the herald now!

Enter Lichas, the herald of Heracles; He brings a group of female prisoners with him, and Iole is among them

DEIANIRA: ²²⁵ Yes, dear women, I can see the procession that is coming toward me – it doesn't escape my sight. And I am happy to welcome you, herald, you who have returned here after so long time absent – and I hope that the news that you bring is welcome.

LICHAS: ²²⁹ But our arrival is good, my lady, and so is the message that I am bringing you. It has all been accomplished and brought to completion. When a man enjoys success, it's only right that he should take some pleasure out of delivering the excellent news.

DEIANIRA: O you dearest of men, please tell me first the news that I most want to hear – am I going to be able to welcome Heracles alive?

LICHAS: ²³⁴ When I left him he was not only strong, but he was flourishing and not afflicted by any malady or sickness.

DEIANIRA: And where was this? Was this in Greece or in some foreign land? Please tell me.

LICHAS: It was at one of the shores in Euboea, where he was in the midst of marking off altars and making offerings and sacrifices to Zeus.

DEIANIRA: Is he doing this to fulfill some vow or promise that he made, or is he obeying the words of some prophet?

LICHAS: ²⁴⁰ It was because of a promise that he made when he conquered and overthrew the country of these women whom you see before you now.

DEIANIRA: And these women then, please tell me – who are they? Who do they belong to? They deserve our pity, if their situation does not deceive me.

LICHAS: ²⁴⁴ Your husband picked them out after he sacked the city of Eurytus – as choice prizes and possessions for himself and in tribute to the gods.

DEIANIRA: Was it to attack this city the reason that he was gone for such an unspeakably length of time, all those countless days?

LICHAS: ²⁴⁸ No, for most of the time that he was away he was kept in Lydia. As he himself tells me, he was not free during this time, but he was instead a slave.

²⁵⁰ There needn't be any hesitation or resentment to tell this tale, my lady, since Zeus is known to have been responsible for this. Anyway, your husband was sold to Omphale,

that barbarian queen, and he served out a full year with her, as he himself told me. And he was so stung by this disgrace that he swore an oath that he would find a way to enslave the man who brought this disgrace on him – that he would make that man, together with his wife and child, all live a life of slavery.

258 And he didn't fail to keep his word, for as soon as he had ben freed from his bondage, he raised an army of volunteers and took them to attack the city of Eurytus. For it was Eurytus that Heracles considered responsible, more than any other mortal, for what he had to endure in his year of slavery.

262 What happened to start it all was this: Heracles had come to the house of Eurytus and was hoping to be welcomed there as an old friend. But Eurytus instead threw insults at him and spoke against Heracles, revealing a great deal of anger that was in his heart.

265 Eurytus said that Heracles might have inescapable arrows in his hand, but added that Heracles was inferior to his own sons and their skill in archery, and he completed the insult by declaring that Heracles was a slave who was subdued by the mere voice of a free man. Then Eurytus became drunk during dinner and he threw Heracles out of his house.

269 This was the beginning of Heracles' anger. And not long after that Eurytus' son Iphitus came to the hill of Tiryns, searching for the tracks of the horses that had wandered away from him. The eyes of the young man were in one place while his mind was in another, and so Heracles seized this advantage, grabbed him, and threw him down from the ridge they were on.

274 It was because of this action that the lord of Olympus, Zeus, the father of all, forced Heracles to be sent out to the countryside and sold like a slave. Zeus could not tolerate what Heracles had done, since this was the only time that Heracles had killed a man by treachery. If he had fought openly and fairly, then Zeus would not have been upset, since he would have gained vengeance on his enemy in a proper and honourable fashion. But the gods don't put up with hubris and foul play.

281 At any rate, Heracles eventually achieved his vengeance after he was released from slavery, for those people who once acted arrogantly toward him now find themselves living in the halls of Hades, and their city is now in ruined and its people enslaved. And these women whom you see before you now come from there, having given up their good fortune for a life that's not to be envied.

285 These were your husband's orders, for me to take these women here and to tell you the good news – and I have carried out his commands loyally and faithfully. As for Heracles, you can be certain that he himself will come as soon as he has made his holy sacrifice to his father Zeus, giving thanks in return for his conquest. In the long story that I have just reported, I'm sure that this is the happiest news by far.

Chorus: 291 O my queen, now your delight is clear and manifest – part of your pleasure is right before your eyes, and the other part you have just heard described.

Deianira: 293 Yes, how could I not rejoice when I hear this news about my husband's successful campaign? Wouldn't I have every right to celebrate? Clearly my happiness must keep pace and be the equal to his triumph. All the same, it is the nature of those who are cautious to still have a bit of fear for the man who is fortunate, in case one day soon he may come to horrible grief.

²⁹⁸ I mean, an incredible feeling of pity comes over me, my friends, when I see these unhappy women in front of me now, homeless and fatherless, taken off as prisoners to a strange and foreign land. Maybe before this they were the children of free men, perhaps they were even the offspring of royalty – but now their life is nothing but slavery.

³⁰³ O Zeus, god of battles and conquests, I hope that I may never see you go against my offspring in such a fashion as this! If you ever do, O Zeus, I hope that I may no longer be alive while it happens. That is the fear that comes upon me when I look upon these women.

(She approaches Iole)

³⁰⁷ Now, young woman, you look so unhappy – please tell me who you are. Don't you have a husband? Or are you the mother of someone? You look as though you've never been treated like this before, but rather as if you are someone from a noble family.

³¹⁰ Lichas, who exactly is this stranger here? Whose daughter is she? Who is her mother, and what is the name of her father? Come, tell me, because I felt the greatest amount of pity for her as soon as I saw her. I have this sense that she alone among these women knows how to feel and suffer.

LICHAS: ³¹⁴ How would I know anything about her? Why would you even ask me about her? Perhaps you're right and she isn't among the lowest people in birth over there – it's possible.

DEIANIRA: ³¹⁶ But is she from the royal house? Did Eurytus have any children?

LICHAS: I really don't know. You see – it wasn't my place to ask questions.

DEIANIRA: And you haven't learned her name from one of her other companions here?

LICHAS: Not at all – I did what I had to do, and I did it in silence.

DEIANIRA: ³²⁰ Then you do us all a favour, you poor girl, poor child – tell us who you are. For it would be a pity for me not to know who you are.

LICHAS: ³²² It would be quite out of the ordinary for her to speak now, I assure you, since she hasn't said a single word on the journey here – not one peep out of her.

³²⁵ For the entire trip she's been constantly weeping, but doing so quietly. The poor girl is trying to find her way through this suffering, and she's been this way ever since she left her ravaged land. Her situation is bad, but she deserves our understanding, compassion, and forgiveness for her silence.

DEIANIRA: ³²⁹ Well, then we should let her be, and let her go into the house just as she wants. She won't receive any new trouble from me in addition to the pain that she already suffers. The misery that she has now is already enough for her to bear, I'm certain of it.

³³² And now let's all go into the house, so that you, Lichas, can head off and do whatever it is that you still need to do, and that I can go inside and start to make the appropriate preparations inside the house.

Exit Lichas and the prisoners, including Iole; The Messenger reaches out to Deianira to hold her back after the others go inside

MESSENGER: ³³⁵ My lady, please wait behind here for a moment. I want to tell you something when everyone else has gone inside. You should know who those women are that are going inside your house, so that you can find out the information that you need to know. For I know everything that you need to know.

Deianira: What is this all about? Why are you trying to stop me from going inside the house?

Messenger: [340] Please stay here and listen to me for a second. What I told you a few moments ago was not a waste of your time, and I think this will also prove to be worth your time.

Deianira: Should I call all the others back here, or do you want to speak only to me and my friends here?

Messenger: I can speak freely only to you and your friends – please leave the others inside.

Deianira: [345] Well, they are all inside now, so please go ahead and give me your story.

Messenger: None of the things this man just told you was true or honest. Either he was lying to you just now, or he was giving a dishonest report when I heard him prior to this.

Deianira: [349] What are you saying? Please tell me everything that you know – and make it clear, for I don't quite follow the tone of what you are implying.

Messenger: [351] I just heard that herald Lichas saying, and there were a lot of men there who could corroborate my story, that Heracles conquered Eurytus and the high towers of his city of Oechalia all for the sake of that girl to whom you were just speaking.

[354] And it was Eros alone, that god of love, that caused him and bewitched him into this act of violence. That is, he didn't attack Eurytus because of his year of servitude for Omphale in Lydia, and it wasn't related to the fact that Iphitus was thrown to his death. No, it was passion, lust, love, that made him do it. And now Lichas is pushing this story aside and is telling a completely different one.

[359] Here's the story that Lichas told outside of the city: when Heracles could not persuade Eurytus to give him his daughter so that he could have her in some secret love, some secret marriage, he then invented some small disagreement, something that would give him an excuse to wage a campaign against the young woman's city. Of course, the city was the one in which Eurytus was king, and so Heracles killed Eurytus, sacked the city, and now he is on our way back home – and he has sent the girl here ahead of him. He sent her here for a reason, my dear lady, and it's not so that she can be a slave. You shouldn't expect that, my queen – that wouldn't be the likely result if he is so enflamed with desire.

[369] This was the reason that I thought I should tell you everything that I heard from Lichas out there, my dear lady. And I wasn't alone in this – many of the men of Trachis heard the same story when we were all gathered around him in the marketplace, and you can certainly question them to see if they'll back up what I've told you. I'm very sorry that what I've told you is not pleasant or agreeable, but nevertheless I have told you the truth.

Deianira: [375] Oh heavens, what is happening to me? Have I welcomed some secret enemy into my house without even knowing it? Oh, this is bad…bad…bad.

[377] Does she really have no name, as Lichas implied when he brought her here, that girl who appears to be so brilliant in her looks and birth?

Messenger: [380] Ma'am, she is the daughter of Eurytus and her name is Iole. But Lichas couldn't tell you anything about her origins, since, as he said, "it wasn't my place to ask questions."

Chorus: To hell with all bastards and scoundrels – but damn him most of all the man who practices a shameful act of evil in secret!

DEIANIRA: ⁣³⁸⁵ Oh no – what should I do, women? The story that I have just heard has left me completely stunned.

CHORUS: You should go and question that man again, that Lichas. Perhaps he'll tell you the truth if you force him to give you an answer.

DEIANIRA: Yes, that's it, I'll do it – good idea. Your advice is excellent.

MESSENGER: ³⁹⁰ And so should I wait here? What would you like me to do?

DEIANIRA: Stay right here, for I can see that Lichas is coming here outside of the house right now of his own volition.

Enter Lichas, from the house

LICHAS: My lady, what would you like me to say when I see Heracles? Please tell me, since I am about to leave, as you can see.

DEIANIRA: ³⁹⁵ How quickly you are rushing off when you were so slow in coming here. We haven't even had a chance to talk again.

LICHAS: Well, if you'd like to ask me anything, please do so – here I am.

DEIANIRA: Are you going you to tell me the truth? Can I trust your words?

LICHAS: Absolutely – as great Zeus is my witness, I'll tell you everything as far as I know.

DEIANIRA: ⁴⁰⁰ What's the name of that young woman you brought? I am referring to the one I addressed.

LICHAS: She's from Euboea, but I don't know who her parents are.

MESSENGER: Hey you, look over here! To whom exactly do you think you are speaking? Do you know who she is?

LICHAS: And who are you to ask me such a question?

MESSENGER: If you were wise you would answer the question that I asked you.

LICHAS: ⁴⁰⁵ I am speaking the woman who has the power of this house – Deianira, the daughter of Oeneus and the wife of Heracles and, if my eyes don't deceive me, it is the woman who rules me that I address.

MESSENGER: There – that is exactly what I wanted to hear you say. You say that she is your mistress and that she is in charge of you?

LICHAS: Yes, it's the truth.

MESSENGER: ⁴¹⁰ Well then, what do you think the punishment should be if you are discovered being disloyal and dishonest with her?

LICHAS: How do you mean "disloyal" and "dishonest"? What kinds of accusations are you making against me?

MESSENGER: Oh, these aren't accusations – this is what I say you are doing.

LICHAS: That's it – I'm leaving. I was a fool to have spent so long listening to you.

MESSENGER: ⁴¹⁵ Not yet – not before you answer some brief questions.

LICHAS: Then speak away, if you feel the need. It's clear that you're not at a loss for words.

MESSENGER: That prisoner, that captive girl, the one you brought into the palace – do you know the one I mean?

LICHAS: Yes, I know – why are you asking me about her?

MESSENGER: ⁴¹⁹ You looked at her just now as if you didn't recognize her, but didn't you recently say that she was Iole, the daughter of Eurytus?

LICHAS: And where am I supposed to have said such a thing? Is there anyone who can come forward and act as witness to say he ever heard me make such a declaration?

MESSENGER: You said it in the marketplace, right in front of a whole crowd of us townspeople. All the men of Trachis gathered around you there when you gave your report.

LICHAS: [425] Oh yes … well … I said that's what I'd heard … but it's not the same thing at all to state what you merely think could be true and what actually is factual and true.

MESSENGER: And what do you mean "think could be true"? Didn't you just swear an oath to all of us over there that you were bringing this girl so that she could be the wife of Heracles?

LICHAS: [429] I said what? As a wife to Heracles? I beg you, my dear madam, please tell me who this stranger is.

MESSENGER: [431] I can answer that myself. I am a man who was there and I heard you say that it was Heracles' desire for the girl that caused him to destroy the city – and that the destruction of the city wasn't connected in any way with that woman from Lydia, but rather it had everything to do with Heracles' love for the girl you just led inside.

LICHAS: Mistress, please send this fellow away. No sensible person should bother wasting his time talking to someone who is clearly irrational.

DEIANIRA: [436] In the name of Zeus whose lightning strikes the topmost fields of Oeta, don't keep the truth from me! Speak to me! You'll find that the woman you'll be addressing is not evil or spiteful, nor am I ignorant as to how men behave – that they don't always take their pleasure from the same place.

[441] Whoever tries to enter the ring like a boxer and trade blows with Eros is a fool. For Eros rules even the gods whenever he wishes, and he rules me as well – so why shouldn't he rule another woman like me? So if I try to blame my husband for being taken away by the sickness of love, then I would be silly and foolish. And I can't blame that girl either, since she has done nothing shameful nor has she done anything to harm me. No, that's ridiculous.

[449] But, on the other hand, if you are telling me lies on his instructions, then you are truly doing something that is dishonourable. And if you have taught yourself to behave in such a way, then you are only going to make yourself look like a liar when you are trying to appear honest. Come, tell me the whole truth. It's a horrible thing for a free man to get a reputation as a liar. And you really can't expect that I won't hear about this eventually, for there are obviously many people around here who will have heard you, and someone will be sure to tell me sooner or later.

[457] And you shouldn't be afraid of hurting me. The only thing that would cause me pain would to be to remain in the dark, unaware. And why is it so terrible for me to know this anyway? Hasn't this one man, Heracles, already had sex with lots of women? And never yet have any of them received insults or threats from me.

[462] And this one here wouldn't receive any bad treatment from me either, even if Heracles should get carried away in his passion for her. For I felt such a great deal of pity for her as soon as I saw her, because it was clear to me that her beauty had destroyed her life and, through no fault of her own, this girl brought ruin and destruction to her own land.

[467] But let all of this fly away into the wind. I tell you that you can be devious and tell lies to anyone that you like, but that to me you should always tell the truth.

Chorus: ⁴⁷⁰ Listen to her – obey her. What she says is right and proper. You'll never have any cause to complain about her later, and you'll win my gratitude and thanks as well.

Lichas: ⁴⁷² Well, my dear mistress, since I can see that you are acting quite reasonably, then I will tell you the whole truth and I won't keep anything hidden. You see things exactly as we mortals need to see them.

⁴⁷⁵ Yes, everything this man has told you is true. A terrible passion for this girl overcame Heracles one day and all because of her your husband decided that he would overturn and conquer her native city of Oechalia with his spear.

⁴⁷⁹ But he didn't tell me to hide any of this from you or to deny any of it – I have to say this in all due fairness to him. But I made did this all on my own, madam, since I was afraid that this would cause you so much pain to hear it. So I was the one who did wrong in concealing this, if you think what I did was wrong.

⁴⁸⁴ But since you now know the full story, I ask you that you show kindness toward this woman, both for his sake and your own sake – and please prove that the words that you said to her previously were spoken in true sincerity. For the man who has excelled in all matters by means of his strength – your husband, I mean – has been completely defeated by his passion for this girl.

Deianira: ⁴⁹⁰ That's how I feel as well, and so I will do just that. I won't choose to add to my troubles by trying to fight against this sickness that has been sent to Heracles by the gods.

⁴⁹² Now let us all go inside the house. I've got some messages for you to carry – and I've also got some gifts that I'd like you to carry off to Heracles in exchange for these gifts that you brought. You must bring them to him. It wouldn't be right for you to leave empty-handed after having brought so much when you arrived.

Exit Deianira, Lichas, and the Messenger into the house

Chorus: ⁴⁹⁷ Aphrodite is a mighty power! She is always able to carry off her victories. I pass over the stories of the gods, and I won't relate how she tricked the son of Cronus, nor Hades who lives covered in darkness, nor Poseidon the great earth-shaker. But for the right to have our lady's hand in marriage, who were the two contestants that fought to make her their bride? Who were the ones that fought those battles that were filled with so many blows and dust?

⁵⁰⁷ One of them was a mighty river, appearing in the shape of a bull, with long horns and four legs – it was Achelous from Oeniadae; and the other one came from Thebes, the birthplace of Bacchus, and he held his spring-like bow, his spear, and his club – he was the son of Zeus. The two of them met together in the middle, both lusting for the bed of that girl. And alone there in the centre was Aphrodite, the beautiful Cyprian – she was there to act as the referee and judge in their contest.

⁵¹⁷ Then there was the thudding of fists and the sound of the bow, and the mix-up of bull's horns – all at once. And legs were mixed up, wrapped around waists, and deathly blows struck foreheads, and groans came from each side. But the girl with her youth and beauty sat down by a distant hill and waited for her future husband, whoever it would turn out to be. I can tell the story just as if I were there. The struggle went on, as I have been saying, but the face of the bride who was the object of their fight waited there most pitiably. And then finally she was ripped away from her

mother, just like a calf that has been lost and wandered away from home.

Enter Deianira

DEIANIRA: ⁵³¹ My dear friends, while our visitor Lichas is inside and talking to those captured girls before he leaves, I have come outside to speak with you without his noticing. Partly I'm doing this so that I can tell you what I have been up to, and partly because I want to get some comfort from you in my suffering.

⁵³⁶ For I have taken in the girl – but I can no longer think of her as a girl, but rather as his wife – just like a captain of a boat takes on cargo that causes outrage in his heart. And now the two of us, both she and I, will have to stay under one blanket for him to embrace when he wishes. This is the reward that Heracles – he who is called so noble and faithful – has sent home to me in order to thank me for having kept the house for so long.

⁵⁴⁴ I don't know how I can really be angry with my husband when he is so clearly suffering from an illness – but what woman could be able to live together with this other girl and share her marriage with the same man? For I can see that she is in the prime of her youth, while my youth is fading away – and the eyes of men love to grab away at the flowers when they bloom while they turn away from flowers once they start to fade. This is the reason that I am afraid that Heracles may not still be called my husband, but that he'll be this younger woman's man.

⁵⁵² But, just as I said before, I know and agree that it's not honourable for a woman to become angry about such matters – and so I'll tell you the plan that I have to bring myself some sense of relief and ease my pain.

⁵⁵⁵ A long time ago I received an old gift from a Centaur, and I keep it hidden in a bronze urn. It was something that I was given when I was a girl – it came from shaggy-chested Nessus when he was about to die. Back then he used to carry people across the deep flow of the Evenus river. He didn't do this with a boat and oars, but rather he ferried them across with his broad arms and shoulders.

⁵⁶² And he was carrying me on his shoulders across that river, back when my father sent me to follow Heracles on that first time that I was sent off to be his bride. And when we were in the middle of the river the Centaur started to put his lustful hands all over me, and so I shouted out. Immediately the son of Zeus turned and shot forth an arrow that went whizzing though the air and right into the chest of the Centaur.

⁵⁶⁸ Nessus fought and made his way to the shore, and as he breathed out his last bits of air he said this to me – "O daughter of old Oeneus, if you listen to what I tell you now, then you'll gain a great reward from being carried by me, since you were my last passenger. If you can find a way to save some of the blood from my wound here, these areas that have been dyed black by the dark clots of the from the poison of the Hydra of Lerna, where your husband dipped his arrows, then you'll find that it will also work as a love charm over Heracles, so that he'll never look at another woman with move love and desire than he has for you."

⁵⁷⁸ I've been thinking about this a lot, my friends, for after the Centaur died I carefully saved and stored the blood in that container and locked it up inside the house. And just now I finally heeded the words of Nessus, for I followed his instructions and dipped this robe in the magic blood – and now everything s ready to happen. It's done.

⁵⁸² I have never learned anything about how to

be rash and commit daring crimes, and I hate the kind of women who do such things. But I am hoping that I'll have found some way to defeat this girl when these spells and charms start to do their magic on Heracles – well, that is what I have done…unless you think that I am doing something wrong. If so, please tell me, and I will put a stop to my plan.

CHORUS: [588] If you have reason to for confidence in this matter, then it looks like you haven't acted badly at all.

DEIANIRA: [590] My confidence in this matter only goes so far, since I have never put it to the test.

CHORUS: But we can only know for certain when we take action. Whatever you may think about this matter, you'll have no way to say for certain unless you give it a try.

DEIANIRA: [594] Well, we'll soon have an answer, for I see that Lichas is already at the door, and he's coming this way. Only please be quiet about this – for one can be ashamed of one's actions when they are done in secret yet still carry them out, since one doesn't actually have to face any public disgrace or shame.

Enter Lichas from the house

LICHAS: [598] And what is it that you would like me to do, daughter of Oeneus? I've already been here too long as it is – and now I'm late and need to hurry back.

DEIANIRA: [600] This, Lichas, is the very thing that I have been looking after while you were inside the house and talking to those foreign women. Right here in this chest I have placed a gift for you to take to my husband – a long fine-woven robe that I made with my own hands.

[604] When you give it to him, it's important that you tell him that nobody should touch this robe before he does, and that he shouldn't let the light of the sun fall on it, nor any sacred fire from any holy altar, until he himself stands visible to all and displays his new robe to men and the gods on the day of sacrifice.

[610] For I made this vow – that if I should ever live long enough to hear or see that he was coming safely home, that I would prepare new and fine clothes for him so that he could make his homecoming sacrifices to the gods in proper and pious attire. And you'll carry with you a sign, so that when he sees it he will easily recognize my seal and know that this gift comes from me.

[614] Now it's time for you to go, and remember that the first rule of a messenger is that you must do what you are told to do and nothing else. If you do your job well, then you'll earn both his gratitude and mine, and so you'll receive twice the honour.

LICHAS: [620] Ma'am, I am your messenger, and if I practice the art of Hermes in the proper way, then I will never fail in serving you.

[622] I'll bring this chest to Heracles exactly as you have given it to me, and I'll repeat the words to him precisely as you said them to me.

DEIANIRA: Good, then you should be on your way right now, since you know how things are in the house.

LICHAS: Yes, I can see everything, and I'll report that all is well.

DEIANIRA: And be sure to remember that I received this foreign girl kindly and welcomed her into this house as a friend.

LICHAS: Yes, that was a wonderful surprise – I was very pleased to see it.

DEIANIRA: [630] And I think that is everything then – so you should go.

Exit Lichas

For I am scared that I would have been speaking too soon if I asked that man to send word as to how much I miss and long for my husband before I know how much he longs for me.

Exit Deianira into the house

Chorus: ⁶⁴⁴ The son of Zeus and Alcmene is hurrying back toward his home, bringing with him the trophies of his conquests after having proved his strength and valour.

⁶⁴⁶ We missed him those twelve long months while he was completely gone from this city, away across the sea, not knowing anything about what happened to him. And his wife, ever loving, ever missing him, spent the whole time worrying about the fate of her husband, wasting away her heart in sadness and fear. But now the great war god Ares has been driven to fury and has released Heracles from his lengthy toils – and this, in turn, has released our lady from her days of stress and worry.

⁶⁵⁵ Oh let the man come, let him come now, and let his ship that has so many oars come here quickly, making no stops along the way before he comes back to this shore, finally leaving behind that island altar out there where we hear that he is sacrificing. Let him come home from there, since we long so much for his return, and let him be united in love with our mistress Deianira, since she has poured out the inducements that were given to her by that Centaur so that her husband may once again fall deeply in love with her.

Enter Deianira from the house

Deianira: ⁶⁶³ Oh women, my friends, I have this great fear that I did something wrong – that I went too far!

Chorus: ⁶⁶⁵ What's wrong Deianira?

Deianira: I don't know exactly, but something makes me nervous. I have this thought that I may soon see that I have done a horrible thing when I was instead trying to do something good.

Chorus: Surely you are not referring to the gift that you sent to Heracles?

Deianira: ⁶⁶⁹ Yes, that's what I mean. I finally see now that I shouldn't throw myself headlong into anything that I still don't understand very well.

Chorus: Please tell us the reason for your fear, if you can.

Deianira: ⁶⁷² A thing just happened, my friends, that if I told you would make you wonder in amazement and desperation. When I was anointing the robe that I sent away as the gift for my husband, I used a piece of cloth to spread the magic ointment on the garment, careful not to touch it myself when I rubbed it all over the robe.

⁶⁷⁴ The cloth that I used to bub in the ointment has disappeared, eaten away by nothing that is in the house but rather completely consumed by itself – and its crumbs now sit there on the top of a stone slab, nothing more than dust. But I want you to know the whole story, so I'll tell you it at an even greater length.

⁶⁸⁰ I neglected none of the instructions that the monster gave me when his side had been pierced by the sharp arrow that my husband had shot into him. Rather I kept his words locked inside my head, not letting myself forget anything that he said to me. And I did exactly what he told me to do. He told me to keep this drug away in a secret place, far away from heat and fire and the rays of the sun, until the time when I could rub it on something – and that's exactly what I did.

⁶⁸⁸ So I applied it in secret, rubbing it on the

robe in a secret, secluded, and dark place deep inside the house, with a piece of cloth that I had. This cloth was really not much more than a tuft of wool that had been plucked from one of the sheep in our flock here. Then I carefully folded the robe, not touching it myself, and I placed it inside a chest before the rays of the sun could touch it, just as you saw. That was the chest that I gave to Lichas, and it's the one he left with, taking it to Heracles.

692 And when I went back into the house I saw something that is too strange for words, almost beyond human understanding. When I was leaving I happened to throw that cloth – the one that was made of sheep's wool that I had used to smear in the ointment on the robe – right onto the hot floor and directly there in the full heat of the rays of the sun. And when that cloth became warm…well…it melted away into nothing and then crumbled into bits on the ground, looking just like the sawdust you see when someone is sawing wood.

701 So the remains just sat there where it fell, but from the ground beneath it a clotted foam started to boil up, looking a great deal like the rich liquid that you see when the blue-green fruit from the vines of Dionysus are poured onto the ground.

705 And right now I have no idea what to think about all of this. I fear that I was foolish and may have done a very terrible thing due to my situation. I finally started to wonder why that monster Nessus would have ever offered to do such a favour for me – and in return for what? – since I was the cause of his death.

709 No, he must have been playing some kind of trick on me, hoping that he could find a way to destroy the man who shot him with the poisoned arrow. But I've come to this realization far too late, when I can no longer do anything with the knowledge. For unless I am wrong, I alone, stupid stupid me, I alone am the one who killed my poor husband.

714 I know that the arrow that Heracles sent at Nessus was so powerful that it even injured Charon, the ferryman of the Hades, and he is immortal – and it kills every man and beast that it touches. This is the very same poison which flowed, all black and oozing, out of the wounds of Nessus – so how can it fail to kill Heracles as well?

723 This is my fear, at any rate. All the same, I have made the decision that if my husband comes to a bad end, then at the same moment I will die along with him. I couldn't bear to go on living and be called an evil woman when my only desire is to be good.

Chorus: Horrible actions always bring about fear – but one should not expect the worst before anything has happened.

Deianira: 725 But when one realizes that their actions are bad and wrong, then there's nothing that can bring back hope or confidence.

Chorus: Yet whenever we make some mistakes through no fault of our own the anger can be softened, and you should gain some benefit and solace from this.

Deianira: 729 It's easy for you to talk like this, since you have no share of the blame – whereas I'm the one who has to live with the evil that I have done.

Chorus: Maybe it's best to be silent now about this, unless you want to say something about it to your son. The boy you sent away to search for your father has just returned.

Enter Hyllus

Hyllus: 734 Mother! I wish that I would have come back and found one of three things – either that you were no longer alive, or that you were alive but someone else's mother other than mine, or that somehow you'd found a better heart than the one you have now!

DEIANIRA: But what is it, my son? What have I done that has made me so hateful to you?

HYLLUS: [739] What have you done? Well, then you should know clearly that on this very day you have killed your husband – and my father!

DEIANIRA: Oh my heavens, what is this thing you are saying, my child?

HYLLUS: I'm saying only what is obvious – for when one has done such an awful thing, then how can you make yourself believe that it hasn't happened?

DEIANIRA: [744] But how can you say this, my child? How on earth did you hear that I did this horrible deed that you accuse me of?

HYLLUS: I saw my father's heavy and horrible downfall with my own eyes – I didn't hear it from anyone.

DEIANIRA: But where did you find him? Were you by his side when this happened?

HYLLUS: [749] If you need to hear about it, then I must tell you the full story. When he returned from having sacked that famous city that once belonged to Eurytus, he walked away with the trophies of his triumph and the best fruits of victory.

[752] On one of the wave-beaten shores in Euboea there is a peak called Mount Cenaeum, and that's where father was, marking off altars along with a grove that he could use for sacrifices to Zeus, his father. And it was there that I first saw him, which gave me a great deal of relief, since I had missed him so immensely.

[756] And just as he was about to start the slaughter of the many beasts to begin the sacrifice, his herald Lichas arrived, just having returned from his home – from here – and he brought with him that robe you made, that robe of death.

[759] He put on the robe just as you asked him to do, and then he sacrificed his first twelve bulls, perfect victims all, the choicest of all the cattle he plundered. Then he continued and brought the number of sacrificed animals to about a hundred – forcing the mixed herd toward the altar.

[763] At first the poor man spoke the prayer in a cheerful and pleasant manner, rejoicing and proud in his new clothes. But as soon as the flame from the pines on the firewood blazed on high and the fire from the bloody sacred offerings became more intense, the sweat started to break out on his skin and the robe started to cling to him on every side. It was attached so tightly to him you would have thought it was the robe on a statue. Then a biting pain shot through him, digging deeply into his bones. Then the poison began to consume him, so bloody and vicious – that evil venom from the blood of the Hydra.

[772] Now he was shouting for that poor man Lichas, who was in no way guilty of your crime, and father asked Lichas to tell him the reason, the plot, that caused him to bring him that robe. That poor envoy – he knew nothing about it and so he told father that it was your gift alone, just as you instructed him to do. When Heracles heard this news, a piercing and agonizing convulsion seized his lungs. Father managed to catch Lichas by his foot, just down there where the ankle meets the socket, and father threw him headlong off that cliff down onto the rocks on the shore below. Where he landed his white brains oozed out of his split-open head onto the stones beneath us.

[783] All of a sudden everyone was shouting, crying for what had just happened to the

man who had died and for what Heracles was suffering at the moment. Because of what had just happened to Lichas, nobody found the courage to come close to Heracles. The pain was dragging him in all kinds of directions. At one moment he would be pushed toward the ground, and at another he would be pushed up in the air. The surrounding rocks were filled with the echoes of his pain – those mountains of Locri and the high cliffs of Euboea.

Eventually he gave up fighting the illness, since there was no point in trying to resist. Then he threw himself on the ground once again in his wretchedness, screaming all kinds of things over and over again. He muttered curses against the disastrous and horrific marriage he had with you, saying that this alliance that he had made with your father Oeneus turned out to ruin his life.

794 Then he lifted up his eyes, which were rolling around in every direction, and through the dark smoke that was encompassing him he managed to see me there in that great crowd of people, while tears were streaming down my cheeks. He looked right at me and called – "O my son, come here! Come to me, and please don't turn away from me when I am in such pain – even if it means that you have to die along with me. My son, lift me out of this, take me away from here, and, if you can do it, put me somewhere that no one can look at me. If you have pity or love for me at all, then you will at least take me out of this country as soon as you can… don't let me die here!"

803 Those were the orders that he gave me, so we found a way to place him in the middle of a boat and we managed to bring him here, although it was difficult, since he spent the whole journey howling loudly as he was seized by the spasms. You'll see him here in a moment, either still hanging on to life or just now dead.

807 These plots and actions, mother, are clearly all a result of your planning and scheming, and I pray that avenging Justice as well as some Fury may find a way to punish you for what you have done. And, if it's right for a son to do so, I curse you. But it must be right for me to curse you, since you are the one who has made it right for me, when you killed the noblest man on earth, the kind of man you'll never see the likes of again!

Exit Deianira, running away

Chorus: 813 But Deianira, why are you leaving so quickly, and why won't you say anything? Don't you realize that your silence only adds weight to the accusations that have been leveled against you?

Hyllus: 815 Oh, just let her go! I hope that a fair wind comes up and sweeps her away, so far away that she is forever removed from my sight! Why should she still hold the name and honour of mother when she has behaved in a way that is unlike that of a mother?

819 No, let her go! She is dead to me now – and I hope that she may soon find the same kind of joy that she gave to my father.

Exit Hyllus

Chorus: 841 The poor woman, poor Deianira - in part she caused the deed, but part of it was put into place due to the will of the Centaur, back at that fatal meeting when she crossed the river. Now that everything is lost and in ruins I think that she laments it greatly – the pale tears must be falling thickly down her cheeks.

851 The flood of tears has broken forth. Such a sickness – oh my! – such a level of suffering has never yet come previously to this glorious hero, never by his enemies… oh, there is so

much sadness, so much pity. Oh, I cry for the black point of his defending spear, which he used to win this new bride from lofty Oechalia. But Aphrodite, such a silent assassin, is revealed as the cause of these things – this is all her doing.

Nurse: Oh me!

Chorus: [863] Am I mistaken, or is that the sound of someone crying inside the house? What am I saying? Of course that's the sound of lamentation – there must be some new form of trouble inside. Look! Notice the old woman who is coming out toward us – it looks like she has some news to tell us, but she is shrouded in a cloud of grief.

Enter the Nurse

Nurse: [871] O women of Trachis, the gift that Deianira sent to Heracles has turned out to be only the start of our sorrows!

Chorus: What new disaster do you have to announce to us, old woman?

Nurse: [874] Without moving her feet my mistress Deianira has set off on her final journey.

Chorus: What? Oh no – surely she hasn't died?

Nurse: Yes, she is dead – now you know it all.

Chorus: You mean she really is … dead?

Nurse: And now you are hearing it for a second time.

Chorus: [880] The poor woman! Please tell us how she died.

Nurse: It was horrible, absolutely horrible the way it happened for her.

Chorus: Tell us how she met her death, woman.

Nurse: She was stabbed by a double-edged sword.

Chorus: [882] What passion, what sickness, took her life with the cruel point of the blade? How could she think of yet another death so soon after the death of her husband?

Oh my, did you see this happen, old woman?

Nurse: Yes I saw it happen. I was standing nearby.

Chorus: [890] How did it happen then?

Nurse: She killed herself – she used her own hand.

Chorus: What are you saying?

Nurse: I'm speaking the truth.

Chorus: [893] Oh heavens, that new bride, the one who arrived before her wedding – she has brought with her a mighty Fury into this house.

Nurse: Yes, and if you had been there with me and had seen what Deianira did, then you would have been moved by even more pity.

Chorus: How could any woman bring herself to do such a thing as this?

Nurse: [899] It was terrible, I agree, but I'll tell you how it all happened so that you can be my witness. When she went into the house all alone and saw her son out in the courtyard making preparations to head out with a bed that could be used to bring back Heracles, she then hid herself where nobody would be able to see her.

[904] She fell upon all the altars in the house, crying out that they would all soon become deserted. And she cried whenever she touched – oh, that poor woman – whenever she touched anything that she once used in the past. She was moving this way and that way all throughout the house, and if she by chance noticed the face of any of her dear servants, she would cry all the more as soon as she saw them, lamenting her own fate and

for the fact that she would no longer have any children.

⁹¹² Then all of a sudden she stopped, and I saw her rush headlong into the marriage bedroom that she shared with Heracles. I stayed in the shadows and watched over her in secret. I could see her in there, rushing about and putting the best sheets and blankets on top of her wedding bed. When she finished preparing the bed, she leapt up and took her position in the middle of the bed.

⁹¹⁹ Hot rivers of tears were pouring from her eyes and down her face, and she said – "O my bridal bed! Goodbye to you, for now and forever, since you will never again receive me to lie up on this bed!" She said those words and with a sweep of her hand she loosened her robe, and her gown opened up far enough to reveal a golden pin that was situated inside, very close to her breast.

⁹²³ And then she uncovered her whole side and her left arm. And that's when I suspected what was about to happen, and so I ran and ran toward her with all my strength, as fast as I could – and I warned her son Hyllus of what she was about to do. And in the very time that I ran there and we ran back to her she had managed to strike herself with a double-edged sword in her side, just below the place where the seat of life resides.

⁹³² Her son screamed when he saw what his mother had done. The poor boy realized that he charged her with this crime and that he was responsible for what she had just done. He learned too late from the others within the house that the Centaur Nessus caused his mother to do this action due to the lies that he told her – and that she herself was completely innocent.

⁹³⁶ Then her poor son – that miserable boy! – gave himself up completely to tears and lamentation. He threw himself on top of his mother's body, covered her with kisses, and held her closely to his side. He groaned and said that he had charged her falsely with the crime, and he wept because now he would be left completely alone, having lost both his father and his mother.

⁹⁴³ This is how things are within the house. If anyone looks too far ahead, if anyone even plans one or two days in advance, then he is acting foolishly, for there can be no tomorrow until we have first passed safely through today.

Exit the Nurse

CHORUS: ⁹⁴⁷ Oh, what shall I mourn for first? Which disaster is the sadder one? In this state that I am in, it's impossible for me to tell.

⁹⁵⁰ There's this one, in the house, that is right before our eyes, and then there's the other one that sits in our thoughts and expectations. To see a disaster and to await a disaster are just the same thing.

⁹⁵⁴ I wish that a blast of wind could come to this house to take me away from this place, to keep me from dying of fright when I look at what has happened to Heracles, that mighty son of Zeus. For they say that he is approaching the house now, in utter agony, the kind of pain that can't be removed – a situation that is beyond belief.

⁹⁶² When I was screaming like that shrill-voiced nightingale, it was for the man who is now here and no longer far away. I can see strangers who are coming near, coming from far away. Where are they bringing him? It looks like they are in mourning for a friend, they are planting their steps so slowly, so silently, so mournfully in the ground.

⁹⁶⁸ Oh, the man himself is silent when he is

carried along. Should I think then that he is dead, or just sleeping?

Men enter from the side, carrying Heracles, and a Doctor accompanies them; Enter Hyllus, from the other direction

HYLLUS: ^{971} O my father! Oh, just look at what has happened to you! I am so miserable! What's going to happen to me? What should I do? Oh gods!

DOCTOR: ^{974} Shh! Be quiet, child – don't arouse the wild pain that makes your father so savage. He is still alive, even though he's lying prostrate on this bed. Please, child, just bite your lips and control yourself a bit.

HYLLUS: What is that you are saying, old man? Is he really still alive?

DOCTOR: ^{978} Yes, he is – but you must be careful not to wake him up from the sleep that is holding him, my boy. For that would only stir up the horrible sickness that is in the briefest of remission.

HYLLUS: But this is such an awful stress, such an awful pain, that is resting on my shoulders. I feel so helpless – and it's driving me insane.

HERACLES: ^{984} O Zeus, where is this place that I have come to? Among what men am I now lying, all worn out by these unceasing pains? Oh gods, why me? These pains are so heavy. This agony, this pain – oh, it's eating me alive!

DOCTOR: ^{988} Now, Hyllus, don't you see how much better it would have been for you to have kept quiet and not disturbed the sleep that was at least giving him a modicum of peace?

HYLLUS: Yes, you were right. Oh, I can't stand to see him suffering like this!

HERACLES: ^{996} O holy rock of Cenaeum, where those altars stand, is this the thanks that I receive for all the sacrifices that I made to the gods on you?

^{1000} O Zeus, what is this outrage that you have inflicted on me? All you give me is torture, and all that I now know is this ever-increasing pain, this madness, and it won't go away. Who is the person who can relieve me of my suffering – any singer, any magician, any doctor who can remove this curse, other than Zeus himself? Even from so far away it would be amazing.

Ahhh! Please just let me be, let me sleep away my misery until it ends – let me sleep my final sleep.

^{1007} Why are you people touching me? Where are you putting me? You are going to kill me, I tell you – you are killing me! You have stirred awake the pain, that part that had gone to sleep.

^{1010} The pain has taken hold of me – ah gods, here it comes again! O you Greeks are so ungrateful! I destroyed myself so many times for you, purging so many beasts from your seas and woods, and yet where are you now to lend me a helpful hand? Is there no one who will bring a fire or a weapon of some kind that will help me end this agony, this horrible pain? Won't someone help me?

^{1015} Oh!! Ahhh! Won't someone please come here now and chop off my head – cut this damn head off my body and end this miserable like that I have to endure! Ahh! Ohh!

DOCTOR: ^{1017} O boy, please come here – you are this man's son. This job is too much for me – it's more than I can manage with my strength. Help me, please, because you have more power, more strength, to preserve him than I do.

HYLLUS: ^{1021} I am putting my hand on him, but it's beyond my power or the power of any other man to find a way to relieve him of this pain. This is the will of Zeus.

HERACLES: [1023] Ahh! Ohh! My son, my boy – where are you? Come here, please – lift me up, help me up…take hold of me. Oh! Ah! The pain is shooting up again, this evil thing – this damn thing is destroying me from inside – this savage unstoppable plague!

Oh! Oh! Athena, it is killing me, torturing me.

[1031] O my son, O Hyllus, please take pity on your father and find a sword from somewhere. Nobody will blame you for this. Strike me right in the chest and help end this pain that your godless mother has inflicted on me. Oh, I wish that I could see her die in the same way, the very same way that she is destroying me!

[1040] Ah! Oh! O Hades, brother of my father Zeus, please find a way to put me to sleep. Bring my day to an end – with a quick death help end my suffering!

CHORUS: [1044] My friends, I shudder when I hear all about the pains that our king has to endure. He's so great a man, yet he's been brought down by such horrible suffering!

HERACLES: [1046] The labours and toils that this back of mine has had to endure are many and savage – it hurts even to speak of those evils. But neither the wife of my father Zeus – that Hera, who tried to destroy me so many times – nor even that bastard Eurystheus himself ever condemned me to an agony as bad as this one here that the two-faced daughter of Oeneus – my so-called "wife" – has set on my shoulders. She tricked me, lied to me, wove this robe with the help of the Furies – and now I am going to die all wrapped up inside of it.

[1053] This sickness that she's thrown my way is clinging to my sides and it's eating away my innermost flesh. It's alive, moving through me constantly, drinking up the channels of my lungs. Already it's drunk up my fresh blood, and my entire body is in ruins, now that I have been conquered by these unspeakable chains.

[1058] Those men who hold the spear of battle down in the plain never did such a thing to me, nor did the earth-born army of the Giants, nor did the violence of the many monstrous beasts I fought, nor the lands of Greece, nor the barbarian nations – nor any country that I ever visited when I was trying to purify myself of my blood-guilt. But a woman, a female who is so unlike a man in every way, she alone brought me down – she didn't even need to use a sword.

[1064] My son, now is the time that I need you to truly become my son – do not honour the name of your mother any more. Go get your mother, and with your own hands take her from the house and bring her here to me. I want to know for certain whether it pains you more to see my body tortured and mutilated than it does to see her body receive its just rewards from me.

[1070] Come on son – bring yourself to do this. Have some pity for me, since I seem pitiable in so many ways, crying out loud and weeping like a girl – nobody can ever say that he has seen me act like this before. In the past I always managed to do what was necessary and I was never reduced to tears, no matter what evils I had to endure. But now, this thing here has turned me into a woman.

[1076] So come here now – come closer, I say, and stand close to your father so that you can see what this misfortune has done to me and what I am suffering. I'll take off my coverings so that you can have a look at my illness. There – just look at me, can you see what has happened to my miserable body! Do you see how horrible, how pitiable I have become?

¹⁰⁸¹ Oh gods, oh gods – this pain is too much! Again and again these spasms of torture are shooting through me. It's passing through my sides, and this ruthless and vile sickness will not leave me in peace.

¹⁰⁸⁵ O lord Hades, please take me to your realm! O father Zeus, please strike me with your lightning! Hurl down your thunderbolt, father, and free me from my misery! Ohh! The pain is feeding on me yet again – it's coming, it's getting stronger!

¹⁰⁸⁹ Oh, my hands, my hands! Oh my back, my chest! Oh, my poor shoulders and arms! Are you the same arms that once defeated that lion in Nemea, that plague on the herdsmen, that creature nobody could approach or confront? And are you the same arms that overpowered the Hydra in Lerna? And were you the arms that defeated that fierce army of those monsters, those Centaurs that had two natures, part men but with feet of horses, so hostile and lawless and overwhelming in their might? And were you once the arms that defeated the beast of Erymanthus, and that beast Cerberus, that three-headed hound of Hades that lives below the earth, once thought to be undefeatable, and the dreaded offspring of Echidna, and that serpent who guarded the golden apples of the Hesperides at the far end of the earth? Are you really the arms that accomplished those labours?

¹¹⁰¹ And I've had my taste of thousands of other labours, and none of them yet has been able to raise a trophy for having defeated me in battle. But now just look at me – my body is torn to shreds, my limbs and joints are barely hanging from my body and I am in such a pathetic state, beaten down and defeated by this horrible affliction.

¹¹⁰⁵ I am called the son of the most noble of mothers, I claim to be the son of Zeus who rules the high heavens – and now just look at what has become of me! But you should know this – even if I am reduced to nothing, a nothing that can't even crawl on the ground, I'll still throw curses at the woman who did this to me, even when I am in a state like this!

¹¹⁰⁹ Just let that bitch come here, so that she'll be able to proclaim to everyone that I punish evildoers both in life and death!

Chorus: ¹¹¹³ O poor unhappy Greece – I can see how great your sadness, how great your mourning will be, if you find yourself deprived of this man.

Hyllus: ¹¹¹⁴ O father, since you have given me the chance to answer you, please be silent for a moment so that I can speak, even though you are so very sick. I'm only asking for what is right. Please give yourself over to me, and for a moment set aside this biting anger that has taken hold of you so strongly.

¹¹¹⁸ Otherwise you will never know how mistaken you are in your lust for vengeance, and how mistaken your anger is.

Heracles: ¹¹²⁰ Speak – say whatever you want and be done with it. I'm sick, my son, and I have no time to deal with riddles.

Hyllus: I have come to tell you about my mother. It's about what she did and how it was an accident.

Heracles: ¹¹²⁴ What? No – damn you! How can you even dare to speak about her, the mother who has murdered your father, and in my very presence?

Hyllus: Yes, because the way things are with her it would be wrong to be silent.

Heracles: No, you are wrong there. For the crime she has committed there should be silence.

Hyllus: But not when you consider what has just happened to her, as you'll soon admit.

Heracles: Go ahead then and speak if you must. But just be careful that you don't prove to be a traitor.

Hyllus: [1130] Then I'll speak. She's dead – she just died.

Heracles: How? Who killed her? I am not sure how to react to this news. It feels like good news, but at the same time it's so bitter.

Hyllus: She killed herself, by her own hand – no one else did this.

Heracles: Oh gods! She died too soon – she should have died by my hand!

Hyllus: Even your anger would fade and your mind would change if you learned the whole story.

Heracles: [1135] What you are telling me sounds strange and terrible. Go on, tell me – what do you mean?

Hyllus: Even though she did a terrible thing, the reasons for her actions were good and noble.

Heracles: So then it's a good thing that she killed your father?

Hyllus: She thought that she was applying a love-charm to your robe – she did it because she saw that new bride Iole arrive in the house.

Heracles: [1140] And who is there in Trachis who is so good a magician who can come up with such a potion?

Hyllus: The Centaur Nessus long ago convinced her to stir up your passion with this drug, this love charm, whenever she felt the need.

Heracles: [1143] Oh no! This is so horrible! So this is how I come to my end. I am lost now, dead – there is no hope at all that is left for me.

[1143] I can't see the light any more. Now I finally know that the end is almost near. My son, you no longer have a father, so go and gather all your brothers, and call on the sad Alcmene, my dear mother who was the bride of Zeus, even though it cost her dearly. I want all of you to hear the final message of the oracle – I want to tell you the last prophecy regarding Heracles.

Hyllus: [1151] What? But you mother is not here. She is now living near to the shore at Tiryns. She has taken some of your children with her there, while I should tell you that some of the others are living in Thebes.

[1155] But, as for those of us who are already here, father – we'll obey you and do anything we must do in order to serve you.

Heracles: [1157] Then listen to me as I tell you what must be done. You have come to the point where you will show what kind of man you really are, Hyllus, you who are said to be my son.

[1159] Long ago my father Zeus revealed to me that I wouldn't be killed by the hand of any living creature, but that I would be taken down by someone who is dead and is a resident of Hades.

[1162] So this beast, this Centaur, has killed me, just as the divine prophecy predicted. He did it while he was dead and while I was still alive. And now I will reveal the new prophecies that are in accord with this old one. I entered the grove of the priests who serve the ancient prophetic oak at Dodona, those priests who live on the mountain there and sleep on the ground. And when I was there I wrote down the prophetic words of my father that the ancient oak spoke with what seemed like so many different voices.

[1169] At that time the oak said that at this very

moment, right now, I would finally find my release from labours – that everything would finally be over. I thought that this meant that I would be happy, but it turns out that it was instead saying that I would die, for there is no need for the dead to engage in any toils.

¹¹⁷⁴ So, my son, since all of this is coming true exactly as it has been predicted by the oracles, you must fight with me in this, and you must not wait and force me to prod you on with harsh and bitter words. But you must instead do exactly as I tell you, and discover all that is noble in yourself by agreeing to follow the most important of all laws – showing obedience to your father.

Hyllus: ¹¹⁷⁹ Father, I am scared at what your words may lead you to say, but I will obey you in whatever you say.

Heracles: Then you must give me your right hand first of all.

Hyllus: Please tell me why you need such a strong pledge. Why do you need me to swear an oath?

Heracles: Are you not going to quickly give me your hand but are you instead going to disobey me?

Hyllus: Here, look – here's my hand. I won't deny you anything.

Heracles: ¹¹⁸⁵ Now swear by Zeus, the great god who is my father.

Hyllus: But what am I swearing? To do what? You need to tell me what I am swearing to do?

Heracles: You need to swear that you'll complete that task that I'll give you.

Hyllus: Yes, of course – I swear, with Zeus as my witness, that I'll do what you ask me to do.

Heracles: And pray that you will receive a punishment if you break your oath.

Hyllus: ¹¹⁹⁰ Yes, I'll pray for that as well – although there is no need to do so, since I will keep my word and so won't face any punishment.

Heracles: Fine. Then do you know Mount Oeta, which belongs to mighty Zeus?

Hyllus: Yes, I know that mountain well – I've often gone there to make sacrifices.

Heracles: ¹¹⁹³ Then your task is to lift my body and take it there, using your own hands and those of your friends. When you have cut down wood from the deeply rooted trees there and collected branches from the wild olives, then I want you to throw my body on top of the pile of wood – and then you must take a torch of burning pinewood and set fire to the whole lot of it.

¹¹⁹⁹ And there shouldn't be any tears or sadness in this, but you'll do this task without weeping or mourning – if you are truly my son. And if you don't do this for me, then I'll wait for you below the earth, a horrible curse against you for eternity.

Hyllus: Oh no – father, what are you saying? What are you forcing me to do?

Heracles: ¹²⁰⁴ This is what must be done! If you won't do it, then you can become the son of some other man – don't call yourself my son anymore!

Hyllus: But father, once more – what are you asking me to do? You are asking me to be your murderer – I'll be polluted by your death, a patricide.

Heracles: No, that's not what I am asking you to do. Rather, I want you to be my healer, the only kind of doctor who can truly heal my pain.

Hyllus: ¹²¹⁰ How can I cure your body by setting it on fire?

HERACLES: If that's the part that bothers you, then at least do all the rest of that which I asked.

HYLLUS: I'll carry you there – there's no way that I can deny you that.

HERACLES: And you'll build the pyre just as I asked you to do?

HYLLUS: ¹²¹⁴ Yes, with the one exception that I will not put my own hands to the final deed you ask. Otherwise I'll do everything else that you asked. I will not let you down.

HERACLES: That will be enough. Now in addition to all of this, please grant me one other small favour.

HYLLUS: No matter whether it is large or small, I'll do it for you.

HERACLES: I suppose you know who the daughter of Eurytus is? The one you mentioned already.

HYLLUS: ¹²²⁰ You mean that girl who is back at the house, right? The one named Iole?

HERACLES: ¹²²¹ Yes, that's her. This, then, is what I ask you to do – when I am dead, if you want to prove your love to me and show your loyalty, remembering the oath that you swore to me, then you'll take Iole as your wife.

¹²²⁴ And don't disobey me in this. Don't let any other man but you take her as his wife, this girl who has already slept with me – you must marry her!

¹²²⁸ Obey me in this. If you fail to do the small things when you have already agreed to do great things it will negate your earlier favour.

HYLLUS: Oh my! It's wrong to argue with a man who is sick, but who could bear to see you thinking the kinds of thoughts you are suggesting?

HERACLES: You sound as if you're going to do none of the things I asked you to do.

HYLLUS: ¹²³³ Well, this girl Iole is the sole cause for my mother's death, she's the reason that you are in the state you're in – so what kind of a person would be happy to do this, unless his mind has been poisoned by the avenging Furies?

¹²³⁶ O father, I think it would be better for me to die than to have to live with her – my greatest enemy.

HERACLES: ¹²³⁸ It seems that this young man will not give me my due respect and honours, when I lie before him dying!

But, I warn you, if you disobey my orders, then a curse from the gods will be waiting for you.

HYLLUS: Oh! It seems to me that you'll soon show how sick you are.

HERACLES: You…you…you are stirring up my agony, my pain, after it had been put to rest for a while.

HYLLUS: Oh, what should I do? I'm torn in so many different directions.

HERACLES: Only because you refuse to listen to your father.

HYLLUS: ¹²⁴⁵ But if I listen to you father, won't that be disloyal as well?

HERACLES: It can't be disloyal if you are doing the thing that pleases my heart.

HYLLUS: So then you are commanding me to do this, and that's what makes it right?

HERACLES: Yes, I command you to do this – and I call on the gods as my witnesses.

HYLLUS: ¹²⁴⁹ Then I'll do it. I won't refuse since you have shown the gods that this deed is in accordance with your will. No one could ever think I am a traitor, father, if I am only obeying your orders.

HERACLES: [1252] You are doing the right thing. Now quickly, before another act of pain comes to strike me, take me to the place where the pyre is to be built and get it made as soon as you can.

[1255] Come on, let's go – hurry. Lift me up. This will be my true rest after all of my labours, the final end of Heracles.

HYLLUS: There's nothing that can prevent these things from being accomplished, since I am doing what you demand of me, father – what you compel me to do.

HERACLES: [1259] Come now, O you stubborn soul of mine, before the sickness comes on again and attacks me – act as if there's a bit in your mouth and don't let any cries of pain escape your mouth.

Come on Heracles, be strong – make it seem as if you're doing something that is a pleasure!

Enter the companions of Hyllus, who lift up Heracles' bed

HYLLUS: [1264] Lift him up, my friends. Show as much compassion for him as I do, for all that has happened to him. You can see how little compassion the gods have shown, considering all that has taken place. These gods produce us and are called our fathers, and yet they can look on sufferings such as these and do nothing!

[1270] No one can see the future. But what is here right now is pitiful and sad for us to see – and it is shameful for the gods. But it's hardest of all on the man there – my father – who is the victim of this disaster.

[1275] You over there, you women of Trachis – come from the house along with us. You have just witnessed some terrible deaths, and some sufferings the likes of which have never been seen before. These things were strange and horrible – and none of these things has happened without the will of Zeus.

Translated from the Greek by Stephen Russell, PhD

Chapter 13
Sophocles
Ajax

THE STORY: In the waning days of the Trojan War, the great hero Achilles is killed, and there is a fight over who will get his arms. The mighty Ajax, "second best of the Greeks," believes that he deserves to take the arms, but after a vote they are instead awarded to Odysseus. Ajax is enraged by this decision, which he sees as an insult to his name. This play is the story of how Ajax responds – it is the story of a fallen hero, and his descent into madness. Apollodorus covers the outline of this story in his *Epitome*:

[E.5.5] The death of Achilles filled the army with gloom and dismay, and they buried him with Patroclus in the White Island in the Black Sea, mixing the bones of the two together. It is said that after his death Achilles now lives with his wife Medea in the Islands of the Blessed. And the Greeks held games in his honour, at which Eumelus won the chariot-race, Diomedes the footrace, Ajax won for throwing the discus, and Teucer won for archery.

[E.5.6] When the arms of Achilles were offered as a prize to the bravest, Ajax and Odysseus came forward to enter their names. The judges were the Trojans or, according to some, they were the Greek allies, and Odysseus was picked as the winner. Ajax was so overwhelmed by anger that he planned a night attack on the army; but Athena drove him mad, and she turned him, sword in hand, against the cattle, and in his frenzy he slaughtered all the cattle along with their herdsmen, mistaking them for Greeks.

[E.5.7] But after Ajax came back to his senses he also killed himself. And Agamemnon ordered that his body could not be burned, and so Ajax is the only man of all those who fell at Troy who lies buried in a coffin. His grave is at Rhoeteum.

CHARACTERS

ATHENA
ODYSSEUS
AJAX
CHORUS (SAILORS FOR SALAMIS)
TECMESSA, THE WIFE OF AJAX
TEUCER, THE BROTHER OF AJAX
EURYSAKES, THE SON OF AJAX
MESSENGER
MENELAUS
AGAMEMNON
GUARDS (OF AJAX)

SCENE: Outside of Ajax's hut, on the coast of Troy.

Enter Athena, who stands to the side, and Odysseus

ATHENA: Odysseus, son of Laertes, as ever I am
  beside you as you creep about in search of an
  edge over your enemies, yet it is confusing to
  find you here by the sea, in the camp of an ally –

Ajax, who holds the last position in the battle lines, guarding the rear of your own troops. You've followed his traces in the sand unerringly like a Spartan tracking hound, and yes – no need to steal a peek – the man you seek is inside that hut, his head and sword hand dripping sweat from the recent slaughter. But tell me why we are here, so I might advise you.

Odysseus: [14] Dearest Athena, nearest to me of all the gods, though I cannot see you I hear your voice clearly. You are not mistaken: I have been following the trail left by an enemy, and now I see it is Ajax the shield-bearer, and no other. Last night he committed a terrible act of treason against us. If it was him. Nothing is certain, surely we can hope... There is still confusion in the matter, so I took it upon myself to find out the culprit personally...

[25] This morning it was discovered that someone had killed the herd of our looted cattle, and with them the guards we posted. Everyone says that man in there is the guilty party. A witness told me he saw Ajax running off alone through the field with his sword dripping blood. Immediately I picked up the trail and... and I am confused. What goes on here?

[34] As ever, your arrival is timely, Athena. Your hand has always guided me surely...

Athena: Yes, I have long walked beside you, eager companion on your long road.

Odysseus: Dear goddess, am I doing the right thing in coming here?

Athena: O yes – this is the man you seek.

Odysseus: [40] What could have inspired him to this frenzy?

Athena: He was upset at the loss of the arms of Achilles – to you.

Odysseus: But why, then, attack the herd?

Athena: His intent was to murder you and your men.

Odysseus: His Greek brothers in arms?

Athena: [45] Yes, and he would have done it if I hadn't intervened.

Odysseus: How did he dare do such a thing? How did he think he'd get away with it?

Athena: At night, in secret.

Odysseus: How close did he come?

Athena: Very nearly all the way: the gates of Menelaus and Agamemnon.

Odysseus: [50] And what prevented him?

Athena: [51] It was me, of course. I diverted his rage toward the spot where the army's stolen cattle and undivided booty were stored, and there he cleaved the spines of the horned beasts on all sides of him, thinking that now, with his bare sword, he was slaughtering the sons of Atreus, Menelaus and Agamemnon, now cutting down one of the other commanders. Yes, I encouraged the man to wander deeper into his own madness, and laid this snare for him.

[61] Once he'd had his fill of killing, he bound up what few cattle remained alive and, still thinking them men, brought the flock back to his own tent, where he tortures them yet. Come, witness his plain madness, and tell the others what you've seen. Have courage.

[71] You in there! Yes, you, Ajax, with all your enemies in chains! I call on you to come outside!

Odysseus: What are you doing? Don't call him out!

ATHENA: [75] Oh, do be quiet: stop acting like such a coward.

ODYSSEUS: For pity's sake, just let him stay inside!

ATHENA: Why? What are you afraid of? Is he not just a man, after all?

ODYSSEUS: Yes, of course, but the hatred he must have borne for me… must still bear…

ATHENA: But isn't laughter sweetest when it's at our enemy's expense?

ODYSSEUS: [80] It's enough for me that he stays inside.

ATHENA: Are you superstitious about gazing on the face of madness, then?

ODYSSEUS: If he were in his right mind, then you know I would face him.

ATHENA: But he could not see you if you stood before him.

ODYSSEUS: Why? Has something happened to his eyes?

ATHENA: [85] It will. He will not see you.

ODYSSEUS: If the gods will it, I suppose it must be so.

ATHENA: Good. Now be quiet and stay put.

ODYSSEUS: Fine, but I'd sooner be anywhere else…

ATHENA: [89] Ajax! Must a friend call you twice?

Enter Ajax from the hut

AJAX: [91] Why, Athena, welcome, blessed daughter of Zeus! I'm very glad that you are here so I can honour you with the spoils of my latest hunt.

ATHENA: [94] That is well said, to be sure, but tell me: did you push your sword all the way through the army of the Greeks?

AJAX: Yes, I can certainly brag on that account, I won't deny it.

ATHENA: Did your mighty sword-hand bring low the two sons of Atreus as well, then?

AJAX: Oh, yes, absolutely – never again will they disrespect Ajax!

ATHENA: Dead then, are they?

AJAX: [100] Yes, yes, the ones who robbed me of the glory that was my due are dead as they come.

ATHENA: Good enough, but what of the son of Laertes? Did he escape your wrath?

AJAX: You want to know what happened to your sneaky little pet?

ATHENA: Of course: your great rival, Odysseus.

AJAX: [105] My dear goddess, that is the best part: he sits bound in chains within the hut, since I am not quite ready to let him die just yet.

ATHENA: What do you plan to do with him? What will it gain you?

AJAX: First, I will lash him to the post in the center of my hut…

ATHENA: Yes?

AJAX: [110]…then I will lash his back to tatters, and then I will kill him.

ATHENA: Surely you will not torture the poor man?

AJAX: Athena, please be content to have your way in all other things: that man will pay the only apt penalty. I will not change my mind.

ATHENA: [114] Well, there it is. If you are so determined to do this thing, then go, set your hand hard to the culmination of all you have planned.

AJAX: [116] I'm off, then! Bless you, dear lady, and I hope you'll always be my ally!

Exit Ajax back into the hut

ATHENA: [118] See, Odysseus, how great is the power of the gods? Was there ever a man that planned more carefully or completely than that one? Or one more skilled at dealing with the ups and downs of his fate?

ODYSSEUS: [121] I can't think of any. And yet I can't help but feel sorry for him, though he is my enemy. He is undone by madness, and I can't look upon him without thinking how easily his fate could be my own, and I finally see that all of us who live are nothing other than ghosts and empty shadows.

ATHENA: [127] Look upon this picture and never say an arrogant word toward the gods, nor think yourself better than another merely because you are stronger or more favoured than they. A single day can bring low all the high things of man. The gods love those who know humility, and hate the wicked.

Exit Odysseus, and Athena disappears; Enter the Chorus

CHORUS: [134] Son of Telamon, who holds the solid earth and sea-ringed isle of Salamis, we rejoice when you prosper, but when you are backhanded by Zeus, or if an insult from the Greeks should reach your ears, we become fearful as the round-eyed dove.

[141] From the night just ending a great noise rises, bringing disgrace upon us. Word is that you visited the meadow where the horses pasture and with your sword destroyed the captured cattle of the Greek troops, yet to be shared.

[148] Slanderous Odysseus whispers it in every ear, persuasive, for the things he says about you are easy to believe, for those who wish to believe them. He who takes aim at a great man has a large target: it would not be so easy to spread such infamy about specks like us, but envy works against the great, though in war small men soon fall without their leadership. For small men are supported by the great as surely as the great are by the small.

[162] But try telling the small man that – they it is who eagerly raise a clamour against you. And without you at our head we are powerless to defend against them. Out of your line of sight they twitter away like a flock of birds, but just like birds they would surely stop their chatter and fly if you were suddenly to appear, as from the shadow of an eagle overhead.

[172] Was it Artemis, daughter of Zeus – O terrible Rumour, mother of shame! – who loosed you at the troops cattle? Perhaps she felt she wasn't sufficiently thanked for some victory, felt cheated of some glory owed, or didn't receive her portion of a hunt? Or could it be the war-god Ares, offended in some wise on the field of battle, who punishes you with this nightmare scenario? For never, lord Ajax, would your own inclination have tempted you so far astray that you would war on cattle – it must be a sickness sent by the gods! We pray that Zeus and Apollo protect us from this evil Greek speech, but if the great kings are telling lies, and if Odysseus, descendant of Sisyphus, is chief among the liars, do not, lord, do not linger longer in this hut by the sea, for it only fans the flame of their speculation.

[192] Please: up, out of your seat, where you have loitered too long in the lull between battles, banking the flame of destruction until it licks at heaven. The spite of your enemies wastes no time, upon this you may rely: they laugh openly at you, with words like sword blades, cutting us deep.

Enter Tecmessa from the hut

TECMESSA: [201] Friends who sailed on the ship of Ajax, fellow descendants of the earthborn race of Erechtheus, we who are so far away from the house of Telamon, yet love it dearly: cry out! For our mighty, strong-shouldered Ajax has gone down, swamped by a dark storm of sickness.

CHORUS: [208] What burden has the night exchanged for day? Please tell us, daughter of Phrygian Teleutas, since mighty Ajax loves you dearly and holds you his bride, though captured as a prize of war. We know you would not tell us anything but the truth.

TECMESSA: [214] How should I speak the unspeakable? For I'm about to tell you of a misery as painful as death. Last night our great Ajax was struck mad, and has since been actively bringing disgrace upon us all. Look inside the tent and see his victims – more properly sacrifices – still leaking blood, all bearing his unmistakable signature.

CHORUS: [221] The unbearable picture you have painted of an out of control man is the very same the Greek leaders are spreading, and makes our worst fear real, however heartily we wish to deny it!

[227] How we dread the inevitable outcome, for everyone knows the man must die who with maddened hand struck down cattle and their guardians.

TECMESSA: [233] Oh no! Then it was from there that he led the cattle in chains? Oh horrible! He slaughtered some of them right away, but others he hacked apart bit by bit, chopping randomly at their sides! Then suddenly he fixed on two white-hooved rams, slit the tongue out of one of them before cutting off its head and throwing it away. As for the other, he tied it to a post and horse-whipped it endlessly, cursing it all the while! What more proof could I need that a god had caused him to do these things?

CHORUS: [245] Now is the time to hide our faces and flee here with all haste: perhaps we might escape by boat, seated among the swift rowers, to wherever the boat will take us. For two kings utter such dire threats against us that we fear death by stoning – for us and for him. We stand to share the punishment of Ajax, who is in the toils of a terrible fate.

TECMESSA: [257] But his madness is over now, as suddenly as it appeared. His anger has ended and he is once again in his right mind, but a new pain has shown itself to him, for what can be worse than when a man looks upon his own misery and realizes he caused it himself?

CHORUS: [263] But this is good news, woman! Madness can be forgiven once it has passed!

TECMESSA: [265] But ask yourselves: which is worse, to rejoice in your friends' destruction, or to share in their pain?

CHORUS: One is as bad as the other!

TECMESSA: Then, now that he is no longer ill, we are doubly troubled.

CHORUS: [270] How so? What do you mean?

TECMESSA: [271] While he was in the throes of madness, at least he enjoyed what he was doing, though for those of us who were in our right minds it was disaster. Now that he is sane again he is afflicted by guilt and shame, and even more desolate than the rest of us – tragedy compounded!

CHORUS: [278] Yes, we see it now. He must indeed have been struck a blow by some god. Otherwise how could his pain be greater now that his sickness is ended?

Tecmessa: Yet that is how it is.

Chorus: ²⁸² But what set him off? We share this grief, so please tell us everything.

Tecmessa: ²⁸⁴ Very well, as you have an interest in this matter. Last night, when all of the lamps had been put out, he took his double-edged sword and stalked off on his insane mission.

²⁸⁸ I tried to stop him, saying – "What is it, Ajax? What are you doing? Where do you go when you haven't been called and no messengers ask for you, not even the sound of the war trumpets? Both armies are asleep."

²⁹² His answer was short and familiar to me – "Keep quiet. It is a woman's place to remain silent. But not Ajax." And he rushed off alone.

²⁹⁴ All I know of what followed is that he returned dragging bulls, herd dogs and sheep, all lashed together. Some of them he cut off their heads, others he turned upside down and killed by breaking their backs, and some of them he bound and tortured, falling upon the menagerie just as if they were men!

³⁰¹ Not long past he ran outside and conversed with some shadow, first damning the sons of Atreus, Agamemnon and Menelaus, then speaking badly of Odysseus, and laughing like hell all the while about the violence he had done defeating them.

³⁰⁵ But eventually, after he came back inside – with time and difficulty – he returned to his senses, and looking around the slaughterhouse, he struck his head and cried aloud, and threw himself down among the slaughtered beasts, clutching his hair and scratching his face.

³¹¹ And then, for a long time, he sat there, not saying a word. Finally he turned to me and in a threatening tone demanded that I tell him everything that had happened, and what depth of trouble he was in now.

³¹⁵ My friends, I was terrified, and told him everything exactly as I had seen and understood it. And as I finished he cried such wracking sobs and moans as I'd never heard from him before. He always told me that crying was for cowards or the weak – in the past his groan was never so shrill, for previously it was the sound of a bellowing bull.

³²³ Now brought low by evil fortune, the man sits not eating, not drinking, there in the midst of that carnage. It's clear that he has something terrible in mind – I can see it.

³²⁸ Please go inside – help him, if you can. A man like Ajax can be swayed by the words of his friends.

Chorus: ³³¹ O Tecmessa, daughter of Teleutas, it's terrible if, as you've told us, the man was driven mad by evil spirits.

Ajax (inside the hut): Oh no, oh no... no no no.....

Tecmessa: ³³⁴ He is getting worse! Do you not hear him?

Ajax (inside the hut): Oh no, oh no... no no no.....

Chorus: It sounds as if he's still mad, or mad again from the sight of what his sickness has done.

Ajax (inside the hut): My son, my son!

Tecmessa: ³⁴⁰ Eurysakes, he's shouting for you! What is he planning? Where are you, son? We are ruined!

Ajax (inside the hut): Teucer! I want Teucer! Where is Teucer? Or is he still fighting while I sit here dying?

Chorus: [344] He sounds more or less coherent. Open the door, and perhaps, when he sees us, he'll feel some compunction regarding our situation.

Tecmessa: The doors are open – see how things stand…

The doors of the hut are opened

Ajax: [349] Oh, my shipmates, my friends, the only ones still loyal to me – look at the waves of blood that lap about my ankles!

Chorus (to Tecmessa): [354] Perhaps you were right – we should come back later…

Ajax: [356] Oh, my only friends, you who brought me here, manning the oars – you and you alone can help end my suffering. Come slaughter me amongst the animals, I beg you!

Chorus: Don't say such things! You can't cure evil with evil, you will only cause more pain.

Ajax: [364] Are you blind? Can't you see the mighty deeds valiant Ajax has wreaked upon his enemies, the defenseless beasts of the field? I am a laughingstock, the shame too great to ever live down.

Tecmessa: Lord Ajax, we beg you –

Ajax: [369] Won't you just leave me alone! You must distance yourself from me. Ahhh….

Tecmessa: In the name of the gods, we beg you, be sensible and listen.

Ajax: [372] If only I hadn't let those bastards slip through my fingers, and made the fields flow with the blood of beasts instead!

Chorus: What profit is there in desolation over what cannot be changed?

Ajax: [379] Oh, Odysseus, it is you who have done this to me, you affliction, dirtiest rat crawling in the army – how you must be laughing at me now!

Chorus: But, Ajax, everyone laughs or suffers as the gods see fit.

Ajax: If only I could see him now, the devil, though I am done for…

Chorus: Hold your proud tongue! Can't you see that it's talk such as this that has landed us in this situation?

Ajax: [387] O Zeus, father of my ancestors, if first you would allow me to destroy that detested trickster and the two ruling kings with him – then I would gladly kill myself!

Tecmessa: [392] If you are praying for that, then ask too that I die with you, for what would become of me after?

Ajax: [394] O Stygian Hades, you shine a dark, seductive light, a gloom that is so bright for me: take me, take me, gather me in to live with you. For I have lost my right to look on the race of the gods, nor would I take any pleasure from human companionship. Goddess Athena is torturing me to death, and so where can I flee? Is there any bolt hole that would have one such as me? All of my great deeds have been washed away, my friends, vengeance fallen upon me by means of this farcical 'victory' in the midst of which I stand, for which the army will relish my murder with their swords in both hands.

Tecmessa: [410] Terrible that a sane man should say such things as he would never have said before today.

Ajax: [412] O waves raging in the sea, goodbye, and goodbye caves of the coast! You've held me fast a great long time hereabout Troy, but no longer will you hold me alive, let everyone beware and understand!

[418] O river Scamander and your nearby streams, so friendly to the Greeks, you'll never see my like again, I dare boast, or a greater

man that the Trojan army has seen come from Greece. Yet now I must do without honour.

CHORUS: [428] We can hardly prevent it, but are not sure this is wise talk coming from one who has fallen on such evil times.

AJAX: [430] Ai-ya! Who would have thought that my name – Ai-yax – would so well foretell my misery? For now I can shout "ai-ya" endlessly and it would never be enough.

[434] My own father sacked Troy with Heracles and returned with all glory, in first place of excellence in the army, with most spoils and honours. I, his son, came to this land with no less strength than he, nor did I achieve lesser deeds with my own hands – yet I am disgraced by the Greeks and will die.

[441] But I am sure of one thing: if Achilles was alive and able to decide which man of all of us would be the most worthy to have his arms, none would have received them before me. Yet the sons of Atreus give them to that scheming liar, spitting upon my own great deeds!

[447] If my mind had not been driven off course, causing my eye to miss the mark, I assure you they would not have lived to fix such a crooked judgment against another man – I'd have been the last.

[450] But Athena – fierce, unconquerable daughter of Zeus – knew what I was up to when I set out against them, grabbed hold and tripped me, caused me to stain my hands with the blood of cattle, not men. So they escaped, and now they are laughing. Yet any coward can escape a better man if the gods choose them over him.

[457] What now? Clearly I am hated by the gods and the army of the Greeks as well, not to mention the entire city of Troy and surrounding plains. Do I go home, cross the Aegean alone, leaving my appointed station and the sons of Atreus? And how shall I look my father Telamon in the eye when I arrive? How allow him to see me return without honours when he won such great prizes in victory? I couldn't endure it.

[466] Should I go instead to the walls of Troy and challenge every last Trojan to hand-to-hand combat, proving my worth to the Greeks by dying there fighting on their behalf? That would certainly make the son of Atreus happy – so that cannot happen.

[470] There must be a way to prove to my aged father that his son is no coward. It's shameful for a man to desire long life when evil surrounds him on all sides. What pleasure is gained from a day when all it does is move you that much closer to death? Any man whose heart beats for empty hopes is no man at all in my opinion.

[479] To be noble one must either live well or die well. That is all I have to say.

CHORUS: [481] Ajax, no one is saying you speak falsely – your words come direct from your own proud heart – but you must give way, allow your friends to prevail over you in this matter, and drop these dark thoughts.

TECMESSA: [485] My lord Ajax, fate is necessity: I myself was born the daughter of a free man, as rich and as powerful as any in Phrygia – but now I am a slave. In this the will of the gods and your own hand were in accord, and so, since I have come to share your bed, I honour you and want what is best for you. Now I am begging you, in the name of Zeus who rules this house, and of the bed in which we were united: please do not abandon me to the jeers of your enemies by making me their captive! For on the day that you die I will be taken by the Greeks and live out the remainder of my life with the invective of my new Greek masters ringing in my ears: "See the concubine of Ajax, our mightiest suicide: once admired, now she is nothing more than a slave!"

504 My destiny is my own, but must I carry it and your shame as well? And, too, think of your father, whom you would be abandoning to bitter old age, not to mention your mother who still has many years left and spends each of them praying that you will come home to her alive. And above all, my lord, pity your son, who deprived of your care will grow up despised and abused.

514 Think of all the sorrow you bequeath to us if you die. There is nothing I can look to other than you. With your own spear you destroyed my home, and another fate took my mother and father to Hades. I have no other country but you, and no currency. You are my life and my salvation.

520 Please think of me if I have ever afforded you a moment's pleasure. Kindness should beget kindness, should it not? A man who would forget a debt of kindness was never a noble man.

Chorus: 525 Ajax, if you have any pity in your heart, you will hear and praise the words of this woman.

Ajax: She will certainly receive all due praise from me, so long as she listens and does as I command.

Tecmessa: Dearest Ajax, you know I shall obey you in every way.

Ajax: 530 Then bring my son to me now.

Tecmessa: But I sent him away because I was afraid.

Ajax: Of my madness, you mean.

Tecmessa: Afraid you would kill him.

Ajax: That would be in keeping with my fate.

Tecmessa: 535 And I was trying to avert it.

Ajax: Yes, yes, good thinking.

Tecmessa: Then tell me what I can do to help you now.

Ajax: Bring me my son and let me speak to him face-to-face.

Tecmessa: Of course – the servants are protecting him nearby.

Ajax: 540 Then what is keeping him?

Tecmessa: Eurysakes, my son! Your father is calling for you! Whoever is watching over him, it is safe now: bring him here!

Ajax: Are they deaf, or merely slow?

Tecmessa: The guard is bringing him now.

Enter a Guard with Eurysakes

Ajax: 545 Lift him up, any son of mine will scarcely be fazed by the sight of newly-spilled blood. Let him be broken in like a horse, trained in the savagery of his father, so that he might be just like him. My son, I hope you'll be more fortunate than I have been, but in all other things my equal. If so, you'll turn out well.

552 But just now I envy you your ignorance, because you can have no idea of the troubles that are at hand. Sometimes the sweetest thing in life is to be innocent, for what you do not know can't hurt you. But a time must come when it will be necessary for you to show the enemies of your father what sort of man you are and who raised you.

558 Until then, enjoy the soft breezes, let your young soul get lost in them, and be a joy to your mother. Neither the Greeks nor anyone else will dare insult you even with me out of

the picture, for my brother, Teucer, will be your tireless protector and raise you well, even if he does wander off to hunt his enemies from time to time. You shield-bearing soldiers, my fellow sailors, I command you to share in this task and communicate my command to my brother Teucer that he should lead this boy to my home, to Telemon and my mother, so that he may care for them in their old age and see them gently into the dark regions of the god below.

[572] Tell him that my arms must not be given to the Greeks to dispose of in some contest where a crooked judge can decide the outcome – and they particularly shouldn't be given to he who has destroyed me. Rather, you my son, Eurysakes – your name means "broad shield", do you know it? – you should take my shield. Grip it tightly by its well-stitched handle and carry its impenetrable thickness, made from seven hides, before you. This shield is yours, my son. Direct Teucer that my other arms be buried with me.

[578] But quick now, take the child inside and lock the gates as best you can. No, don't cry in front of the hut – women are so prone to weeping – any good doctor will tell you that a boil that needs it is best lanced quickly.

CHORUS: [583] It is frightening to see you in such haste – your words have too sharp an edge.

TECMESSA: [585] O my lord Ajax, what does your wild heart drive you to now?

AJAX: Do not question me. Control your tongue, woman.

TECMESSA: I beg you in the name of your son and of the gods not to betray us!

AJAX: [589] You weary me! Don't you understand that I no longer serve the gods?

TECMESSA: Blasphemy!

AJAX: Tell it to someone they haven't betrayed!

TECMESSA: Won't you be persuaded?

AJAX: You've said far too much already!

TECMESSA: Only out of terror, my lord!

AJAX: Just shut the gates. Quickly!

TECMESSA: In the name of the gods, soften your heart!

AJAX: [595] You disappoint me if you think, after all this time, that you can teach me to change my character, especially now. You knew who I was when I took you for my wife.

Exit Tecmessa, Eurysakes, and Guard; Ajax following behind

CHORUS: [596] Famed island of Salamis, caressed by the sea, blessed of the gods, always bright, never fog-bound! For us it's been such a long, miserable time so far away from you. We no longer count the months, and make our beds here worn thin by the passage of time and the sad expectation that one day soon we'll go, not home, but to Hades, the dark destroyer.

[609] Ajax is with us here and will not be cured – best friend and protector turned the most formidable of our innumerable enemies! Alas, his spirit shares lodgings with a divine-sent madness. Long ago, Salamis, you sent him forth valiant to glorious war, but now that he feeds his lonely thoughts he is a source only of grief to his friends, while his former feats, excellently achieved, have all fallen away, leaving him friendless in the eyes of the sons of Atreus, miserable as they are.

[621] Doubtless, when his ancient mother hears tell he is sick with disease that routs the mind – cry sorrow! – she must match the piteous plaint of the nightingale or hold the shriek

deep within, beat her fists against her breast, and tear out her thin grey hair.

⁶³⁵ For better hidden away in Hades beneath the earth is the man who suffers from the empty sickness, for though his inheritance from his father's family was better than that of any of the toiling Greeks he no longer has the temper that he grew up with but is become a stranger to himself. Pity his poor father: how sad the madness of his son, which he is yet to know and has no cause to expect, for it is a ruin never known to afflict any in his family before.

Enter Ajax, carrying his sword, followed by Tecmessa

AJAX: ⁶⁴⁶ Time, being long, eventually sees the springing up of every happenstance, and just as surely sees them buried again. And, too, nothing is immutable: even the most hardened oath and resolute intention can be conquered by time.

⁶⁵⁰ Even I, who was once so steely – as unbreakable as iron – for the sake of a woman have softened my words. I pity her for making her a widow and my son an orphan, leaving both in the hands of my enemies.

⁶⁵⁴ So I'll go to the bathing place in the meadow by the shore and there wash away the filth and blood that coats me, that I might escape the anger of the goddess. From there I'll go to some out of the way place, and hide my sword, this most hateful of weapons. I'll dig a hole in a place nobody can find, and Night and Hades can keep it safe for me down below.

⁶⁶¹ Ever since I got this sword as a gift from Hector, my worst enemy, I haven't had anything good from the Greeks. The proverb is true, then – the gifts of enemies are not gifts at all and bring no profit.

⁶⁶⁶ In future I shall know better how to yield to the gods, and learn to respect the sons of Atreus again. They are the rulers, after all, one ought to bend to their will. Of course one should. Even the most formidable of powers must yield, in time, to authority. Terrible winters piled with snow must give way to fruitful spring, and even eternal night stands aside so that day might light its torch. The blast of the wind puts the raging sea to sleep, and not even all-encompassing Sleep holds forever those it has bound.

⁶⁷⁷ Recognizing this, how could I not learn moderation and restraint? I shall learn it, for just now I see that an enemy should be hated only so far if he may later be a friend. Though as to that, there are friends and there are friends, and where some are concerned it is wiser not to put too much stock in the harbour of their friendship, and friends like those should expect a like amount of friendship in return.

⁶⁸⁴ But matters at hand will now be well. As for you, woman, pray to the gods that I can put this right.

Exit Tecmessa

⁶⁸⁷ And you, my brothers in arms, honour me the same way that she does and, if my brother happens by, ask him to care for us and be loyal to you until my return. I am going where it's necessary for me to travel, but do just as I say and perhaps you may soon hear that, though I am unhappy now, I have been saved.

Exit Ajax

CHORUS: ⁶⁹³ We tremble with delight! We soar on wings of spiraling joy! O Pan, o Pan, O sea-roaming god, appear to us from Mt. Cyllene's snowy brow, our lord who makes the gods dance, so that in our company you may dance the rapid Mysian and Cnossian steps that you invented! And may lord Apollo, the Delian god, come over the Icarian sea to keep company with us, undisguised, well-disposed to us for all time!

706 Ares has lifted the coins from off our eyes, letting in again, O Zeus, the white light of a happy day dawning. Ajax has forgot his sorrows and once more performed with full sacrifices the rites of the gods, paying greatest reverence to them and their divine law! Time extinguishes all things and relights them again; now we can truly say nothing is impossible, when, beyond our hopes, Ajax has been translated from anger against the sons of Atreus.

Enter a Messenger

Messenger: 719 Dear friends, I must report that Teucer has arrived from the mountains of Mysia. He went directly to the tent of generals in the midst of the camp and was abused on the way by the mass of the Greeks. Surrounding him, they hurled invectives and insults at him, threatening to stone to death the brother of the lunatic who conspired with the enemy. Their swords were in their hands when the elders stepped in and put an end to it.

733 But where is Ajax? It's important your commander know everything that has happened.

Chorus: 735 He left a short while ago a changed man, with a whole new outlook.

Messenger: Uh-oh. It seems I have been too slow getting here.

Chorus: 740 What do you mean?

Messenger: Teucer instructed me that Ajax must not be allowed to leave his hut before he has a chance to speak with him.

Chorus: But he's already gone, as we told you, and in good spirits, left to make peace with the gods, his anger set aside.

Messenger: 745 It will do him no good if Calchas' prophecy is true.

Chorus: What now? What do you know about this that we should know?

Messenger: 748 The way I heard it, Calchas slipped out of council in order to whisper in Teucer's ear that Ajax must not come out of his tent as long as there is daylight – that is, if he wanted to see him alive again. For the anger of the goddess still drives him, if only for this one day. Or so the prophet said. He also said: "The unwise mighty are brought low by terrible afflictions fit for mortals who have somehow convinced themselves they rank with the gods. On the day he left home, Ajax was given good fatherly advice, but he would not listen: 'Son, strive for victory with your spear, but always win with the help of a god.' But the prideful boy boasted: 'Father, with the gods on his side, anybody might win glory: but it takes a real man to do without them.' And on another occasion, Athena offered him assistance against the Trojans and he told her to go stand near the rest of the Greeks! For where he was standing the line would never break! Thus he incurred the wrath of the goddess. He does not see that he is just a man."

778 But take heart. If he is still alive today, perhaps you might still save him – with Athena's help. This is what the prophet told Teucer, and Teucer sent me to tell you. But as Calchas is a wise prophet, if you dally, that man is good as dead.

Chorus: 784 Poor Tecmessa, daughter of an ill-starred family, come hear what this man has to say and cease rejoicing.

Enter Tecmessa and Eurysakes

Tecmessa: What now? Why have you recalled me from my sweet relief?

Chorus: [789] This fellow brings disturbing news of Ajax.

Tecmessa: O no….well, man, what is it? Surely we've had disaster enough for one day?

Messenger: I don't know how things stand for you personally, but as for Ajax, if indeed he is no longer inside...

Tecmessa: He has gone, yes – what are you saying?

Messenger: [795] Teucer sends word advising against it.

Tecmessa: But where is Teucer, and why did he say it?

Messenger: He'll be here soon, but sent me ahead, for he believes Ajax must die if he leaves the protection of the hut today.

Tecmessa: [800] How do you know all of this?

Messenger: From the prophet Calchas.

Tecmessa: [803] No! My friends, please save me from this new disaster! Some of you fetch Teucer here as quickly as possible; the rest go east and west of the harbour and find my husband wherever his black mood has led him! He has deceived me! He cares nothing for what happens to us, my son – what am I to do? One thing is certain: whatever it is, it must happen now, and I'll go as far as my strength will take me. Let's go! Hurry! There is no time for standing about when you're striving to save a man who is in a hurry to die!

Chorus: [813] We're on our way! The speed of our feet will be exceeded only by the conciseness and brevity with which we explain to you exactly how exceedingly fast we are leaving! Which is to say: fast! Okay, we're off, right................... now!

Exit Tecmessa, Eurysakes, the Messenger, and the Chorus; Enter Ajax

Ajax: [815] The killer stands where his thrust will cut the deepest, if he has the time for such calculation. This sword was a gift from Hector, the man most hateful to my sight. Now I will ask this hostile Trojan land to hold it for me very firmly, point up, newly sharpened on the iron-eating whetstone, so that it might be kind and give me a quick death.

[823] So. I am ready. This is my will. I call on you first, O Zeus, as is right, to help me. It's not a large boon that I ask. Please send some messenger to bring the news to Teucer, so that he will be the one to lift me up after I have fallen on my sword, and not one of my innumerable enemies, who would only use my body as food for dogs and birds.

[831] I also call on Hermes, guide of the underworld, to please put me gently to sleep when with a quick movement the point of the sword is pushed through my ribs.

[835] I call on the everlasting virgins, the holy Furies with their long strides, who always observe all human suffering, so that they may witness how I have been destroyed by the sons of Atreus. Please snatch those evil men away in a manner that's fitting for them. Just as they see me falling a suicide, let them perish at the hands of their closest relations! Come, swift avenging Furies – feed on the whole army! Spare no one!

[845] Helios, the Sun-god, who drives his chariot over the steep heaven, when you see my homeland, pull up a moment and announce my death to my old father and the wretched woman who nursed me. No doubt my

Tecmessa: mother's cries, when she hears of this, will echo throughout the entire city.

⁸⁵² But what's the use in moaning? The deed must be done, and with speed! Death, come visit me... and I shall return the favour...

⁸⁵⁶ I greet you Helios, shining light of the present day, for the very last time.

⁸⁵⁹ Holy soil of my home island Salamis, foundation of my father's home and hearth; famous Athens, and the people who grew up there with me; and these springs and rivers; and the wide Trojan plains... Farewell O my nurses! This is all that Ajax has to say to you. The rest I shall say to those in Hades below.

Exit Ajax; Enter the Chorus in two parts, from opposite sides

Chorus A: ⁸⁶⁶ Trouble upon trouble! Where have we failed to look? No place seems likelier than any other! But listen! Do you hear that?

Chorus B: That was us over here, your shipmates.

Chorus A: What news?

Chorus B: We've searched the entire west side of the harbour.

Chorus A: ⁸⁷⁵ And what have you found?

Chorus B: Trouble and toil, and little else.

Chorus A: Nor does the man make his presence known anywhere on the eastern side.

Chorus: ⁸⁷⁹ Which of the toiling sons of the sea who spends their time in endless hunting, or the goddesses of Olympus, or of the flowing rivers of the Bosphorus, might tell us they see that fierce-hearted man approach and from which direction? For we cannot see the stricken man.

Enter Tecmessa and the body of Ajax

Tecmessa: ⁸⁹¹ Oh no... oh no.... oh no...

Chorus: Who comes crying out from the woods?

Tecmessa: This is our ruin!

Chorus: ⁸⁹⁵ It is Tecmessa, his ill-fated bride, the captive of his spear, lost in grief.

Tecmessa: I am destroyed, friends.

Chorus: Tell us.

Tecmessa: Here is Ajax newly-slaughtered, sword hidden deep in his own belly.

Chorus: ⁹⁰⁰ Oh no... Our way home... Lord Ajax, you have killed your shipmates along with you. Poor man! And poor woman, too...

Tecmessa: This is how it is – all we can do now is cry.

Chorus: ⁹⁰⁵ But how did this happen? By whose hand...?

Tecmessa: By his own hand, this is clear, his sword fixed firmly in the ground to receive him.

Chorus: ⁹⁰⁹ We are ruined. We didn't see, and now you lie covered in your own blood, having died alone and lonely, without the solace of your friends, and we deaf to your cries.

Where shall unbreakable Ajax lie? Ill-omened name...

Tecmessa: ⁹¹⁵ He shall not be seen! I've hidden him with my cloak, for none of his friends could bear to look upon him while the blackened blood flows from his nostrils and the gaping wound that he inflicted on himself.

⁹²⁰ What should I do now? Which of his friends will lift Ajax up? Where is Teucer? If he were to arrive now he'd be just in time to bury his brother.

⁹²³ Oh, Ajax, for a man like you to have such

an end. Even your enemies should cry to see it.

CHORUS: ⁹²⁵ Immovable man: so finally you fulfill your inevitable destiny, bringing a final close to your interminable moaning through both day and night, and your passionate hatred for the sons of Atreus. That was the beginning of our trouble, when competition was declared for the arms of Achilles.

TECMESSA: ⁹³⁶ No... No... No....

CHORUS: It's true and blameless pain that twinges your heart.

TECMESSA: No... No... No....

CHORUS: ⁹⁴⁰ We understand, you loved him so.

TECMESSA: You understand it – I have to live with it.

CHORUS: ...You're right.

TECMESSA: ⁹⁴⁴ Next we'll be slaves, my poor, poor son – those are the manner of people who rule us now.

CHORUS: No, surely that would be unthinkable, even for the ruthless sons of Atreus. The gods will prevent them from doing so!

TECMESSA: ⁹⁵⁰ None of this would have happened if not for the gods!

CHORUS: It is true, they've placed a heavy burden on your shoulders.

TECMESSA: All this is the work of Pallas Athena, terrible daughter of Zeus, to please her dear Odysseus.

CHORUS: ⁹⁵⁵ No doubt our celebrated hero is enjoying a good laugh at Ajax's maddened suffering... What fun! Ha ha! And chuckling right along with him, the sons of Atreus.

TECMESSA: ⁹⁶¹ Let them rejoice at the misfortunes of this man! Though they had no use for him while he was alive, they will certainly regret the loss of his spear. Petty men don't know what they've got until it's gone.

⁹⁶⁶ His death, as painful to me as it is sweet to the Greeks, was for Ajax a pleasure – for with this he has deprived them of their victory. How will they laugh when the gods are the ones who killed him, not men?

⁹⁷¹ Let Odysseus enjoy his futile jeering, for Ajax cannot hear it anymore, and only to me is it a source of sorrow!

Enter Teucer

TEUCER: Oh no!

CHORUS: ⁹⁷⁵ Everyone be still. Hear the voice of Teucer, who cries out at this disaster.

TEUCER: Dearest Ajax! Face of my brother! Have you done as Rumour says you did?

CHORUS: The man is dead, Teucer – we can tell you that.

TEUCER: ⁹⁸⁰ If this is true, my fate hangs heavy as well.

CHORUS: Since it is so...

TEUCER: Oh no, no brother....

CHORUS: ...you may well lament.

TEUCER: This pain strikes deep.

CHORUS: Yes, it's terrible sharp.

TEUCER: But what of the boy? Where in this Trojan country is his son?

CHORUS: ⁹⁸⁵ He is alone, beside the huts.

TEUCER: Then bring him to me as quickly as possible, in case one of his enemies should try to snatch him up like the cub of a lion who has strayed too far from its mother. Quickly! All men mock their enemy when he lies at their feet.

Exit Tecmessa

Chorus: [990] While he was yet alive, Ajax asked that you care for his child, just as you are doing now.

Teucer: [992] This is the most painful sight these eyes have ever seen. No other road on which I have stepped has caused me as much pain, dearest Ajax, as the one I entered upon when I heard what happened to you. Swift Rumour passed among the Greeks saying you were dead. When I heard it I shuddered, but now I see it with my own eyes the sight of you destroys me. Ay-ax! Ai!

[1003] Uncover him so that I may see this evil in its entirety.

Ajax is uncovered

[1004] I can hardly bear to look at that proud face with its bitter courage; how many miseries, Ajax, have you invented for me by dying? Where can I go, and to what people, when I failed you so utterly in your time of need?

[1008] I'm sure our father will be delighted to see me when I arrive home without you. Of course he will – the man never cracks a smile at good tidings, let alone bad. What will he not say to me? What vile names won't he hang on me, just a bastard born from an enemy's concubine? Coward and weakling at the very least, or worse, betrayer. He'll say I wished control of the family and to rule Salamis. The old tyrant. I expect I'll be sent into exile, reduced by his words to the level of a slave instead of a free man. And that's just the treatment I may expect in the bosom of our family. Here at Troy...

[1024] Oh...what should I do now? Drag you off that spike, for a start, I suppose. That Hector is quite the killer – even dead he managed to put his sword in you. Just think of it! Hector, tied to the back of a chariot with your belt and dragged to death; then you, Ajax, end by falling upon Hector's sword. Was this sword not forged by some Fury, that belt not made by Hades? For it's the gods who have caused these things, sure as I'm standing here, and anyone who thinks otherwise can keep it to himself.

Chorus: [1040] Please, don't linger over your eulogy, but consider how we can hide this man in a grave, and what threatens to happen next if you fail to do so. For an enemy is on the horizon, and when he arrives he'll surely lick his lips over our misfortunes, as evil men are wont to do.

Teucer: Who is it that approaches?

Chorus: [1045] Menelaus, whom we sailed here to help.

Teucer: Yes. I recognize that cock-walk even at this distance.

Enter Menelaus

Menelaus: You! Leave that body where it lies, I command it!

Teucer: The enormity of that request is so sheer I wonder you even bother making it.

Menelaus: [1050] It is my decision, and that of my brother Agamemnon, who is in charge of the army.

Teucer: And on just what grounds do you dare make it?

Menelaus: [1052] Because this man has proven a worse enemy than the Trojans – a traitor who plotted to murder the entire army in its sleep! If the gods had not interfered, all of us would be lying dead in his place! Therefore no man will lay Ajax in the grave: instead, he will be food for the birds that fly along this sandy coast. No, don't bother making a show of your fierce anger: we couldn't control him while he was alive, but we shall certainly master him now that he is dead, whether you will it or no, and make an example of him. We take charge of his body now because at no time previous did we even have his ear.

¹⁰⁷¹ For it is the mark of a low nature when a man of low rank refuses to obey his betters. Anarchy soon reins in a city where transgression carries no fear of reprisal; likewise, regulations governing an army must be seen to have teeth.

¹⁰⁷⁷ Every man must know that, large and powerful though he may be, he stands to lose it all in an unguarded moment. Only when a man always feels the eyes upon him – fear and shame – is he truly safe. And that is why, if any man commits an outrage and gets away with it, the city, however powerful, and however long it has stood, begins to crumble.

¹⁰⁸⁴ Fear is there to protect us, for we mustn't be allowed to think that if we do whatever we will that we won't be punished. And turnabout is fair play – this man fairly brimmed with insolence in life, now it is my turn, and he won't cheat me by dying. So I order you before all those here not to bury him – and if you do, be prepared to join him!

Chorus: ¹⁰⁹¹ Menelaus, after such a wise speech, do not lower yourself to mistreating the dead.

Teucer: ¹⁰⁹³ Men, never again should you be shocked when a low-born man acts badly, if a noble will stoop to uttering so crooked a speech. Let me say it straight: do you really claim ever to have ruled over this man? Did he not sail away from Salamis as his own master to be an ally to the Greeks? By what right were you his commander, and by what authority do you rule the troops that accompanied him from home? You came here as ruler of Sparta, not us. You can lay no more claim to ruling him than he could have claimed to ruling you. In fact, if memory serves, you sailed here under another's orders, not as general of the assembled forces, so tend to your business of ordering about those actually under your command – spout your pompous drivel at them. But as for him, whether you or the other general wish it or no, in spite of your threats, I will bury Ajax.

¹¹¹¹ He didn't join this expedition in order to reclaim your wife, like those poor, overworked fools of yours, nor at the behest of a nonentity like you – he came because of the oath he had made.

¹¹¹⁵ Go on, then, clear off, and come back when you've got more heralds, and maybe the general as well. I'll listen no further to a man like you.

Chorus: These words seem ill-advised. True they may be, but they cut too deep.

Menelaus: ¹¹²⁰ Seems rather sure of himself for a mere archer.

Teucer: It's not a vulgar skill.

Menelaus: You'd be better suited to boasting if you carried a shield.

Teucer: You're pretty well armored, why don't you try me?

Menelaus: I wonder: are you as fierce as your tongue?

Teucer: ¹¹²⁵ Outraged justice inspires courage.

Menelaus: Is it just, then, to honour the man who murdered me?

Teucer: Murdered? How strange that you should be dead, yet still standing here talking our ears off...

Menelaus: The gods spared me: so far as Ajax was concerned I was dead at his hand.

Teucer: Then how do you, of all men, have the audacity to dishonour the gods?

Menelaus: [1130] How dishonour?

Teucer: You can ask that, when you stand here demanding that the dead go unburied?

Menelaus: Yes, my enemies – that is the will of the gods!

Teucer: Did Ajax ever really stand before you as an enemy?

Menelaus: He hated me, and I hated him – you know this.

Teucer: [1135] Of course he hated you – you rigged the jury against him in the matter of Achilles' armor.

Menelaus: That was the decision of the vote, not mine.

Teucer: Ah, but it was you who did the tally.

Menelaus: ...These words will go hard for you.

Teucer: I don't think I'll feel more pain than I cause.

Menelaus: [1140] I have only one thing to say to you: this man will not be buried.

Teucer: And I have only one thing to say in reply: he will.

Menelaus: [1142] I once knew a man with a tongue as bold as yours. He convinced sailors to go to sea when a storm was expected, but soon shut up when the wind and rain blew up: just lay huddled beneath his cloak and made the sailors step around him as they scurried about. Never said a word. I expect it will be the same with you and your big mouth. Never fear, your storm is coming.

Teucer: [1150] I, too, once knew a man, a moron who liked to show up at funerals and harass the mourners, until one day someone who looked a lot like me, with a short temper not unlike my own, looked him dead in the eye and said – let's see if I remember it right – something like: "If you insist on disrespecting the dead I'm going to put an arrow in you." Yes, I see it all quite clearly now, as if it were yesterday, and, in fact, now I recall that the idiot looked exactly like you. Not being too subtle for you, am I?

Menelaus: [1159] That's it, I'm leaving. Why trade insults with fools when it's so much easier simply having them killed.

Teucer: [1161] Good – get lost. It's an even bigger waste of time dignifying your windy words.

Exit Menelaus

Chorus: Now hard battle is inevitable! Hurry, Teucer, find a place to lay your brother down, a tomb to be remembered by men forever.

Enter Tekmessa and Eurysakes

Teucer: [1168] Here come his wife and son, just in time for the burial rites.

[1171] Child, come here – kneel and embrace your sire. Sit in supplication with three locks of hair in your hands – one from me, one from your mother, and one from your own head... the gift of the suppliant.

[1175] Should anyone from the army try to pull you away from this body, may he die badly and be himself unburied, an exile from his own country, and may the whole of his family be cut down along with him as I now cut off this lock of my hair.

[1180] Hold onto the body with all your might, my boy – protect it, and let no one move you.

¹¹⁸³ And as for you (*to the Chorus*): stand near and act like men. Support him until I come back – I go to prepare his grave, come what may.

Exit Teucer

Chorus: ¹¹⁸⁵ What then will it be, the number of the wandering years which strand us seemingly forever in wide Troy, suffering the endless torment of battle-sufferings, a sad reproach to the Greeks?

¹¹⁹² I wish that he had gone instead to Heaven, or into Hades that is common to all, whoever it was who first taught the Greeks to war with hateful weapons and share the pain that brings only more pain, in a round! For that was the man who ruined them, and robbed we poor soldiers of garlands and deep draughts of wine, deprived us of the sweet sound of pipes and the pleasure of sound sleep at night. He cut us off from the passion of love, and now we lie uncared for in the morning, hair strung with thick dew to remind us where we've wakened once again, in miserable Troy.

¹²¹¹ Previously relentless Ajax was our defense against missiles and terror in the night,; but now he is given up to hateful fate what spoils – what treasure now – will be a soldier's portion? We long for the wooded bay of Salamis, our home caressed by waves, that we might sail out and greet holy Athens!

Enter Teucer

Teucer: ¹²²³ I am returned in haste because I spotted Agamemnon rushing toward us. It seems that fool, too, has a few choice words for us.

Enter Agamemnon

Agamemnon: ¹²²⁶ You there! I am informed that you've been gaping your stinking trap like you think you can slander my house and survive it! Yes, I'm talking to you, son of that slave-bitch! Doubtless, had you been born of noble woman you'd be speaking even more boldly and walking taller than you do as a nobody standing in defense of his nothing brother.

¹²²⁹ You say that Menelaus and I came here neither as generals over either you or the Greeks, and that Ajax sailed as his own commander. Pretty talk from a low-born slave! Who is this paragon that you trumpet so loudly – where did he go, where did he stand that I did not stand myself? Do the Greeks have no other men but him? It was an evil day for us when we decided there would be a tournament for the arms of Achilles, for since then, despite the decision of the judges, Ajax and Teucer have been revealed the sorest of losers.

¹²⁴⁶ If such behavior as you counsel were permitted, then no laws would stand upright, for it would mean taking what has rightfully been earned by the just and bestowing it instead on the second-rate. This will never happen. The brawniest man is not necessarily the best – rather, he of sound mind makes the ideal citizen. An ox has the broadest back, but must be whipped down the straight and narrow road. It is this very remedy I prophesy for you, and presently, if you don't listen to reason. This man here is already a ghost and perhaps beyond reach, but you shouldn't forget I can still lay hands upon you.

¹²⁵⁹ Be reasonable – behave according to your class, or failing that task a free man with arguing your case, for the nonsensical babble of a barbarian cannot sway me.

Chorus: ¹²⁶² Please, gentlemen, be reasonable: you will never receive better counsel than that.

Teucer: [1266] It amazes me how quickly the memory fades of the debts we owe the dead. Despite the innumerable times you fought beside him, Ajax means nothing to you now, everything he did for you thrown away and lost just as if it never happened.

[1272] For you, of all people, to speak such foolish words... Have you somehow forgotten the day you were hemmed in by a shower of spears, while fire wreathed the masts of the ships and Hector leapt among the trenches? Who was it alone that came to your defense? Wasn't it he who you claim never set foot anywhere that you didn't? Did he do this because you ordered him? Did he face Hector in single combat on your order, or was it decided by lot? And was his token the heaviest he could find, that would sink to the bottom of the helmet, or was it the lightest and most eager to spring from the pot? That is the kind of man he was. And I stood beside him, I the slave, born of a barbarian mother.

[1290] Fool, how dare you look me in the eye and speak such idiocies. Have you forgotten, too, that your grandfather was old Pelops, a Phrygian barbarian? And that Atreus, your father, served his brother Thyestes the unholy meal of his own children? You are the child of a Cretan mother, who as a girl was caught with a lover and sent by her father to be food for fish. And you dare chide me about my origins? My father, Telamon, received the royal daughter of Laomedon as his bride as due prize for being first in courage and valour in the army by Herakles, son of Alcmene herself. As the son of two equally noble parents, how could I bring shame on my blood, by allowing you to profane my brother, who now lies in such distress?

[1308] Be sure of this: if you cast him aside you do the same to his brother, his wife, and his son. Better I should die fighting on behalf of my brother than to do so for that wife of yours – or should I say the wife of your brother?

[1313] You would do better to look to your own affairs and leave mine to me – for, if you think to be bold with me and mine, one day soon you'll wish you had been a coward.

Enter Odysseus

Chorus: [1316] Lord Odysseus! You're just in time, if you've come to salvage this situation!

Odysseus: What's all this, then? I could hear you bellowing over this brave warrior's corpse from all the way down the beach.

Agamemnon: [1320] Yes, well, then did you also hear the disgraceful things his brother has been saying?

Odysseus: It is easy to forgive a man who merely returns an insult.

Agamemnon: Of course he is insulted! He has earned it! His actions toward me were shameful!

Odysseus: [1325] What harm has he done you?

Agamemnon: He defies me, and insists on burying this corpse!

Odysseus: ...Might a friend speak his mind to you, yet remain a friend no less than before?

Agamemnon: [1330] Of course, Odysseus – speak! I would not show sense otherwise, regarding you as I do my greatest friend of all the Greeks.

Odysseus: [1332] Then listen to me. In the name of the gods, do not leave this man unburied. Do not allow hate to rule and compel you to tread all over justice. Ever since I won the arms of Achilles, Ajax loved me least of any man in the army – but even so, never will I deny that he was the best of us who came to Troy, excepting only Achilles himself.

¹³⁴² It is not right for him to be dishonoured by you. If you do that, then you do no harm to him, but great damage to the laws of the gods.

AGAMEMNON: Odysseus, do you fight for this man, against me?

ODYSSEUS: Yes, though I did hate him – when it was right to hate him.

AGAMEMNON: Is it any less fitting for you to wipe your feet on him now he is dead?

ODYSSEUS: O son of Atreus, I beg you, do not reduce yourself to taking unfair advantage.

AGAMEMNON: ¹³⁵⁰ It is not an easy thing for a ruler to follow the law and show pity.

ODYSSEUS: Nor to honour friends who give good advice?

AGAMEMNON: A good man must abide by the will of those in power!

ODYSSEUS: Stop. You would rule better in this case by yielding to your friends.

AGAMEMNON: Remember the kind of man for whom you are attempting to do a favour, Odysseus. Do you forget what he meant to do to all of us?

ODYSSEUS: ¹³⁵⁵ He was my enemy, it's true – but he was once noble.

AGAMEMNON: What do you suggest? That we honour him?

ODYSSEUS: His excellence moves me far more than hatred does.

AGAMEMNON: The man was unstable.

ODYSSEUS: Yes, and many men who appear stable later turn out duplicitous.

AGAMEMNON: ¹³⁶⁰ And you think such people should not be made examples?

ODYSSEUS: It's not in me to abide an inflexible nature.

AGAMEMNON: ...You will make us all look like cowards.

ODYSSEUS: On the contrary, you will look like men of justice in the eyes of all the Greeks.

AGAMEMNON: Are you sincerely telling me that I should let this body be buried?

ODYSSEUS: ¹³⁶⁵ Yes. For every one of us will also one day come to this same end.

AGAMEMNON: The whole world over, every man looks only to his own self-interest... It is short-sighted, Odysseus.

ODYSSEUS: For whom, then, is it more fitting that I should work than myself?

AGAMEMNON: Very well, then – but let it be called your ruling, not mine.

ODYSSEUS: That's fine – if you abide by it, you will still be acting justly.

AGAMEMNON: ¹³⁷⁰ Just understand this: to you I would give even greater favours than this one, but that man remains the enemy of us all whether he lies here or is stowed underground. Do what you will...

Exit Agamemnon

CHORUS: ¹³⁷⁴ Odysseus, after this, anyone who says you are not wise is a fool.

ODYSSEUS: ¹³⁷⁶ And now I announce before you all that, as much as I was once his enemy, now I am Teucer's friend. I wish to aid in burying the dead, taking part in every phase, neglecting none of the things that should be done in honour of the best of men.

Teucer: [1381] Noble Odysseus, I can give you only thanks. You have completely reversed my expectations of you. While he lived you were the most hated of all the Greeks to my brother, yet you alone stood by him after his death. You do not give way to impious laughter at having outlived your enemy, unlike that insane general and his brother. They it is I pray that the father who rules Olympus, and the unforgetting Furies, and Justice, who can do all things, will destroy. But for your part, Odysseus, son of aged Laertes, I cannot allow you to touch his grave, for fear of offending the dead man. But you may take part in all the rest, and if you want to bring along anyone else from the army, we won't mind.

[1398] I'll dig the hole myself, but you should know that as far as I am concerned you are a good man.

Odysseus: [1400] That's fine. I respect the wishes of the family and withdraw.

Exit Odysseus

Teucer: [1402] Quickly! Too much time has passed already. Some of you dig a hollow trench with your hands, and others erect a tall tripod in the middle of the fire for the sacred bath. And someone go and fetch the armour from his hut that he used to wear beneath his shield.

[1409] You boy, Eurysakes, with all your strength, gather your father lovingly to you and help me raise him. Careful – for his body is still warm and may drool black blood. Come, everyone who claims to be a friend, and bend to your work for the sake of this man, for there was no better man than Ajax, when he was alive. This is what I say.

Chorus: [1418] Mortals can understand many things when they see them. But before he sees them no one can be a prophet of what will be. Man can make laws, but must judge each case on its own merits.

Translated from the Greek by Stephen Russell, PhD

English by Jonathan Allen and Stephen Russell

Chapter 14
Euripides
HELEN

THE STORY: What? Was the whole Trojan War just a cruel joke that the gods played on mankind? Apollodorus, in his *Epitome*, provides us with the outline of the story that we see in Euripides' *Helen*:

[E.6.29] Menelaus, with a total of five ships under his command, arrived at Sunium, a headland of Attica. And when he was driven away from there by winds toward Crete, he drifted far far away, and he wandered up and down the coasts of Libya, Phoenicia, Cyprus, and Egypt, where he collected a great deal of treasure. According to some accounts, Menelaus discovered Helen at the court of Proteus, the king of Egypt. These accounts say that until that time Menelaus only had a phantom of her, one that was made of clouds. And after wandering for eight years he sailed back to Mycenae, and there he found Orestes, who was there after having avenged his father's murder. And then from there Menelaus went to Sparta, where he regained his own kingdom – and having been made immortal by Hera he then went to the Elysian Fields with Helen.

CHARACTERS

HELEN
TEUCER
CHORUS (OF CAPTIVE GREEK WOMEN LIVING IN EGYPT)
MENELAUS
OLD WOMAN (A SERVANT OF THEOCLYMENUS)
SERVANT (OF MENELAUS)
THEONOË (SISTER OF THEOCLYMENUS)
THEOCLYMENUS, KING OF EGYPT
MESSENGER (A SERVANT OF THEOCLYMENUS)
SERVANT (OF THEONOË)
CASTOR AND POLYDEUCES (THE DIOSCURI, GODS AND BROTHERS OF HELEN)

SCENE: Egypt, near the mouth of the Nile and in front of the gates of the royal palace belonging to the Egyptian king Theoclymenus. In front of the palace we can see the tomb of his father Proteus. Helen is sitting next to that to that tomb as a suppliant.

HELEN: Here the Nile flows, that great river with its fair nymphs! It is fed by the melting of pale snows and this river, and not the rains sent from Zeus, is what soaks the fields of Egypt with moisture. Proteus, while he was still alive, was the king of this land – and he lived on the island of Pharos, but he was lord of the whole of Egypt. He married Psamathe, one of the nymphs of these waters, after she left her marriage to Aeacus. In her marriage to Proteus she had two children – a boy who received the name Theoclymenus (because the boy's father honoured the gods throughout his lifetime), and a fine girl called Eido when she was young and the delight of her mother. But when she became older and came to the womanly age of marriage they changed her name to Theonoë, which means "divinely-inspired," for she understands how things are and how things will be – everything that divination can bring. Her ancestor Nereus gave her this power of divination.

[16] As for me, my homeland is glorious Sparta. My father was Tyndareus, although there is this story that Zeus changed himself into a swan and then, in that form, he flew to visit my mother Leda. He set it up that he was fleeing an eagle and so he turned to my mother to save him – and he won her love by this act of treachery, if this story is reliable.

[22] That's where I come from and that's the story of my birth. My name is Helen, and I'll tell you the truth about all that's happened to me and all that I've suffered. Three goddesses came to the remotest part of Mount Ida – Hera, Aphrodite, and Zeus' virgin daughter Athena. They came there to see Alexandros – the man some people call Paris – and the reason for that was that they wanted him to judge which one of them was the most beautiful.

[27] Aphrodite offered Alexandros marriage to my beautiful self – if this curse of mine can ever be called beauty – as a reward if he picked her as the most beautiful. He did pick her, of course, and so that goddess won the contest. Thus that shepherd Paris left his herds behind and set out for Sparta, to take me as his wife … as his reward.

[31] But Hera was angry that she lost to the other goddesses, and so she made sure that Paris' marriage with me was as empty as the wind, for she didn't give that son of Priam me, but rather she gave him a breathing image of me that she made from the sky to resemble me. And now Paris believes that he's holding me – but it's all in his imagination, his empty dreams, for he doesn't have me at all.

[36] And then Zeus decided to add still more troubles to these troubles of mine. He gave war to the peoples of Greece and those poor Trojans to relieve mother earth of the burden of all these people and so that he could find out who the bravest man in Greece really was. And I was put forth by the Greeks as the prize and reason for the invasion in this war against the Trojans – though it was not me all, just my name.

[44] Myself, I had been long since snatched up by Hermes, who took me away into the sky and covered me with clouds, for Zeus had not forgotten me. Hermes set me down in this house of Proteus – a man Zeus judged to be the most virtuous on earth, and he placed me here because he knew that Proteus would protect my honour until Menelaus could come and get me.

[49] And here I am in Egypt, while my poor husband gathered an army and went to the towers of Troy so that he could try to win me back by force. Many lives were lost next to the Scamander river – all because of me. And now I, who have suffered so much already, am cursed by men, and everyone believes that I've betrayed my husband and caused the Greeks to bring about this great war.

[56] What's the reason for me to keep going on living, then? There's only one that I can think of: I heard a prophecy from the god Hermes, who said that one day I'll live again in those famous plains of Sparta with my husband, and that my husband will realize that I didn't really go to Troy and that I didn't share my bed with anyone other than him. As long as king Proteus was still alive I was safe from marriage, but now that he's dead and lies buried underneath the darkness of the earth, his son is now pursuing me, wanting my hand in marriage.

[63] This is why I am out here clinging as a sup-

pliant to the grave of Proteus, honouring the husband I once had in Menelaus. I'm hoping that the dead king can find some way to keep me safe and free from the advances of his son. Even if my name causes all men in Greece to throw curses my way, I'm not going to allow my body to become contaminated by disgrace here in Egypt.

Enter Teucer

Teucer: [68] I wonder who the master of these well-fortified walls is? Wow – this house seems to be worthy of comparison to that of Plutus – the god of wealth himself. Everything here looks so royal, and its halls are so wide and impressive!

[71] O my gods, what am I looking at? In front of me I see the deadly image of a woman who is most hateful to the Greeks – the woman who ruined me and all of us! May the gods forever hate you for being the exact double of that evil Helen! If I weren't standing on foreign soil right now, then I'd take my unerring arrow and shoot you right through the heart, just because you look so much like that daughter of Zeus!

Helen: [78] O you poor man, whoever you are, why do you turn back from me? Why would you blame me, and hate me, for all of the troubles that she caused?

Teucer: [80] I apologize – it was wrong of me to so easily give way to anger. You see, the whole of Greece hates Zeus' daughter Helen. Please excuse me for what I just said to you, my lady.

Helen: But who are you, and what has brought you to this land?

Teucer: Lady, I am one of those unfortunate Greeks…

Helen: [85] Then it's no wonder that you hate Helen as much as you do! But tell me what your name is and where you come from. How should I address you?

Teucer: My name is Teucer, and my father is Telamon, and Salamis is the island where I grew up.

Helen: And why have you come so far to this land of the Nile?

Teucer: [90] I'm in exile, and I've been driven far off from my native land.

Helen: Oh, that's so horrible for you! Who sent you into exile?

Teucer: It was none other than my father, Telamon. Does a man have any closer relative than his father?

Helen: But why would he do such a thing? Clearly there is a great deal of unhappiness in your story.

Teucer: My brother Ajax died when we were in Troy – that proved to be my undoing.

Helen: [95] But why? Surely he didn't die by your sword?

Teucer: No – he died when he leapt on top of his own sword.

Helen: Was he driven mad? Would a sane man ever do such a thing?

Teucer: Do you know of a man called Achilles, the son of Peleus?

Helen: Yes, I heard that he once came to ask for Helen's hand in marriage. Or, at least that's the rumour that I've heard.

Teucer: [100] His death caused all of his friends to fight over who would get his armor.

Helen: But how could the death of Achilles bring harm to Ajax?

Teucer: When another man won the arms of Achilles, that's what drove him to kill himself.

Helen: But his suffering has caused damage to your life as well?

Teucer: Yes – because I didn't die along with him.

Helen: [105] Does that mean that you also went to that famous city of Troy, stranger?

Teucer: Yes – I helped destroy the city, but in bringing Troy to ruin I ended up destroying myself.

Helen: Do you mean that the city has already been destroyed by fire?

Teucer: Yes, that's right. You can no longer even tell for certain where its walls once stood.

Helen: Poor Helen – it's your fault that all those Trojans died!

Teucer: [110] And many Greeks died there as well. The whole place was a site of great evil.

Helen: How long has it now been since Troy was destroyed?

Teucer: Almost seven years – seven times for planting seeds and seven harvests.

Helen: And how much time did you spend at Troy?

Teucer: Myself, I was there for many months, but the war lasted ten years in total.

Helen: [115] And so you must have been able to capture that woman from Sparta? You did get Helen, right?

Teucer: Yes, we did. Menelaus grabbed her by the hair and dragged her away.

Helen: But did you actually see the poor creature, or did you only hear about it?

Teucer: I saw her with my own eyes, just like I'm looking at you right now.

Helen: Think back for a moment – you might have witnessed some divinely sent illusion… a trick sent by the gods…

Teucer: [120] Oh, please let's talk about some other topic – I'm so sick of talking about Helen.

Helen: Sorry, but I just want to know whether you're really convinced that what you saw is absolutely correct.

Teucer: Listen, I saw her with my own eyes – and what my eyes see, my brain also sees.

Helen: So is Menelaus now home with his wife?

Teucer: Actually, no. They aren't in Argos, nor are they anywhere near the bank of the Eurotas River, which runs near their home.

Helen: [125] Oh no! That's so horrible! I mean, it's so horrible for those two, that is.

Teucer: No, you're right – it's terrible. The rumour is that Menelaus and his wife have both vanished.

Helen: But didn't all the Greeks sail back home together?

Teucer: That was the plan, but a storm came up and drove them all in different directions.

Helen: Where were they on the sea when all of this happened?

Teucer: [130] They were just making their way through the middle of the Aegean.

Helen: Has anyone heard whether Menelaus made his way to land after that?

Teucer: No – in Greece they're saying that he's dead.

Helen: Oh gods no – then I'm done for! But what about the daughter of Thestias – is she still alive?

Teucer: Do you mean Leda? No – she's dead and gone.

Helen: [135] How? Did she die because of the shame that Helen brought upon her?

Teucer: That's what I hear – they say that she herself put a noose around her own fair neck.

Helen: And are the sons of Tyndareus still alive or have they died?

Teucer: They're dead, and not dead – there are two different accounts.

Helen: Which is the prevailing story? Oh gods, how miserable all of these stories are making me!

Teucer: [140] A lot of people say that they've been turned into stars and that they're now gods.

Helen: That's at least some small bit of good news. But what is the other story about them?

Teucer: [142] According to that tale, they killed themselves out of shame for what happened to their sister Helen.

[143] But enough with these stories – I don't want to add more misery and tears to my current pains. I came to this royal palace because I wanted to see Theonoë, the prophetess of the god. I want you to see if you can arrange a meeting for me with this Theonoë – I want to learn by prophecy how I can sail my ship and reach the island of Cyprus. Apollo gave me the prophecy that I must live on that island, and that I should establish a city there and call it new Salamis in honour of my far-off native land.

Helen: [151] If Apollo has said that this is your destiny, then you should just sail away at once, stranger – the journey will show you the way.

But you really need to leave this land quickly before the son of Proteus, the king of this country, sees you here! Right now he's off hunting wild beasts with his hounds, but he kills every Greek that he can catch hold of.

You really shouldn't try to find out why he does this, and I won't tell you – for what good would it do you to know this?

Teucer: [158] Thanks for all your good advice, my lady, and I hope that the gods will treat you well in return for all the kindness you have shown me.

[160] I swear, even though you resemble that Helen in terms of your appearance, your heart is nothing at all like hers – for you actually have a heart. As for her, I pray that she dies a painful death and that she'll never get back to the streams of the Eurotas! But may your fortune always be good, my lady, for you are kind and good.

Exit Teucer

Helen: [164] Oh, as I begin the long lament for my troubles, what will be the strain of my song, or what Muse will I call to help me, or with what tears or sadness or signs of sorrow shall I start? Oh gods – why me!

[167] O you winged young girls, O you virgin daughters of the earth – I mean you Sirens, if only you could come here and bring a Libyan harp, some pipes, some lyres, and spend some time with me in my terrible moment of grief. With tears of your own you could sing of my unhappiness – you could sing woes that would match my woes, and songs that would match my songs.

[173] You could help me sing such sadness that Persephone might hear me down in the land of the dead, and so that she'll welcome my songs of sadness, the ones I'm dedicating to all those who are now in Hades all because of a war fought over me.

Enter the Chorus (of captive Greek women living in Egypt)

Chorus: ¹⁷⁹ I was down near the shining blue water, and I placed my coloured wash to dry out in the bed of young rushes on the shoots of tender grass, there in the tender glare of the sun. It was there that I heard a noise that stirred my pity, a lament too sad even for a lyre, a sharp voice of pain uttered by some wife. It's the kind of sound a Naiad would make if she were caught in the hills while she tried to flee – such a cry of pain when she screams that she's being raped by Pan in some rocky valley.

Helen: ¹⁹¹ Come, hear me out, O you spoil, O you booty, O you who've been taken by some barbarian ship, you women from Greece. I've got some news. A sailor has come here from Greece, and he brought a message that has tears upon tears. He said that the ruins of Troy have now been overcome by a hostile fire – and that it was all because of me. Oh, I'm the killer of so many, because of my name and the destruction that comes with it.

¹⁹⁹ He tells me that my mother Leda has died, killing herself due to the pain she feels because of my disgrace; that my husband is lost, wandering on the sea, and presumed gone; and my brothers Castor and Polydeuces, the twin glories of our country – they have disappeared as well, vanished… leaving behind the plain where their horses trampled, leaving behind their wrestling grounds by the reeds of the Eurotas river, the place where all the young men like to run and ride and work.

Chorus: ²¹¹ O what a miserable fate, what a sorrowful destiny you've met, my lady! It was a destiny of pain that claimed you for its own on that day when Zeus flashed through the upper air with the snowy wings of the swan so that he could visit your mother and produce you.

²¹⁷ What trouble is not yours? What have you not suffered in your lifetime? Your mother is now dead, and Zeus' twin sons, your brothers whom you loved, don't receive good fortune, you can't go home to see your native land, and throughout all the cities of Greece the tale is told that places you in the bed of the Trojan prince, my lady. And now we hear that your husband has died on the deep sea and he'll never bless the halls of his ancestors – and that he'll never bless the bronze temple of Athena with his presence.

Helen: ²²⁹ What man was it of the Trojans, or was it someone from Greek soil who cut down the pine that brought so many tears to Troy? This was the timber that Priam's son shaped into that damn ship – the one that was driven with barbarian oars and brought him to the place where I lived. He came to seek my unfortunate beauty, so that he could win me as his bride.

²³⁸ And with him came that treacherous goddess Aphrodite – so murderous and bringing death to all the Greeks.

²⁴¹ But then Hera, that great goddess who sits upon the golden throne and who sleeps in the arms of Zeus and is greatly revered – she sent out Hermes, that swift-footed son of Maia, to do her bidding. I was gathering fresh flowers, picking them and placing them within the folds of my dress so that I could bring them to decorate the bronze shrine of Athena – I was doing all this when Hermes caught me and swooped me up and took me through the heavens to this unholy land.

²⁴⁶ Oh, why me? He made me a prize of war for both the sons of Priam and all the Greeks, and my name is falsely cursed beside the streams of Simois river near Troy.

Chorus: ²⁵² You suffer from a lot of pain – I know this quite well. But it's best if you try to bear the harsh necessities of life as lightly as you can.

HELEN: ²⁵⁵ Dear women, to what kind of fate have I been attached? No woman, either Greek or barbarian, ever gave birth to a white shelled egg that one usually sees from birds, but men say that this is how Leda produced me from Zeus. Did my mother give birth to me so that I could be a monstrosity in the eyes of men? In any case, my life and fate have indeed become monstrosities – partly this is because of Hera, and partly this is because of my beauty.

²⁶³ For my part, I wish I'd been wiped clean like a painting and made plain instead of beautiful, and I wish that the Greeks would forget the evil name that I now have and that they'd only remember what's good about me, just as now they can only remember me with evil thoughts!

²⁶⁷ Whoever receives from the gods just a single strain of luck, and all of it bad, he has a hard and sad lot, but he still has to endure it.

²⁶⁹ However, the sorrow that surrounds me is much more complex than that. First, I've done nothing wrong but I have earned an evil reputation – and it's worse to be hated for wrongs that you haven't done than if the charges were true. Second, the gods have placed me far away from my native land and have sent me to live with barbarians.

²⁷⁴ I'm deprived of my friends and family and I've been forced to become a slave, even though I was born of free parents. In lands that belong to barbarians every man is a slave except for the one man who claims to be king. There was one anchor that steadied me in my misfortune – the hope that my husband would one day come here and rescue me from my misery. But that hope is now gone, for he's no longer alive, but has died.

²⁸⁰ My mother is dead too, and I'm the reason for her death. I know that such an accusation is unfair, but I deserve such unfairness. My daughter Hermione, who is the glory of our house, who was the glory of my life – she surely has no husband and will grow old unmarried. The two Dioscuri, my brothers, said to be the sons of Zeus, are no longer alive. So all my luck has been turned to misery and for all intents and purposes I'm dead, even while I'm still alive.

²⁸⁷ And the worst thing of all is that if I should ever reach home I would find the gates of my palace locked against me, since the men there would think that Helen of Troy died with Menelaus. If my husband were alive, then I could become recognized by him through some signs that no one else but he would recognize.

²⁹² But as it is, that will never happen, and he'll never return home. So why should I even go on living? What fate is there left for me? Should I choose a marriage as an escape from my problems and then live with a barbarian husband here? Should I sit with him at his rich table? However, when a woman is married to a man she dislikes, even her own body becomes repugnant to her.

²⁹⁸ In this case death is the best option. How can it not be right to die? But to commit suicide by hanging is unseemly – it doesn't even look good when a slave does it. No – death by the sword is the more noble and glorious suicide, and the movement from life to death will only be a short time… but it's often hard to find the important spot that will end life quickly. That's how far I have sunk in the depths of my misery – while other women are made happy by their beauty, my beauty is the very thing that has destroyed me.

CHORUS: ³⁰⁶ Helen, you shouldn't be so sure that this stranger, whoever he is, told you the truth when he spoke to you.

HELEN: But he told me quite clearly that my husband was dead.

CHORUS: People say many things as if they're facts that are later proven to be false.

HELEN: ³¹⁰ Yes, but they could just as easily be true.

CHORUS: You're speaking like this because you're pushing yourself to believe the worst and not the best.

HELEN: Of course – I'm very frightened, and anxiety surrounds me on every side.

CHORUS: How do those people feel about you inside the house? Do they show any good will toward you?

HELEN: Everyone here is a friend of mine, except for the one who's hunting for my love.

CHORUS: ³¹⁵ Do you know what you should do? You should leave your place next to this tomb here…

HELEN: What the hell are you saying? What is this advice that you are giving me?

CHORUS: ³¹⁷ You should go into the house and find the daughter of the Nereid – Theonoë, I mean – and then ask her whether your husband is still alive or dead. After all, she knows all things. And then when you have learned the truth, you can cry or celebrate in accordance to whatever news you happen to hear.

³²² But before you know for certain, what good does it do you to feel such grief? Come on, take my advice – get up from this tomb and go find the young woman. She'll tell you everything you want to know. I mean, since she's here already in this house, then she can tell you what you need to know. So why would you even look anywhere else?

³²⁷ I'm willing to go along with you into the house and stand by your side while you hear the girl's prophecy. It's important that we women help one another.

HELEN: ³³⁰ My friends, I accept your advice. Please, the lot of you go into the house first, just ahead of me, if only so that you can gain a sense of what awaits me in there. I'll follow directly behind you.

CHORUS: I'll do this – and I won't hesitate at all. You won't need to ask me twice.

HELEN: ³³⁵ O miserable and unlucky day! Oh, what story full of tears and sadness will I hear?

CHORUS: Oh, don't be such a Cassandra and only give prophecies of grief and sorrow, my friend. Don't predict the worst before you need to.

HELEN: ³⁴⁰ My dear poor husband – what has happened to him? Do his eyes still look on the light above? Does he still see the chariot of the sun and the stars at night when they trace their paths, or is he below the earth and among the dead, suffering that everlasting and irrevocable fate?

CHORUS: Whatever happens tomorrow – lean toward the good.

HELEN: ³⁴⁸ I call upon you, I ask you to be my witness, O Eurotas river – so pale with your washed reeds. I ask you to take note that if the news of my husband's death turns out to be true – and how is this not clear already? – then I swear that I'll fasten a deadly noose around my neck or I'll thrust a deadly sword of bloody death into my flesh with enough force to kill myself. I'll serve as a sacrifice to the three goddesses and to that son of Priam, who once tended his cattle up there in the hollow caves of Mount Ida.

Chorus: ³⁶⁰ I pray that your misfortune may be turned away and go somewhere else. I want your luck to be good again.

Helen: ³⁶² O poor unhappy city of Troy! You were destroyed, you suffered so much, and all for deeds that were never done. The gifts that lady Aphrodite gave me brought forth so much blood, so many tears, and pain on top of pain, tears on top of tears – so much suffering.

³⁶⁷ Mothers saw their sons die, and young women, sisters of the dead men, cut their hair and threw their locks into the Trojan river they call the Scamander to honour their dead brothers. And Greece too has cried aloud in lamentation – she has struck her head with her hand, and the bloodying stroke of her nails has made blood run down her tender cheek.

³⁷⁵ O Callisto, you lucky girl from so long ago! You left the bed of Zeus with limbs that go on all fours, having been turned into a bear. How much better your lot is than mine! Since by taking the form of a shaggy beast, with its violent eye, you have removed from yourself the ability to feel pain.

³⁸¹ And you too, O Titan daughter of Merops – you're also blessed, because Artemis once chased you away from her group of followers and transformed you into a stag with golden horns.

³⁸³ But my beauty and loveliness have ruined so much – ruined the citadel of Troy, ruined the Greeks, and so many men on both sides were ruined by death.

Exit Helen and the Chorus into the palace; Enter Menelaus, in torn clothing

Menelaus: ³⁸⁶ O Pelops, who once competed in the famous chariot race against Oenomaus in the Pisa field at Olympia – how I wish that when you were cooked and turned into a feast for the gods, when you were still young and unmarried, I wish you'd lost your life before you ever had a chance to give life to my father Atreus!

³⁹¹ Atreus married Aërope and they produced both Agamemnon and me, Menelaus – what a glorious pair we were! I don't think this is a boast, but I'm sure that I took the greatest army that the world has ever seen with me when we sailed over to Troy. We did this not as tyrants leading slaves, but as commanders leading the young men of Greece, all of whom were willing and eager to participate.

³⁹⁷ It's possible for us to now call out the names of all those who died and those who managed to escape the dangers of the sea and make it home safely carrying information about their dead comrades. But as for me, I'm stuck wandering in my misery over the waves of the gray sea – and I've been doing this for the whole time since I left the fallen towers of Troy. I'm desperate to reach my home, but it seems clear that the gods don't want me to do this. I've sailed to all the desolate and unfriendly landing places in Libya, and whenever it looks like I'm getting closer to my home country, the wind forces me back again and never gives me a favourable enough breeze that allows me to arrive home.

⁴⁰⁸ And now I've been shipwrecked here… and I don't know what to do. I lost so many of my companions and I've been driven to this shore. My ship has been broken up against the rock and is now in bits and pieces. The only thing that remains intact is its keel, and by some unexpected chance I managed to sail here on that keel with Helen, whom I took from Troy by force.

⁴¹⁴ I've no idea what this land or its people are called. I was too ashamed to be seen in public and mingle with the crowds, because

I didn't want anyone asking about these rags that I'm wearing and my bad luck – so I kept myself hidden out of embarrassment. When a great man happens to fall upon hard times, he falls into a state that is completely new and unfamiliar, and this is a far worse situation than it would be if he'd been accustomed to rough times.

^{420} I'm in really rough shape. For I have neither food nor any clothing to cover my body. You can tell from one look at me that I'm just wearing remnants of the sail from the ship. My former clothing, so fine and so luxurious, has all been swallowed up by the sea. In a cave over there I've hidden the wife who was the cause of all my troubles while I come here – and I forced the last survivors of my friends to keep guard over her.

^{428} So I've come to this place alone, trying to get something for my friends over there that they can use – something… anything that they need. I approached because I saw this house, which obviously belongs to a wealthy man – its walls are so impressive and it's surrounded by such huge gates. From a wealthy house such as this there's hope of obtaining something for my sailors, while from a poor house we wouldn't likely be able to get any benefit or help even if the people there were willing to give it.

^{435} Hey in there! Gatekeeper! Someone please open up the house so that you can carry the message of my grief back inside! Hey – is there anyone in there?

Enter an Old Woman from the palace

OLD WOMAN: ^{437} Who is at our gates? Go away – leave this house! Don't stand there in our courtyard and bother my master! Otherwise you'll be put to death. From the sounds of you, I think you're a Greek – and Greeks aren't allowed here.

MENELAUS: ^{441} Old lady, that's fine – I'll do what you say, so you can say these words in a less harsh tone. I'll obey you – just please don't be so angry!

OLD WOMAN: Go away now! It's my job, stranger, to ensure that no Greek comes near this palace.

MENELAUS: ^{445} Hey – keep your hands off me! Stop trying to shove me!

OLD WOMAN: It's your own fault. You're forcing me to do this, since you won't do what I tell you to do.

MENELAUS: I want you to go inside and bring this message to your master…

OLD WOMAN: You'll end up regretting it, I think, if I take your message inside.

MENELAUS: … say that I have come here as a shipwrecked sailor, a foreigner – but one that's important, noble, and under the protection of the gods.

OLD WOMAN: ^{450} So if you're so special, why don't you go to some other house and leave this one alone?

MENELAUS: No – I'm going to go inside this one. Do what I tell you!

OLD WOMAN: You're being a complete nuisance – and I warn you that you'll be forced out of here really quickly.

MENELAUS: Oh gods, where are all my famous military campaigns now, the ones that brought me so much glory?

OLD WOMAN: You may be considered a great man back in your homeland, but you aren't one here.

MENELAUS: ⁴⁵⁵ Oh, why do I have to endure such undeserved condescension?

OLD WOMAN: Why are you even bothering to cry? Do you expect that you'll be able to win someone's pity?

MENELAUS: I'd earn the pity from someone in my old city.

OLD WOMAN: So then go away and find someone from there who'll feel sorry for you!

MENELAUS: But what land is this? Who owns this palace?

OLD WOMAN: ⁴⁶⁰ This is the palace of Proteus – and this land is Egypt.

MENELAUS: Egypt? Oh no – what a long distance I've sailed! I'm so far from my home!

OLD WOMAN: And do you have some kind of problem with the land of the Nile?

MENELAUS: There's nothing at all wrong with the Nile – I was lamenting my own fate.

OLD WOMAN: Lots of people have troubles – you're not the only one.

MENELAUS: ⁴⁶⁵ The king that you mentioned – is he in the house?

OLD WOMAN: That's his tomb right over there. His son is now the king of the land.

MENELAUS: And where is he? Is he at home or has he gone somewhere?

OLD WOMAN: He's not at home – but he hates Greeks more than he hates anyone.

MENELAUS: What have the Greeks done to him that I should be punished for it?

OLD WOMAN: ⁴⁷⁰ It's because Zeus' daughter Helen is in this palace.

MENELAUS: What are you saying? What's this? Please tell me again.

OLD WOMAN: The daughter of Tyndareus, who used to live in Sparta.

MENELAUS: Where did she come from? How did she get here? Please explain!

OLD WOMAN: She came here from Sparta.

MENELAUS: ⁴⁷⁵ Huh? When did this happen? Has my wife been stolen from the cave that I placed her in?

OLD WOMAN: ⁴⁷⁹ If you really need to know, stranger, she came here before the Greeks left for Troy. But you have to leave this house. Something has happened here to throw everything into confusion, and you're arriving at an extremely bad time. If my master happens to catch you here, then death will be the only welcome that you will receive.

⁴⁸¹ You know, I myself rather like the Greeks, in spite of those harsh words that I just said to you. I was just afraid of what the master might do to me.

Exit Old Woman into the palace

MENELAUS: ⁴⁸³ What on earth can I make out of all this? She's telling me about brand new troubles that come hard on the heels of my old ones. I came here bringing the wife I took from Troy, and she's now being guarded for me in a cave, and yet I hear that there's this other woman now, who has the same name as my wife, and she's living in this house.

⁴⁸⁹ The old woman here said that this "Helen" was Zeus' daughter. Is there some man named Zeus who lives near the banks of the Nile? No, no – there can be only one Zeus, and he lives up there in the heavens. And where on earth is there a Sparta other than the one that has the waters of Eurotas flowing past it with its lovely reeds? And Tyndareus is the name of just one man – there can't be two people with that name. Are there other lands with the names

Sparta and Troy? I have no idea what to make of this. I suppose that there are many men in the wide world who share the same name, and the same must be true with respect to women and cities. So maybe this is nothing so amazing after all.

⁵⁰⁰ But I'm not going to run away because of the supposed danger that the servant woman just mentioned. There's no one who's so uncivilized and so heartless that he won't help me out and give me food once he hears my name. I mean, the fire of Troy is famous, and so am I, because I'm the one who lit it – I'm Menelaus, famous throughout the whole known world. I'm going to wait for the master of the house. I have two options in front of me. If it turns out that he is a cruel fellow, then I'll hide myself and make my way back to that wreck of a ship. But if he shows some signs of kindness, then I'll ask him for whatever my current situation requires.

⁵¹⁰ Of all the evils that I have to endure, this one is the worst – that I'm a king and I have to beg other kings to help me find some way of staying alive. But this is what has to be. I wasn't the first one to say it, but a wise man once said that nothing has more power than cruel necessity.

Enter the Chorus and Helen from the palace

CHORUS: ⁵¹⁵ I've heard from the prophetic young woman Theonoë – she told me exactly what I wanted to hear when I entered the palace, for she told me that Menelaus has not yet been covered by earth and hasn't yet gone down to the depths of gloomy Hades. He's still somewhere on top of the stormy seas, still trying to find a way to reach the harbours of his native land – and the poor man spends his time wandering, without any friends, taking his ship to all sorts of places ever since he set sail from Troy.

HELEN: ⁵²⁸ And I'm also returning along with you – back once more to the shelter that is this tomb. I heard the news form Theonoë, and it was good indeed. She knows the truth about things, and she says that my husband is still alive and looking at the light of day, but that he's endlessly driven back and forth across the sea, and that he'll finally come home, tired out from all his wandering, after he has reached the end of his troubles.

⁵³⁵ But one thing that she didn't say was whether he'll be ok when he reaches home. I didn't ask her specifically about this because I was so happy to hear the news that she told me when she said that he's alive and safe. She also says that he's actually quite close to this land here, that he's a shipwrecked castaway with few friends left. O, when will you get here? You will be such a welcome sight when you arrive!

⁵⁴¹ But oh – oh no – who is this man here? Is it possible that I am about to be ambushed by someone who's carrying out the orders of Proteus' godless son? Quick, I have to hurry to the tomb and run as fast as a galloping colt or a Bacchant from the god. The fellow who's waiting for me is savage and fierce from the looks of him.

MENELAUS: ⁵⁴⁶ Hey! You there – the one who's trying so desperately to reach the steps of the tomb and those altars where the burnt offerings are placed. Stay for a moment! Why are you running from me? You should know that when I saw your face I was struck by amazement and disbelief.

HELEN: ⁵⁵⁰ Oh no, women – this means violence! That man is trying to stop me from reaching the safety of the tomb. He's planning to take me and give me to the king that I don't want to marry!

MENELAUS: No – I'm no thief, and I'm also not someone who acts as a servant-boy for evil men.

HELEN: But you're dressed just as crudely as a villain would be dressed.

MENELAUS: [555] Just please… don't be afraid of me. Stop where you are.

HELEN: Fine, I can stop now, since I finally have my hands on the tomb.

MENELAUS: Who are you, my lady? Whose face am I looking at when I look at you?

HELEN: And you, I can ask you the same question – who are you?

MENELAUS: I have never seen a greater resemblance in my life.

HELEN: [560] O gods! It's a gift from the gods to recognize your own!

MENELAUS: Are you a Greek woman or are you native to this place?

HELEN: I'm Greek – but I want to know more about you.

MENELAUS: You are more like Helen than any woman I have ever seen.

HELEN: And you are more like Menelaus than any man I've ever seen. I… I don't know what to say.

MENELAUS: [565] So you recognize me then, even though I'm in most unfortunate circumstances?

HELEN: O dear – you've come at long last to the arms of your wife!

MENELAUS: Wife? What wife do you mean? Take your hands off my clothes.

HELEN: I'm referring to the wife that my father Tyndareus gave you.

MENELAUS: O Hecate, you goddess of the night – please send me better dreams than this!

HELEN: [570] But I'm not a dream from the goddess of the crossways. You're looking at your Helen.

MENELAUS: But I'm just one man – I can't have two wives.

HELEN: To what woman other than me are you married?

MENELAUS: The woman I left in the cave – the one I brought back with me from Troy.

HELEN: You have no other wife than me. I'm your only wife.

MENELAUS: [575] Is it possible that my mind is solid but that my eyes are bad?

HELEN: When you look at me aren't you convinced that you're looking at your wife?

MENELAUS: You definitely look like her – but I don't know what to say for certain.

HELEN: Just look at me – why do you need any more proof than that?

MENELAUS: You look very much like her – I can't deny that.

HELEN: [580] And who would know her better than you?

MENELAUS: My problem is that I have another Helen – over in the cave.

HELEN: That was just an image of me – I never went to Troy.

MENELAUS: And what kind of craftsman can make a living person?

HELEN: It was made from the upper air – it was the gods who made that artificial wife for you.

MENELAUS: [585] Which one of the gods made her? What you say is amazing to me.

HELEN: Hera did it – she made a substitute for me so that Paris would not get the real me.

Menelaus: What do you mean? Were you both here and at Troy for the whole time?

Helen: A name can be in many places, but a body can only really be in one.

Menelaus: Oh, I wish all of this would stop! I had enough grief already when I arrived here.

Helen: [590] What? Are you going to leave me and take your phantom wife away with you?

Menelaus: I send you my congratulations for resembling Helen so much.

Helen: Oh, this is horrible! I've finally found you, my dear husband – but I can't keep you any longer!

Menelaus: I trust my many years and hardships at Troy – not you.

Helen: [594] Oh, is there any woman who's more unfortunate than I am? My dear husband is deserting me, and I'll never reach Greece again, never again reach my native city!

Enter a Servant of Menelaus

Servant: Menelaus, it's been really hard to find you! I've roamed up and down this barbarian land looking for you. The soldiers you left behind sent me for you.

Menelaus: [600] What's wrong? You aren't being attacked by these barbarians, are you?

Servant: Something really strange has happened – something so strange that I can hardly find words to describe it.

Menelaus: Tell me – you must be bringing some surprising news, if you're hurrying her like this.

Servant: I have to tell you that your countless labours and adventures have all been in vain.

Menelaus: I've heard this kind of sob story before – what's your news?

Servant: [605] It's your wife – she's disappeared, swept up and away from us and out of sight into the recesses of the sky. She's vanished into the high heavens!

[607] She left the secret cave where we were guarding her, saying only this before she vanished – "you poor Trojans and all you Greeks. Day after day you killed one another for my sake by the banks of the Scamander river. But it was a trick on you that Hera devised – all of you thought that Paris had Helen, which he never did. I've just completed the task that I was placed on this earth to fulfill – now it's time for me to go back to my father the sky. The unlucky daughter of Tyndareus has been wrongly vilified – she doesn't deserve any blame."

[616] Oh ... hey ... what's this? Hey there! There you are, daughter of Leda! So this is what happened to you! I was just bringing the news to your husband that you'd departed for the starry heavens. I had no idea that you had wings. But I really have to ask you not to make fun of us like that again – the troubles that you gave your husband and his men at Troy provided more than enough stress.

Menelaus: [622] This is the same story that she just told me! Her words are true after all! O what a wonderful day – this is the day that I've longed for, for it has brought you, the real you, back into my arms once again!

Helen: [625] O Menelaus, the man I love the most, it's been far too long, but now joy has finally returned to us!

[627] My friends, I'm filled with such joy now that I finally can greet my husband and put my arms around him after all these days have passed by!

Menelaus: [630] And I'm so happy to have you again. There's so much I want to say to you, but I don't know where to begin. My heart is jumping for joy, the hair on my head is standing on its ends, and tears are starting to fall from my eyes! I'm so happy to throw my arms around you and take you in my arms.

HELEN: [636] Oh my husband! It's such a joy to finally look at you again!

MENELAUS: I'm the happiest man alive! There's nothing left for me to wish for, for I have my wife again – the glorious daughter of Zeus and Leda.

HELEN: Yes, I'm the woman whom the boys with the white horses, my brothers, led with the bridal torch. It was a marriage that was called blessed – and these words were not false in the past.

MENELAUS: [641] And those words are not false now, for heaven is leading you to an even better fate than the one we had before.

HELEN: Yes, the evil that kept us apart for so long, my husband, eventually turned to good and brought us back together. I pray that I can enjoy this new blessing for a long time!

MENELAUS: [646] I hope the same for me as well. Your wish is my wish, for it's not right in a couple if one person is happy and the other person isn't.

HELEN: My friends, my friends – no longer do I have to feel bad about all that has happened in the past. I have my husband with me now – the man I've waited so long for… since those long years at Troy… so many years!

MENELAUS: [652] Now you have me, and now I have you. It was hard to live through those many days without you, but now I recognize that it was all heaven's hand at work. The tears I'm crying are those of joy – they are filled more with gratefulness than they are with pain and sorrow.

HELEN: At this stage what can I really say? Who could have even hoped for this? I am finally holding you in my arms, never having expected to be able to do so ever again.

MENELAUS: [658] And I hold you as well, when I thought you had gone to that city near Mount Ida and the pitiful towers of Troy.

But how in the name of the gods were you taken away from my house?

HELEN: Ah, it's a painful story that you're asking me to tell…

MENELAUS: Please tell it to me. The gods caused this to happen, so it's right for me to hear it.

HELEN: [665] The tale I'm about to tell makes me feel nothing but revulsion.

MENELAUS: All the same, please tell it to me – to hear of a trouble that is over and done with can be a type of pleasure.

HELEN: I wasn't carried away to the bed of a young barbarian prince, wasn't carried on the beating of his oars, wasn't carried away on the wings of desire for an unholy marriage…

MENELAUS: Then what was the divine power, what was the fate that stole you from your country?

HELEN: [670] It was the son of Zeus and Maia, Hermes – he was the one who brought me here to the land of the Nile.

MENELAUS: This is so strange! Who told him to do this?

HELEN: I have so often wept for this, and even now again my eyes are filled with tears. It was the wife of Zeus who destroyed me like this.

MENELAUS: [675] Hera? But why did she want to cause us so much pain and trouble?

HELEN: There was a danger there for me in that bath and those gushing springs where the goddesses made themselves beautiful and where they came to be judged.

Menelaus: Why did Hera decide to make this judgment such a sorrow for you?

Helen: ⁶⁸⁰ She wanted to take me away from Paris…

Menelaus: I don't understand – what do you mean?

Helen: Aphrodite promised me to Paris and so Hera didn't want him to actually get to have me.

Menelaus: Oh, you poor woman!

Helen: And so Hera sent me in my misery to Egypt instead.

Menelaus: Then she gave him the image to replace you, if I heard you correctly.

Helen: ⁶⁸⁴ But there have been so many sorrows back at home. Oh, my mother! Mother – so much suffering, so much pain!

Menelaus: What do you mean?

Helen: My mother is dead. She tied a noose around her neck because she was so ashamed at my impious marriage.

Menelaus: Oh no! But what about our daughter Hermione – have you heard anything about her? Is she still alive?

Helen: ⁶⁸⁹ She's alive, but she spends her time grieving for my non-existent disastrous marriage – and she passes her days in tears, unmarried and childless.

Menelaus: O Paris, you've completely destroyed my home!

Helen: ⁶⁹² Yes, all of this has been horrible for you, and it has caused the death of countless other bronze-armored Danaans.

⁶⁹⁴ But I was sent far away from my country by heaven – far from my city, and far from you. I was unfortunate and cursed by men for having left your house and your marriage bed – even though I did not leave it – and for supposedly joining a marriage filled with shame.

Menelaus: But if the rest of your life is fortunate from now onward, then it will offer comfort and solace for all that happened in the past.

Servant: ⁷⁰⁰ Menelaus – please tell me what's making you so happy. I've heard some bits and pieces of it here, but I don't fully understand it myself.

Menelaus: Well then, old man, you should take part in this conversation with us.

Servant: Wasn't this woman the reason for all our troubles in Troy?

Menelaus: ⁷⁰⁵ No, not this woman. The gods played a trick on us. The whole time both the Trojans and we were holding merely an image of her that had been made out of the clouds.

Servant: What do you mean? Are you saying that we went to Troy for nothing – for a fucking cloud?

Menelaus: This was the doing of Hera, and it all stemmed from the anger of the three goddesses.

Servant: But is this woman who's standing here now really your wife?

Menelaus: ⁷¹⁰ Yes, it's her – you can take my word for it.

Servant: ⁷¹¹ Young lady, the ways of the gods are so complex and hard for us to predict! It turns everything now in this direction, and then suddenly in another direction. One man has troubles now but later he'll find happiness and blessings from heaven, while another man, who's had no trouble for the most of his life, suddenly dies a very painful death, since nobody can retain his fortune forever and make it last.

⁷¹⁶ You and your husband had your share of troubles – you with your reputation, and he with all the pains and struggles of war. No matter how hard he worked, all his hard fighting was fought for nothing. But now we can see that he finally receives a blessing without having to do anything at all – all by a stroke of great luck.

⁷²⁰ So, my lady, you haven't brought shame on your old father or your brothers the Dioscuri, for you didn't do any of those things that the rumours accuse you of doing. Now I can sing your marriage song once again. Now I can once again think of the wedding torches that I carried beside you when you rode in your wedding chariot – with your husband by your side. You left a blessed house to gain another noble one when you married your husband.

⁷²⁶ Only an evil man doesn't revere and respect his master, doesn't rejoice at his successes, and feel bad with all his sorrows. Even if I were a slave, I would always hope to be one of the good slaves – one with the heart of a free man even if I lacked the title of a free man. It's much better to do that than to join two misfortunes in one person – that is, to have an evil heart and hear yourself referred to as the slave of another man.

MENELAUS: ⁷³⁴ Old man, you've done great service for me in battle. Now I want you to share in my good fortune. Please go off and find all of my friends who are left – all those people who were guarding that ghost in the cave – and tell them how you've found things here and how our fortune now stands.

⁷³⁹ Tell them to stay there on the beach and to watch for the outcome of the trials that that I fear will be mine and Helen's. If somehow I can manage to steal her away from this land, tell them that they should be ready and waiting for us so that we might join our fortunes together and be able to get clear of all these barbarians, if we can find the strength.

SERVANT: ⁷⁴⁴ I'll do as you say, my lord. I'm just thinking about how worthless prophets are – how they're such liars! There's no truth in the flame that comes from sacrifice or in the cries that come from birds. How stupid it is to think that birds can offer any guidance to mankind!

⁷⁴⁹ I mean, our prophet Calchas never said a word to the Greek army, and apparently the Trojan "prophet" Helenus didn't say anything to the enemy troops – they both kept silent when they saw that so many of their colleagues were dying for the sake of a mere cloud. A city was destroyed, and so many people died – all for nothing.

⁷⁵¹ I suppose you could reply by saying that "But that was because the god did not want the truth to be known." If that's the case, then why do we even bother to consult the prophets? It seems that we should sacrifice to the gods directly and ask them directly for blessing – and leave prophecy and prophets alone. The whole art-form was invented as a scam, a way for charlatans to make a bit of money – "prophets love their profits," as they say. But none of these phonies would have ever become rich performing their magic tricks if there were no one willing to pay them. It seems to me that the best way to tell the future is to use common sense – to be intelligent and plan ahead.

Exit the Servant

CHORUS: ⁷⁵⁸ My own opinion of the prophets and prophecy is the same as this old man's. If a man has the gods on his side and if they are

Helen: his friends, then that is the best prophecy that his house can have.

Helen: [761] So everything has been peaceful here in Egypt up to this point. But, my dear husband, please tell me how you survived the battles in Troy. I realize that it will do me no good to hear it, but I still feel a great desire to hear about the troubles that affect my husband.

Menelaus: [765] That single question of yours requires a huge answer. How should I tell you about the many shipwrecks we had on the Aegean, or the false fires set by Nauplius on the Euboean, or all the cities in Crete and Libya that I visited, or even the lookout place of Perseus? If I were to give you all the information you want about my story, then I'd be suffering all the more by the act of having to retell it. It would be just as bad as when I suffered the real experiences, and so I would feel the pain a second time.

Helen: [772] What you've said was more than I asked for. But maybe you can tell me one thing and leave out all of the rest – how long have you been wandering over the waves of the sea?

Menelaus: [775] It's been seven years that I've been going around on the sea, added to the ten years that I spent in Troy.

Helen: My poor husband – what a long time! You lived through all of that, and survived everything – only to die here.

Menelaus: To die here? What do you mean by that? Your words cut me deeply, my wife.

Helen: [780] O Menelaus – you need to get away from this place as quickly as you can, or you'll be killed by the man who rules this palace!

Menelaus: What have I done to deserve such treatment as that?

Helen: Your arrival was unexpected – and you'll be seen as a hindrance to my wedding.

Menelaus: What? You mean that someone's going to try to marry my wife?

Helen: [785] Yes, and that action will commit an outrage against you and your rights, and it will be an outrage against me.

Menelaus: Is it a king or some warlord or some wealthy nobleman?

Helen: It's Proteus' son – the ruler of the land.

Menelaus: Now I understand why the woman at the gate spoke to me the way she did.

Helen: Which barbarian gates were you standing in front of?

Menelaus: [790] These ones right here. And I was driven away from them as if I were a beggar.

Helen: You weren't begging for food, were you? Oh, this is so bad for me!

Menelaus: That's what I was doing, but I did not call it "begging."

Helen: Then now you know the whole story about his attempt to marry me.

Menelaus: Yes, I hear that – but it's not clear whether you've been able to prevent him.

Helen: [795] I assure you that he has never placed a hand on me – my body belongs to you.

Menelaus: How can I be sure of what you say? It's wonderful news if it's true.

Helen: Do you see this tomb here? Do you see this miserable and sad place where I've been sitting?

Menelaus: I can see a couch that's been made out of leaves – but what does this have to do with you?

Helen: This is where I've been taking refuge as a suppliant to avoid marriage with him.

MENELAUS: [800] It doesn't look the same as our Greek tombs – is this how they look here?

HELEN: It may seem different, but this tomb has protected me just as much as a Greek temple would.

MENELAUS: So there's no way for me to take you home from here by boat?

HELEN: A sword is waiting for you, not my bed.

MENELAUS: Oh, I've become the unhappiest man alive!

HELEN: [805] Don't waste your time feeling ashamed. You should take flight immediately and get away from this land.

MENELAUS: And leave you behind? No chance – I destroyed Troy for your sake.

HELEN: Yes, you should leave – it's better that you do that than be killed because of your wife.

MENELAUS: You make me sound like a coward, like someone who's unworthy of the fall of Troy.

HELEN: Perhaps you want to kill the king here. It won't be possible.

MENELAUS: [810] You mean that his body is so powerful that it can't be pierced by a sword? Is he made of steel?

HELEN: You'll see – but a wise man doesn't try to do things that are impossible.

MENELAUS: And so should I just hold out my hands to him and quietly let him put me in shackles?

HELEN: Your situation now is desperate – we need to come up with a clever plan.

MENELAUS: Yes, it's better to die while trying to do something than it is to die doing nothing.

HELEN: [815] We do have one hope – a single way that could lead to our salvation.

MENELAUS: How so? Does it involve bribery? Doing something daring or forceful? Or using clever argumentation?

HELEN: We need to make sure that the king never hears of your arrival here.

MENELAUS: I'm sure that he won't know who I am. And who could possibly tell him?

HELEN: Inside the palace he has an ally who is as powerful as any of the gods.

MENELAUS: [820] What? Is there some ethereal voice that's living in the innermost part of the house?

HELEN: No, it's his sister – her name is Theonoë.

MENELAUS: Her name means "divinely-inspired," doesn't it? It's a rather ominous name at any rate. Tell me what she does.

HELEN: She knows everything, and she'll tell her brother, the king, that you're here.

MENELAUS: Then I'm done for. There's no way that I'll be able to escape detection.

HELEN: [825] But what if we throw ourselves on her mercy and try to persuade her…

MENELAUS: Persuade her to do what? What is the hope that you are raising in me?

HELEN: We'll ask her not to tell her brother that we're in this land.

MENELAUS: And after we persuade her, then we can escape?

HELEN: Yes, we'll easily be able to do that – with her help. But if we try to do it without her knowledge, then we'll never be successful.

MENELAUS: [830] Then this should be your task. You need to arrange this, for it's best for a woman to deal with a woman.

HELEN: I'll grab hold of her knees in supplication.

Menelaus: But just wait – what if she's unwilling to listen to us and help us?

Helen: Then you'll be killed, and I'll be forced into a miserable marriage with the king.

Menelaus: That would mean you'd be betraying me. Mentioning force only provides an excuse for the shameful action.

Helen: 835 No – I've sworn a sacred oath, in your name!

Menelaus: Do you mean to say that you'll die? That you'll never take a new husband?

Helen: Yes, I swear that I'll die before that happens, and with the same sword. And I'll lie next to you.

Menelaus: Take my hand, then, and make your promise.

Helen: There – I've got your hand. I swear that if you are killed then I'll die as well.

Menelaus: 840 And I swear that if I lose you then I will die as well.

Helen: But if we die this way, how could we do it in such a way that we would win glory and people would remember us?

Menelaus: 842 I'll kill you right on top of this tomb here, and then I'll kill myself. But first I'll put up a brave fight for your sake and for our marriage. I'll take on anybody who wants to try me. There's no chance that I'll ever bring shame to my Trojan reputation or disgrace myself by returning to Greece without you. I'm the man who took Achilles away from Thetis, I witnessed the suicide of Ajax, that great son of Telamon, and I saw Neleus' son Nestor lose his own son in battle. Isn't it only natural that I think it right to die for the sake of my wife?

851 Oh, it's something that I have to do. And if the gods are kind, they'll cover the man who fights bravely and is killed by the enemy with earth that lies very lightly upon him. But cowards – the gods toss the cowards out onto the hard mounds of earth.

Chorus: 855 Oh gods, I pray that you can find a way to let the race of Tantalus find happiness at last and escape from all this misery!

Helen: 857 Oh this is horrible! Our luck has run out, Menelaus – we are ruined! The prophetess Theonoë is coming out of the palace. I can see that the bolt is starting to open and the house is making sounds of the door starting to open.

860 Run! But where can you run? Oh, what's the use? Whether she's here or somewhere else, she still knows about your arrival. Oh, it's all over for us now! My poor husband, having escaped from the horrors of Troy, once again you're going to be attacked by a barbarian sword.

Enter Theonoë with attendants

Theonoë: 865 Lead the way, all of you servants. Carry the torches, let them shine, and cleanse the recesses of the sky with sulfur so that I can breathe the pure air of the heavens!

868 And you over there, in case anyone has polluted this path by walking on it with an unholy foot, treat it with the purifying flame and touch it with the torch so that I can make my way through. When you've done the appropriate service to the gods, the things that are fitting for my position, then take the fire back into the house.

873 Helen – there you are. And what about my prophecies? Are they not true, exactly as I told you? Of course they are, for your husband has returned. There he is, right beside you, plain as day to see – having lost all his ships and with your image having disappeared back into the sky.

⁸⁷⁶ You poor man, think about all the dangers you had to escape in order to arrive here. And yet you still have no idea whether you'll be able to go home or whether you'll stay here. In point of fact, on this very day there is a great disagreement among the gods about you as they all gather about the court of Zeus. Hera, who used to be your enemy, is now acting as your friend and is trying to bring you and Helen safely home so that the whole of Greece can learn that Paris' marriage, that gift of Aphrodite, was no marriage at all.

⁸⁸⁴ But Aphrodite is now working to prevent your coming home. She doesn't want to be placed in a position of disgrace when it's discovered that she bought the name of beauty in that contest and received a lie in return – a marriage to Helen that was not the real thing.

⁸⁸⁷ The outcome to all this resides with me. Should I, as Aphrodite wants, tell my brother of your arrival here and thus bring an end to your life? Or should I stand on the side of Hera and save you by keeping this a secret from my brother, who ordered me to tell him when you arrived?

⁸⁹² Which one of you, my slaves, will go and tell my brother that this man is here so that my future will be made safe?

HELEN: ⁸⁹⁴ O young woman, I fall at your knees as a suppliant. I'm begging both for myself and for this man. I'm at my wit's end. I've barely had him back in my life, and now I face the very real danger of never seeing him again. Please, I beg you, please don't tell your brother that my husband has come back to my arms!

⁹⁰⁰ Save him, please! Don't sacrifice your own good name for the sake of your brother just in order to buy him wicked pleasures that he doesn't deserve and are contrary to justice.

⁹⁰³ The god hates violence, and he's ordered all men to obtain their goods and property fairly, without stealing. Unjust wealth must be left alone. The sky belongs to all mortals in common, and there is the earth for us to live in, and on this earth no man should hold other men's property or take it by force to try to fill his own home.

⁹⁰⁹ For me it was hard, and it was also a kind of blessing, that Hermes brought me here and gave me to your father Proteus to keep me safe for my husband. And now my husband is here and he wants to take me home. How can he do that if he's killed? And how can your brother give back a living woman to someone who's dead? It's time to consider that the god and your father have the same desire, the same right – and it's their wish that I should be returned to my husband. Would the god and your father want you to give back your neighbour's goods or not? I think they would. And that's why you shouldn't regard your foolish brother more highly than your wise father.

⁹¹⁹ If you really are a prophet and believe in the gods, but yet you'll still corrupt the just actions of your father merely so that you can uphold the unholy actions of your brother, then it's an absolute disgrace that the gods give you the power to see the present and the future but they don't show you what justice really is. It's shameful to know the past, present, and future – but not to know justice!

⁹²⁴ I'm in such a state of misery from all the problems that surround me. Please save me from this! Count this as one more just deed that you'll have done. Every man hates Helen – every single one. It's been reported throughout the whole of Greece that I abandoned my husband and went to live in the golden houses of Troy. But if I reach Greece once again and can walk again in Sparta, men will see that

they went through all of this due to the shenanigans of the gods and that I wasn't a traitor to my family after all. They'll give me back my future and I'll be able to find a husband for my poor unmarried daughter. I'll be able to escape the life of a beggar that I have here and I'll be able to enjoy living my life – as a queen – in my own home.

⁹³⁶ If my husband Menelaus were killed and burned somewhere on a pyre, I would be honouring him with my tears even though he would be far away. But he's here – he's alive and is standing safely in front of me. And so am I then going to be robbed of him? No, please no, young woman! I beg you, please grant me this favour and imitate the ways of your just and righteous father. The best renown for children is to be born from a noble father and to be equal to him in character.

Chorus: ⁹⁴⁴ Helen, the pleas that you are making bring out my pity and compassion. But I want to hear what Menelaus will have to say in defense of his life.

Menelaus: ⁹⁴⁷ As for me, I can't bring myself to fall at your knees and fill my eyes with tears. Such cowardly behavior would bring disrespect and shame on everything that happened at Troy, even though some people say that it's the mark of a nobleman to cry in the midst of disaster. All the same, I won't choose such noble tears – if tears are noble, that is. Instead I'll try to act bravely.

⁹⁵⁴ If you think that it's best to save the life of a stranger who is properly and justly trying to recover his wife, then give her back to me and save my life along the way. But if you won't do this, it won't be the first time that I've felt miserable. No – it will just be a continuation of the suffering that I've been enduring for a long time now. But, and mark this well, it will prove that you are an evil woman.

⁹⁵⁹ But the words that I think are worthy of me and are fair and honest and will touch your heart most closely – I'll say these words, as is appropriate, to the tomb of your aged father, addressing the dead king.

⁹⁶² Old sir, you who live within this monument of stone, I ask you for the return of my wife to me, the woman whom Zeus sent to you to keep safe for me. Give her back to me! Since you're dead, I know that you yourself can't be the one who gives her back to me. I'm aware of that. But this woman here, your daughter, will not think it right that her father, whom I have called from the dead, receives such a bad name when it used to be so good and virtuous. Everything, including your reputation and memory, is now within her power.

⁹⁶⁹ O Hades of the underworld, I call on you as well! As payment you've already received many bodies killed by my sword – all because of this woman. I ask you to either give my dead soldiers all back to me alive or please force this young woman here to show herself equal to her divine father by giving my wife back.

⁹⁷⁵ But if you Egyptians are going to rob me of my wife, I'll tell you what she left unsaid. Young woman, you should know that my wife and I have bound ourselves together by an oath. The first part of that oath states that I will fight against your brother. Simply put, either he or I will have to die. But if your brother refuses to meet me in combat and if he tries to capture the two of us by starving us here as suppliants at this tomb, then we've resolved to die here, for I'll kill my wife and then thrust this two-edged sword through my own heart. I'll do it right on top of this tomb, so that streams of our blood will seep down into the grave of your father. We'll both lie here as

two corpses, side by side, upon this marble tomb – and it'll be a shame for your father, and it will harm you, forevermore.

⁹⁸⁸ Neither your brother nor any other man will ever marry her. I'll take her away from here. We'll either go back to our home or to the grave.

⁹⁹¹ But why am I even doing this? If I'm turning into a woman and using tears, then I'll be pathetic and no longer a courageous man of action.

⁹⁹³ So kill me, if that's what you think's best. You won't kill a man who has disgraced himself. But you'll be better off if you listen to my words and arguments – for you'll behave honourably and justly, and I'll get my wife back.

Chorus: ⁹⁹⁶ It's up to you, young prophetess, to act as the judge on what has been said. Make your judgment, and try to judge in a way that will please everyone!

Theonoë: ⁹⁹⁸ It's my nature to lean toward fairness and piety. I have to think of myself and not pollute the name and reputation of my father. I won't do a favour for my brother that will also bring me a bad name.

¹⁰⁰² Built within me there is a great temple to Justice, and it's this devotion to all that is right and just, Menelaus, that I've received as my inheritance from Nereus – and I plan to keep it always. Therefore, since Hera plans to treat you well, I'll place my vote alongside of hers.

¹⁰⁰⁶ As for Aphrodite, I pray that she won't be offended. But she really holds no sway with me, for I plan to remain a virgin my entire life.

¹⁰⁰⁹ And as for the comments you just made about my father and his tomb, I have the same opinion as you. That is, I would be acting unjustly if I did not return your wife. Yes, you're right – if my father were alive, he would have given her back to you and you to her. In fact, all men will have to face punishment for deeds done above the ground when they finally go below to Hades. Even though the mind of a dead man is not really alive in the way we understand it, it will forever have the capacity to feel when it has been thrown into the eternal upper airs.

¹⁰¹⁶ But to keep my story brief, let me just say that I'll keep quiet, as you've asked me to do, and I won't allow my good advice to be used by my brother to help him in his shameful lusts. In many ways I'm even doing him a favour, even though he might disagree, if I can move him to become good and god-fearing instead of evil and impious.

¹⁰²² Now it will be up to the two of you to find some means of escape – I'll merely stand out of the way and hold my tongue. You should begin by praying to the gods. Pray to Aphrodite to allow you to reach home, and pray to Hera as well, asking her to remain true to the goodwill she is now showing both of you, the goodwill that will save you.

¹⁰²⁸ O father, you're long departed from this earth, but as far as I have the power to affect things, you'll never be called a wicked name but will only ever be praised for your goodness and virtue.

Exit Theonoë with her attendants

Chorus: ¹⁰³⁰ Unjust men never really end up enjoying good fortune. Our hopes for safety lie in good and righteous behaviour.

Helen: Menelaus, this young woman has saved our lives for the moment. From this point onward we must think clearly and come up with a way for us to both reach Sparta safely.

Menelaus: ¹⁰³⁵ Listen then – you've lived in this house for a long time and have no doubt become familiar with the servants of the king.

Helen: That's true, but what do you mean? Do you have some idea as to how we can use this to our mutual advantage?

Menelaus: [1039] Do you think that you could persuade one of the chariot-keepers to let us have a chariot?

Helen: I could do that. But what kind of an escape could we make even if we do get a chariot? We're on barbarian soil and we don't know our way around here.

Menelaus: You're right – it would be impossible, hopeless. Hmmm… well then… what if I hide in the palace and kill the king with my double-edged sword?

Helen: [1045] His sister would never let you get away with it. She's a prophetess, remember, so she'd know what you're up to, and so she'd tell him that you were planning to kill him.

Menelaus: And we have no ship to use to make an escape by sea. The boat that we did have is now at the bottom of the sea.

Helen: I think I have an idea. Just give me a listen and decide whether a woman can have a clever idea. Are you willing to be reported dead even though you're still alive?

Menelaus: [1051] It sounds like a bad omen. But if we're going to gain some advantage by this tale, then tell me what you have in mind. You can tell people that I'm dead even though I'm still alive.

Helen: Then I'll act as if I am in mourning in front of this godless young king. I'll chop off my hair and go about wailing, just like women do when they've lost a loved one.

Menelaus: [1055] But how is that going to help us escape with our lives? I can't see how this plan is going to actually help us.

Helen: Since I'll say that you died at sea, then I'll ask the king that he let me bury you in effigy in the sea.

Menelaus: [1059] Suppose he agrees to this – how can this plan help us win an escape if we still don't have a ship?

Helen: I'll ask him to provide a ship so that we can throw your funeral fineries overboard and into the grave of the deep sea.

Menelaus: That seems like a good idea, but there's one potential problem – what if he tells us to perform the funeral rites on land? Then the whole plan will come to nothing.

Helen: [1065] We'll have to say that it's not our custom in Greece to give a land burial to those who've died at sea.

Menelaus: Another great suggestion! Then I'll travel along with you on the same ship and help throw the things overboard.

Helen: [1069] Yes, it's very important that you are there as well – and your sailors who escaped the shipwreck with you should be there too.

Menelaus: Once I can take possession of the anchored ship, my men will stand behind me and we'll fight with our ready swords.

Helen: At that point you'll be in charge of everything. I only hope that the winds will offer us fair sailing and that the ship will sail quickly away!

Menelaus: [1075] I'll make sure that the ship moves quickly. The gods are finding a way to help our troubles come to an end. But who will you say has told you the news of my death?

Helen: You will. You will say that you sailed with the son of Atreus, that you saw him die, and that you were the only one to survive.

MENELAUS: ¹⁰⁷⁹ Well, these rags that I'm wearing on my body now will seem to back up that story well.

HELEN: The loss of your good clothing worked out well, although it seemed like bad luck when it happened. However, that misfortune may just turn out to be a blessing.

MENELAUS: Should I go inside the house with you or should I sit quietly here next to the tomb?

HELEN: ¹⁰⁸⁵ Just stay here. If he tries to use violence against you, then you can use this tomb and your own sword to protect you.

¹⁰⁸⁷ I'm going to go into the house, cut my hair, and change the white clothes that I'm wearing – and instead I'll put on black clothes of mourning. And I'll make my cheeks look all bloody from scratching them with my nails due to mourning.

¹⁰⁹⁰ This contest that stands in front of us is a great one, and I can only see two possible outcomes – either I'll have to die if my trickery is discovered, or I'll save your life and we can both go home.

¹⁰⁹³ O divine Hera, sister and divine wife of Zeus, please help these two pitiful creatures in our time of trouble! We beg you, lifting our arms straight up toward the heavens, where you live among the stars.

¹⁰⁹⁷ And we beg you as well, Aphrodite, daughter of Dione, who won that prize of beauty by making the bribe of marriage with me as the reward. Please, Aphrodite, please don't destroy us! You've already treated me horribly enough when you gave my name to those barbarian Trojans, even though you didn't give them my real body. But if you're planning to kill me, at least let me die in my own country. Why do you have such thirst for mischief and trouble? Why do you bring about such passions, lies, devices full of treachery, love-magic, and murders in the homes of decent people? If you could only be moderate, then I must confess that you'd be the most pleasant of the gods for mortals.

Exit Helen into the palace

CHORUS: ¹¹⁰⁷ I send out my cry to you, O you who sit deep in the forest and keep on with your house of song. I call out to you, O bird most gifted in music, you nightingale, one called Philomela, the songbird with so many tears. Please come to me, O you who sing your song of sadness through your colourful beak. Share in my sadness as I sing about the horrible sadness of Helen along with the miserable fate of the daughters of Troy, and all that they suffered at the hands of the Greek spearmen. Sing about how that young man sped so swiftly over the gray sea with his barbarian oars, the one who brought the sons of Priam with him – that Paris who took you, Helen, as his bride from Sparta, for that ill-fated marriage, when he was brought there by the will of Aphrodite.

¹¹²² Many Greeks died from the sword and from the great boulders that were tossed at them – all of their deaths were in vain, it seems. And their unhappy wives express their misery by cutting off their long hair, for their bedrooms and homes can no longer be filled with bridal love and desire.

¹¹²⁶ There were also many Greeks who were killed by one of their own – I mean Nauplius – who sent out his bright gleam around water-encircled Euboea. He was a solitary rower, and he led them to crash to their deaths on the Aegean rocks at Caphereus when he lit his false torches, signals of rocky peril that the others misread as beacons of safety.

¹¹³² It was at that point when Menelaus was

driven off course to lands that have no harbours and where men dress in strange clothing. It was then that the storm winds pushed him away from Greece and his homecoming, taking his prize, his phantom wife, with him – the cause of all that fighting, the divine phantom made by Hera.

^{1137} What mortal has the ability to search out and tell what's a god and what's not a god and what lies somewhere between the gods and men? Perhaps he has found some remote and obscure way to the absolute, and that he's seen the gods, and that he's come back again, with the outcome constantly wavering and unexpected. Is there anyone who can hope for such a fortune?

^{1144} You, Helen, are the daughter of Zeus – your father came on wings to Leda, and when she took that bird in her arms the seed of your birth was planted. Yet you are hated throughout Greece – you're called a traitor, you are said to be faithless, lawless, and godless. I don't know whether I can ever find a reliable and true word about the gods from mortals.

^{1151} All men are fools, whoever tries to gain renown for valour through the use of the spear in the heat of battle, stupidly winning a release from all your toils in death. If contests of blood will always be used to solve problems, then hatred and war will never cease among the cities of men. Hatred and war could have been spared from the halls and bedrooms of Priam's Troy if it had been only possible, Helen, for men to bring an end to the quarrel they fought over you with reason and words. But now so many men in that battle have been sent to Hades down below, those walls overrun by violent flames, just like the lightning from Zeus – and you, Helen, you endure sorrow after sorrow, and you were luckless in your grievous sorrows.

Enter Theoclymenus, with servants and hunting dogs

THEOCLYMENUS: ^{1165} O tomb of my father, I send my greetings to you. I buried you so close to my gates, dear father, so that I – your son, Theoclymenus – can always greet you and share a word with you when I enter and leave my house.

^{1169} You servants – take the dogs and all of the hunting supplies into the house. I want to have a private word with my father.

^{1171} Now, father, we're alone. I've often found many horrible things to say about myself as criticism, wondering why we don't put evildoers to death. And now I've just learned that a Greek man has slipped though our guards and gates, and he has shown his face here. It's clear to me that he's either a spy or he has come here to steal Helen away from me. I want us to find him and kill him – let's hope we can catch him quickly!

^{1177} But what is this? It looks like I've come here too late and the whole thing has already happened! Tyndareus' daughter Helen is nowhere to be seen. She's left her place inside the tomb, and she must have been carried out of this land.

^{1181} Hey, you servants over there near the gates! Open up the gates, open the stables, and bring out the chariots. If I can somehow stop her, then the wife I desire won't be able to be secretly stolen away from my land.

Enter Helen from the palace

^{1184} Oh, just wait! I see that the woman I'm looking for is in fact still at home and that she hasn't fled. Helen, why is it that you've changed from your white clothing into black attire? And why did you take a knife and cut the long hair from your lovely and noble head? And why are you crying, making your cheeks wet with such fresh tears? Did some bad dream come to you in the night that forces you to do weep like this? Or have you heard some news from your homeland that is filling your heart with sorrow?

HELEN: [1193] My lord – for that is the name that I'll use to address you from now on – my life is in ruins. There is nothing left for me, and I'm dead!

THEOCLYMENUS: [1195] But what's happened? What's this trouble that has come over you?

HELEN: It's... it's my Menelaus. How... how can I say it? He's... he's dead!

THEOCLYMENUS: [1197] I don't take any pleasure in the news that you're bringing me, even though it works to my advantage.

How do you know that he's dead? Have heard this from my sister Theonoë?

HELEN: Yes – and I also heard it from someone who was there when he died.

THEOCLYMENUS: [1200] Really? Is there someone here who can confirm the truth of Menelaus' death?

HELEN: Yes, there is – and I wish he'd go to hell for having brought such horrible news to me!

THEOCLYMENUS: Who is he? And where is he? Tell me more – I want to have a clearer picture of all this.

HELEN: It's that man over there... the one who is sitting so despondently near the foot of the tomb.

THEOCLYMENUS: Oh my gods! Just look at the rags he's wearing for clothing!

HELEN: [1205] I think my husband must have looked like this recently – I feel so sorry for him!

THEOCLYMENUS: Where is this man from? And how did he arrive on our shores?

HELEN: He's Greek – one of the many Achaeans who sailed with my husband.

THEOCLYMENUS: And did he say how your husband died?

HELEN: Yes. It was a most horrible way – death at sea.

THEOCLYMENUS: [1210] In what sea did it happen?

HELEN: He was tossed into the cliffs of Libya – the ones that have no harbour.

THEOCLYMENUS: Then how did this guy over there survive? He was in the same ship.

HELEN: Sometimes the lower classes have more luck than their superiors.

THEOCLYMENUS: And so where are the remains of his ship?

HELEN: [1215] They're in a place where I wish that this man had died instead of my husband!

THEOCLYMENUS: Yes, Menelaus is dead – I understand. But how did this man get here? In what boat?

HELEN: He says that some sailors found him and rescued him.

THEOCLYMENUS: And what happened to that curse of an image that was sent to Troy instead of you?

HELEN: You mean the image that was made out of cloud? It went poof and vanished into the upper air.

THEOCLYMENUS: [1220] O Priam and Troy – your deaths were so pointless!

HELEN: I also share this same miserable fortune with the sons of Priam.

THEOCLYMENUS: Did this man bury your husband or did he leave him unburied?

HELEN: He's not buried yet – Oh, this is so terrible! So unbearable!

THEOCLYMENUS: So that's the reason you cut your long blonde hair?

HELEN: [1225] Yes – Menelaus is just as dear to me now as he was when he was alive.

THEOCLYMENUS: It's understandable that you're filled with tears.

HELEN: It's all ruined for me – my life is over!

THEOCLYMENUS: But don't be too impetuous – it's possible that the report of his death may be wrong.

HELEN: Do you think that it's so easy to fool your sister?

THEOCLYMENUS: No – of course not! But what's going to happen now? Are you still planning to make this tomb your home?

HELEN: Even though he's dead, he's still alive in my heart. Shouldn't he be remembered with honour?

THEOCLYMENUS: Why do you keep trying to provoke me? Why don't you just let the dead lie there in peace?

HELEN: But wherever a husband is, the wife should also be there.

THEOCLYMENUS: [1230] Is your running away from me a sign of being faithful to your husband?

HELEN: You don't have to worry about that now. You can begin the wedding arrangements.

THEOCLYMENUS: This is good news! I've been waiting a long time for this, and I'm really glad to hear finally hear it.

HELEN: Here's the thing we must do – we have to forget about the past.

THEOCLYMENUS: How so? In what way? A kindness should always be answered with another kindness.

HELEN: [1235] Let's make peace between ourselves. Please forgive me for everything.

THEOCLYMENUS: Of course! The quarrel that we had – consider it over! It's gone, taken flight, vanished!

HELEN: But let me go down on my knees and ask you this, if you're my friend…

THEOCLYMENUS: Why are you assuming this pose as a suppliant? What would you like me to do for you?

HELEN: I want to go give my dead husband a burial.

THEOCLYMENUS: [1240] How? Isn't your dead husband missing? How can you bury a man when you don't have his body? Are you going to bury a shadow?

HELEN: The Greeks have a custom whenever someone is lost at sea and is presumed dead.

THEOCLYMENUS: What do you do? It seems to me that the descendants of Pelops are quite skilled in such things.

HELEN: We hold a burial ceremony for the one who has died and we bury him in effigy.

THEOCLYMENUS: That's fine – then bury him. Feel free to raise up a funeral mound anywhere you like.

HELEN: [1245] That's not quite the way we bury sailors who died at sea.

THEOCLYMENUS: How do you mean then? I can't keep up with all your Greek customs.

HELEN: We take out to the sea everything that the dead will need.

THEOCLYMENUS: What should I give you then that you can use for your dead husband?

HELEN: This man over here knows more about it than I do. I was fortunate up until now, for I've never experienced such a thing before.

Theoclymenus: ¹²⁵⁰ You over there! Yes, you stranger – you've brought us some good news.

Menelaus: Well, it's not good news to me or to the man who died.

Theoclymenus: Tell me – how is it that you bury those who die at sea?

Menelaus: We bury him a lavishly as the dead man's wealth will allow.

Theoclymenus: It's settled then. You can take whatever you'll need for this burial at sea. Tell me what you'll need this this case – don't worry about the cost.

Menelaus: ¹²⁵⁵ The first thing we'll need is the blood of an animal so that we can make an offering to the dead.

Theoclymenus: What kind of animal. Just let me know, and it will be done.

Menelaus: Umm…you can decide for yourself… whatever you provide will do…

Theoclymenus: Among us "barbarians," it would most likely be a bull or a horse.

Menelaus: That sounds fine – just make sure that it isn't disfigured or flawed in any way.

Theoclymenus: ¹²⁶⁰ Our herds are large and rich – we won't have any problem in finding a suitable victim for this sacrifice.

Menelaus: We also like to provide some clothing to cover the body, even though we lack a body for such a funeral.

Theoclymenus: You'll get it. Is there anything else that your customs demand?

Menelaus: Yes. We'll need some bronze weapons – Menelaus really loved the spear.

Theoclymenus: The weapons we'll give you will be worthy of a descendant of Pelops.

Menelaus: ¹²⁶⁵ And we'll also need food – plenty of food that comes from this rich soil here.

Theoclymenus: What do you mean? How will you be able to throw all of these things into the sea?

Menelaus: We'll need a ship so that we can row out into the depths, and we'll need some skilled rowers as well.

Theoclymenus: How far out from this land will you have to go?

Menelaus: Just as far as the place where you can barely see the waves beating on the shore.

Theoclymenus: ¹²⁷⁰ Why on earth does Greece observe a custom like this?

Menelaus: We do this so that the waves and the tide will not wash everything back to the shore. That would be a type of pollution.

Theoclymenus: Very well then – I'll make sure that you have our fastest Phoenician ship, and there'll be plenty of oars.

Menelaus: That sounds excellent – Menelaus would be very pleased with that.

Theoclymenus: And can you do this by yourself, or do you need her to go with you?

Menelaus: ¹²⁷⁵ This ceremony must be performed either by the mother, the wife, or the children.

Theoclymenus: You mean to say that it is Helen's job to bury her husband?

Menelaus: It's the pious thing to do – we shouldn't cheat the dead of their due.

Theoclymenus: ¹²⁷⁸ Fine – she can go with you and do this. It'll be better for me if I can encourage my wife's piety. Go into the palace and you can choose whatever clothing you'll need to make your sacrifice for the dead man.

¹²⁸⁰ Once you've performed this service for

Helen you won't be sent away empty-handed. Since you've brought good news to me, you'll receive clothing to replace your rags. We'll do that right now, in fact. And we'll give you some food as well – we'll give you plenty of supplies so that you can return to your homeland. I can see that your present situation isn't very pleasant.

1285 And you, poor Helen, don't let yourself become worn down in longing for what's no longer possible. Don't spend too much time grieving for Menelaus. His life has ended, but you're still here, still alive – and no amount of weeping will ever be able to bring him back.

MENELAUS: 1288 Now you know what you have to do, young woman. You should pay attention to the husband you have and stop paying any attention to the one who's no longer relevant. That's the best option for you in these circumstances. As for me, if I can make it back to Greece safely, then I'll put an end to all those slanderous things that have been said about you – as long as you prove yourself to be a good wife to your husband from this point onward.

HELEN: 1294 It shall be so. My husband will find no reason at all to complain about me, and you yourself can serve as a witness to that.

1296 So, poor man, it's time for you to go inside, bathe, and then put on some fresh clothes. I'll start treating you with the appropriate level of kindness right away, for you'll perform the rites for my dear Menelaus in a better spirit if you receive proper and respectful treatment from me.

Exit Menelaus, Helen, and Theoclymenus into the palace

CHORUS: 1301 Once upon a time the Mountain Mother of all the gods – some call her Rhea, others say Cybele, but at this point she was just called Demeter – rushed forth on her swift feet in the wooded valleys and the overflowing streams of water and the deep-resounding waves of the sea. She was running so hard, looking for her young daughter, the girl we call "the maiden" for we may not say her name aloud.

1308 The roaring cymbals, their sharp and piercing notes – they were all clear when Demeter yoked her chariot to the wild beasts and sped off to find her missing daughter – her precious daughter who'd been ripped away from the circles of dancing that she was engaged in with those other young girls, her dear friends.

1314 Next to the mother stood storm-footed Artemis, ever ready with her bow, and grey-eyed Athena with all her weapons at her side. They set out to help Demeter as she searched for her missing daughter. But Zeus, the great god who rules all things – he was looking down from his high throne in the heavens and he brought about a different fate.

1319 When the mother came to the end of her aimless rushing around, and when she stopped her search for her dear daughter who'd been so sneakily taken away from her, she came to the snowy peaks where the nymphs of Mount Ida make their home and in her grief she threw herself on top of the rocks and snow and the grassless fields there.

1326 And it was then that she took away the fertility from the lands everywhere – she was determined to destroy the human race. For the flocks and herds of animals she no longer provided the foods of grass and leaf. The cities were running out of food, the gods had no sacrifices, and on their altars no offerings were made. She was moved to such sorrow for her missing daughter that she dried up the fresh springs that pour forth from deep in the ground, and there was no longer any water left to drink.

¹³²⁸ When she stopped all eating and all feasting by the gods and mankind, Zeus spoke up to soften the anger of the Great Mother. He said – "Go, you lovely and noble Graces, and go all of you Muses. Go to Demeter who's been made so angry by the disappearance of her daughter. Drive out her grief with loud cries and push her sorrows away with dancing and singing." It was at this point that Aphrodite, the loveliest of all the blessed gods, took up the rumbling voice of bronze and the drums made of stretched hide. The mother goddess took the deep sounding pipe and the clashing drum in her hands, delighting in their loud cry.

¹³⁵³ We must always revere her, and the holy flames that we light in our halls must always have sanction – we must always show true reverence to the sacrifices of this goddess. The power of her spotted dress of deerskin is great, and the ivy that is wound around the holy hollow reed also has power. And the noise in the air of the shaken wheel of the bull-roarer, twirled in a circle, the long hair leaping in Bacchic joy for Lord Bromius, the great Dionysus – it has so much strength and power, as do the nightlong feasts of the goddess when the moon with her chariot shines forth in the dark gloom of night.

Enter Helen from the palace

HELEN: ¹³⁶⁹ My friends, everything that happened in the house has been good and favourable for us. Proteus' daughter Theonoë joined with us in covering up the arrival of my husband and didn't tell her brother that he's here. Rather, when she was questioned she replied that Menelaus was dead and no longer saw the light of the sun.

¹³⁷⁴ For his part, my husband happened upon a real piece of luck, for he's carrying the weapons that he is supposed to throw into the sea. Right now his noble arm is fitted inside the handle of the shield and he's wearing it on his powerful shoulder. The spear is in his right hand, and he's pretending that he is going to use these items to honour the dead man – the dead man who's really himself.

¹³⁷⁹ And what's most convenient of all for battle is that he's carrying all kinds of other weapons with him, which will soon make so many barbarians turn back and run when we get on board this ship. I took off the shipwrecked rags that he'd been wearing and gave him fine new clothes, and I bathed him as well, with fresh water that I took from the stream.

¹³⁸⁵ But look – the prince is coming out now, the one who thinks that he has me safely in his possession and that he's soon going to marry me. I'll have to keep quiet about this once again. And I call on all of you, my friends, to help me in this deception – I need you to stay on my side and hold your tongues. If somehow we can make our way out of here, then we'll do our best to come back and rescue you as well.

Enter Theoclymenus and Menelaus from the palace

THEOCLYMENUS: ¹³⁹⁰ Servants, I want you to get to work and do exactly what this stranger tells you to do. So take these offerings to the ship so that they can be used for a funeral at sea.

¹³⁹² Helen, if you think that what I say is not bad and improper, then I'd like you to do as I say and stay here on the shore. Whether you're on that ship or not, you'll be doing your duty to your husband in both cases.

¹³⁹⁵ You see, I'm afraid that you'll be filled with an intense desire to throw yourself into the waves, especially when you're forced by

this ceremony to remember the joy that you had with your former husband. I know how excessively you mourned for him.

HELEN: ¹³⁹⁹ O my new husband, it's only natural that I honour my first marriage and the love that I gave him when I was his bride. And, yes, for the love of my husband I would even go so far as to die. But what kind of favour is it to him if I join him in death? Please – just let me go out there and give him his funeral offerings in person, as is right and appropriate.

¹⁴⁰⁵ I pray that the gods will give you all the blessings that you deserve, and I'm sure that this stranger here joins me in my prayer, for all the help that you've given us in this matter! For all the kindness you're showing me and Menelaus you'll soon find me the kind of wife that you deserve to have. All of this is the gift of fortune. But please tell someone to give us the ship so that we can carry out these offerings and then I'll be deeply happy.

THEOCLYMENUS: ¹⁴¹² Very well then. You, slave – go prepare a Sidonian fifty-oar ship. Make sure there are some solid rowers on board as well.

HELEN: But shouldn't the one who's actually conducting the funeral be in charge of the ship? I mean, this stranger here is the one who knows about all of these rituals.

THEOCLYMENUS: ¹⁴¹⁵ Of course – I'll make sure that my sailors do everything that he says.

HELEN: Please give them the order again so that they'll clearly understand your instructions.

THEOCLYMENUS: I'll give them the order over and over again – as long as it takes for them to understand.

HELEN: Oh thank you so much! And I hope that the task that I have in mind will bring you as many joys and blessings as it will me.

THEOCLYMENUS: Now now… don't waste your time with too much crying.

HELEN: ¹⁴²⁰ This day will reveal the full extent of my love for you!

THEOCLYMENUS: I still think that such care for the dead is a wasted effort.

HELEN: But what we do in this world, I think, has some effect in the other world.

THEOCLYMENUS: You'll find me no worse a husband than Menelaus.

HELEN: I can ask no more than that. The only thing I need now is the blessing of fortune.

THEOCLYMENUS: ¹⁴²⁵ But that's really within your own power – just be certain to show your good will toward me.

HELEN: Thankfully I won't ever need to be taught how to love my friends.

THEOCLYMENUS: Do you want me to come along with you and help out with this funeral?

HELEN: Oh, there's no need at all for that! There's no need at all for you to act as a slave for your own slaves.

THEOCLYMENUS: ¹⁴²⁹ Very well then. I'll leave all the rituals of the descendants of Pelops to you. My own house is free of blame and free of stain, since Menelaus did not die here.

¹⁴³¹ But now I'm going to send one of my slaves back into the palace so that they can prepare all the appropriate wedding decorations. The whole land here should be filled with the sound of happy singing so that my marriage to Helen will be truly blessed and enviable.

¹⁴³⁶ Now, stranger, go out into the sea and deliver all these offerings into the arms of Helen's former husband. Then please hurry back to the shore again with my wife. You'll be my guest at the wedding feast – and then you

can either set out for your home or you can stay here and have a happy life.

Exit Theoclymenus into the palace

MENELAUS: [1441] O Zeus, you who are called father and the wisest of all the gods, please look down on us and rescue us from our troubles and our pains. While we try to pull ourselves from the brink of disaster, please reach out to us and touch us with the tip of your finger – if you can only do this, then we'll surely achieve the good fortune we long for.

[1446] We've suffered so much already, and in the past few years I've said some rather unpleasant things about the gods. I don't deserve to always endure such misery, but I should once again be allowed to walk upright and like a man. If you can find a way to grant this one favour to me it will make me happy for the rest of my life.

Exit Menelaus and Helen

CHORUS: [1451] O swift ship of Sidon, that city in Phoenicia! You are an oared ship and so dear to Nereus' waves. You lead the graceful dolphins in their lovely dance whenever the sea is calm and windless.

[1457] I pray that the daughter of the great sea – I mean grey-eyed Galeneia, the daughter of the windless calm – might find a way to say, "You'll freely spread your sails and be pushed along by the breezes of the sea. But you, O sailors, you'll still need to take hold of your pine oars – so do that carefully, O sailors, and bring Helen home safely to the pleasant harbor that was once settled by Perseus.

[1465] I hope she'll find the daughters of Leucippus there by the river, or perhaps she'll find them in front of the temple of Pallas, when she arrives back home during the season of the dances. Or maybe it'll be in the midst of the revels for Hyacinth and the nightlong celebrations. Hyacinth was at that one time killed by Phoebus Apollo, who errantly tried to throw that round discus. And from that time afterward Zeus ordered the land of Lacedaemonia – the place we call Sparta – to perform a day of sacrifices in honour of the young boy who died. And she may have the chance to see the young daughter she left at home, young Hermione, for whom the marriage torches have yet to be lit.

[1478] I wish that we could fly through the air and take our wings to Libya, where the lines of birds go when they flee the wintry weather of the north. They fly obediently, listening to and obeying the whistle of their old leader, who is their shepherd and leads them to the rainless and flat places of the area, screaming out his directions.

[1486] And you birds with the long necks, you who share your path with the racing clouds, go fly beneath the Pleiades in the middle sky, go fly toward Orion so high in the night sky, and shout out your news as you settle down on the banks of the Eurotas – tell everyone that Menelaus, has defeated the Trojan town of Dardanus and is finally on his way home.

[1495] I hope that you may go riding through the bright air, sitting on top of your swift horses, you twin sons of Tyndareus, who live above among the whirling of the bright stars. Come down as saviors to your sister Helen, come down over the salty spray and the dark-blue waves of the sea, and bring from Zeus the kinds of winds that blow friendly for sailors. Remove from your sister's name the shameful reproach of the barbarian marriage, a shame that she's had to endure so long. It came to her as a punishment for the dispute on Mount Ida, even though Helen herself never visited the land of Troy, and she never saw its towers that were once built by Phoebus Apollo.

Enter the Messenger (a servant of Theoclymenus); Theoclymenus enters right behind him

MESSENGER: [1511] My lord, this is the worst possible news for our house. The trouble you are about to hear from me is so strange and disturbing.

THEOCLYMENUS: What is it?

MESSENGER: [1514] You'll need to plan for a marriage to someone else – Helen has left our land!

THEOCLYMENUS: How can this be? Did she fly away on wings, or did her feet still touch the ground?

MESSENGER: It was Menelaus who took her away from here. He was the one who was here with her – he came here and brought you news of his own death.

THEOCLYMENUS: [1519] What you've said is horrible! But what ship took them away from here? Your story is so hard to believe.

MESSENGER: He took the ship you gave him as your guest. He took the men that you gave him and then left. There – that's exactly what took place in a single breath.

THEOCLYMENUS: How could all of this take place? It's beyond my belief that a single man can overpower so many sailors, that he defeated all those sailors who went with you…

MESSENGER: [1526] Zeus' daughter Helen left the palace and prepared to head off to sea, just as you saw, and while she walked toward the ship she was very loudly and cleverly mourning for her husband – who was actually right next to her and by no means dead.

[1530] When we reached the docks and all of your boats, we took a brand new Sidonian ship that was fitted with fifty oars. And then we did our various duties in preparing to launch the vessel. One man took his place near the mast, while others went down to the benches and took hold of an oar. Someone put the white sails in their proper place, and the steersman prepared himself right next to the rudder.

[1537] While your men were doing all these things to get ready, some Greeks, Menelaus' crew, who must have been waiting for this moment, came down to where we were on the beach. Their clothes had been ripped to shreds because of shipwreck and, although they were strong and good looking men, they were also completely filthy.

[1541] Menelaus saw them and called out to them, and he made a false show of pity for our sake. He said to them – "You poor men! What Greek shipwreck did you emerge from? Come along here and help me bury the son of Atreus, who has died at sea. The daughter of Tyndareus here is going to give him a funeral in effigy."

[1546] The Greeks then poured forth fake tears and got on board with offerings that they said they'd throw overboard to honour Menelaus. At this point we started to become suspicious, for we took note of the large number of passengers that we had just taken aboard. But we had your commands in mind so we didn't make any objection – you were the one who caused all of this by putting that foreigner in charge of the ship.

[1554] We easily brought all of the other things on board, because they were light. But the bull refused to make its way on the plank. He bellowed loudly and arched his back. He looked at all of us very fiercely through his horns, warning us not to place a hand on him. But Helen's husband called out – "Come on, all you who once captured Troy, pick up the bull in our Greek way! Place him on top of your young shoulders and set him down in the prow!" And here he drew his sword and said that this bull "would serve as an offering to the dead man."

¹⁵⁶⁵ Those Greeks obeyed his command, picked up the bull, and set him down in the middle of the rowing benches. And while they did this, Menelaus persuaded the horse to get on board by stroking its neck and forehead.

¹⁵⁶⁹ Finally, when everything was on board and the cargo was set down in its proper place, Helen climbed down the ladder with her small steps and she sat down in the middle of the rowing benches, with Menelaus sitting right beside her – the man who was supposedly dead. The rest of the Greeks sat down to the right and left of them, almost as if they were making a formation, with their swords cleverly hidden beneath their coats.

¹⁵⁷⁶ We all turned the sea into white foam when we obeyed the orders and moved our oars in unison. When we reached a point when we were not too far from land, nor too close to it as well, our steersman asked – "Stranger, should we keep on rowing, or is this far enough? You're in charge of the boat."

¹⁵⁸¹ And Menelaus responded by saying – "This is fine right here." Then he took his sword in his right hand and went up to the front of the prow. He stood there readying to sacrifice the bull. He didn't make any prayer for the dead Menelaus, but as he cut its throat he said – "O Poseidon, you who live in and rule the sea, and all you holy daughters of Nereus, please bring me and my wife safe and unharmed from this land to the shores of Nauplia!" The streams of blood leapt out of the animal's neck and into the water – which was no doubt a good omen for the foreigner.

¹⁵⁸⁹ Then one of us shouted – "This voyage is a trick! Let's row back to land! You, give the order to turn this boat around! You, put the rudder in reverse!" But the son of Atreus, having completed the sacrifice of the bull, shouted out to his friends from where he stood. "O you chosen men of Greece, the time for delay is over! Get up now, kill these barbarians, and throw them from this ship and into the sea!"

¹⁵⁹⁵ Your steersman shouted the equivalent order to your sailors – "Quick! Grab anything you can use to fight with! Take a piece from the boat, break off a part of a bench, or even a bit from an oar! Smash the heads of these foreign enemies!"

¹⁶⁰⁰ Everyone stood up – one side carried oars and pieces of wood in their hands, and the other side was carrying swords and other such proper weapons. The ship ran with blood. Helen urged them on from the back of the boat, shouting: "Where is the glory that you won at Troy? Show these barbarians what you're made of!"

¹⁶⁰⁴ They all fought very hard, and some men went down and some men kept their feet, but the ones who fell you could see were dead. Menelaus was clothed in armor, so he watched to see where his friends might need the most help, and that's where he took himself and the sword that he held in his right hand, forcing all of his enemies to flee, with the result that many of them leapt from the ship into the sea. He swept the rowing benches clean of your sailors, then he went up to the rudder and made the steersman turn the ship toward Greece. They put up the mast, and then a favourable wind came, blowing them toward home.

¹⁶¹³ They are long gone from this country. Myself, I escaped death by jumping into the sea near the anchor. I was near to death when I was rescued by a fisherman who picked me

up and brought me here so that I could bring this news to you.

1617 The best trait for a man to have, it seems to me, is to be judicious and skeptical whenever they hear news that sounds too good to be true.

Exit the Messenger

Chorus: My lord, I would never have expected that Menelaus could be here without your and our knowing it – but I guess he was here all the while.

Theoclymenus: 1621 Oh, I'm ruined, destroyed by the trickery of a woman! My bride's escaped! If it were possible for me to make a pursuit and catch that ship, then I'd make the effort and teach those foreigners a lesson.

1624 But I don't think that I will be able to catch them, so instead I'll punish my sister, since she's the one who betrayed me. She saw that Menelaus was in the house and yet she chose not to tell me. I'll make sure that the bitch will never use her prophecies to deceive anyone else.

Enter a Servant (of Theonoë)

Servant: 1627 Hey! You there, master – where are you going? You look like you're on the verge of committing murder.

Theoclymenus: I'm going exactly where justice is leading me – so get the hell out of my way!

Servant: No – I won't let go of your clothing. What you're going to do is a horrible wrong!

Theoclymenus: 1630 You're nothing but a slave, and do you imagine that you can control your master?

Servant: I'm going to try, and perhaps I'll succeed, since I have sense and I mean you well.

Theoclymenus: In my eyes you don't, unless you let go of me right now.

Servant: No – I can't allow you.

Theoclymenus: I'm going to kill my hateful sister…

Servant: She's not hateful – she's pious and god-fearing.

Theoclymenus: …she's betrayed me…

Servant: But her betrayal was an act of justice. She committed a righteous act.

Theoclymenus: …she gave my bride to someone else…

Servant: Yes, to someone else whose claim that was stronger than yours.

Theoclymenus: 1635 Who has any right to that which is mine?

Servant: The man who first received her from her father.

Theoclymenus: But chance then gave her to me.

Servant: Yes, and chance just took her away from you.

Theoclymenus: You are in no place to act as a judge of what belongs to me.

Servant: Oh yes I am – if I'm in the right and have justice on my side.

Theoclymenus: So now I'm no longer the ruler – rather, I'm ruled.

Servant: You are still in charge – but only to act properly and with justice, not to do wrong.

Theoclymenus: It seems to me that you have a death-wish.

Servant: 1639 Then kill me! You can kill me if you want, but I won't allow you to kill your sister. It's a wonderful and glorious thing for a noble slave to die on behalf of their mistress.

Enter Castor and Polydeuces ex machina

Castor: ¹⁶⁴¹ Stop this anger, Theoclymenus, ruler of this land! Stop this anger that's driving you off into every direction. It is the two Dioscuri who are talking to you, the ones whom Leda once gave birth to – the same Leda who gave birth to Helen, the woman who has just fled your home.

¹⁶⁴⁶ This marriage that you're so angry about was never meant to happen. It was fated that Helen would live in your house – but only up to this point. Now that Troy has finally been destroyed and she lent her name to the gods so that it could happen, she'll live here no longer. She has to once more be joined to the same man in the same marriage, return home, and live with her husband in Sparta.

¹⁶⁵⁴ And your sister Theonoë, that daughter of the Nereid, hasn't done you any wrong in honouring the laws of the gods and the righteous commands of her father. So take your dark hand away from your sister – you need to realize that she acted virtuously in all of this. We would have gladly saved our sister long ago, for Zeus turned us into gods. But we were overruled by Fate and the other gods, who made a decision long ago that this is how things would be.

¹⁶⁶² That's what I have to say to you. The rest of what I have to say is for my sister Helen. Sister, for I know that you can hear me – sail on, I tell you. Sail on with your husband – you'll receive a favourable breeze. We, your two brothers, will come riding along side on the waves and we'll bring you home safely as your guardian divinities.

¹⁶⁶⁶ When you finally come to the last part of your life and you let out your final breath, then you'll be called a goddess and you'll receive libations in the company of your brothers the Dioscuri, for just like us you'll receive gifts from mortals. That's what Zeus wants.

¹⁶⁷⁰ That place where Hermes, that son of Maia, first brought you on your journey through the heavens from Sparta – I mean the place known at Attica – that place will from this point onward be known by mortals as Hellenic, since that is the Greek word for "captive." That is the Hellenic ["Greek"] land where you were stolen away from your home.

¹⁶⁷⁶ As for Menelaus, your husband the wanderer, the gods have decreed that he'll live on the Island of the Blessed once his time on earth is up – for the gods don't hate those who were born noble, since those men often have to endure more suffering than men who are of lesser importance.

Theoclymenus: ¹⁶⁸⁰ O sons of Zeus and Leda, I'll let go of my anger in this matter that involves your sister. And I won't do anything to harm my sister, and Helen may go home in peace, if that is the will of the gods.

¹⁶⁸⁴ You should know that you're brothers to a sister who is both very brave and virtuous. I send my praises to you for the sake of Helen's noble heart. There aren't many women who are as noble as her.

Exit Enter Castor and Polydeuces into the sky; Exit Theoclymenus and the Servant (of Theonoë)

Chorus: ¹⁶⁸⁸ Zeus and the court of Olympians sometimes rule in ways that may surprise us. Often we don't get the verdict we anticipate. But whatever happens is their will, so that must be what happened here...

Translated from the Greek by Stephen Russell, PhD

Chapter 15
Sophocles
Electra

THE STORY: This play is still another version of the revenge of Orestes and Electra.

CHARACTERS

OLD SLAVE
ORESTES
ELECTRA
CHORUS (YOUNG WOMEN FROM ARGOS)
CHRYSOTHEMIS

CLYTEMNESTRA
PYLADES
SERVANT
ATTENDANTS

SCENE: This play takes place in front of Agamemnon's former palace.

Enter Orestes, Pylades, and the Old Slave

OLD SLAVE: O son-of-Agamemnon, that man who led the Greek armies in Troy, now you can finally look on the sight that you've been longing to see.

⁴ This is the ancient city of Argos, the one you've been yearning for, the area that once belonged to Io, that daughter of Inachus, who was chased away by Hera's gadfly.

⁶ And over here, Orestes, you can see the market place of the wolf-killing god Apollo; and here to the left is the famous temple of Hera; and you can believe your eyes, for right now you're looking at golden Mycenae and the tragic house that belongs to the sons of Pelops.

¹¹ This is the house from which I once carried you on that day when your father was murdered. I took you from the hands of your sister, and I kept you safe and raised you to become a strong young man, so that one day you'd be able to avenge your father's murder.

¹⁵ And so now, Orestes and Pylades, you need to decide quickly what you should do, for the sun is already starting to come up, and the dark night and its stars are leaving. Before any men get up and come out of his house, you two need think about what we need to do – now is the time for action.

ORESTES: ²³ O you dear man, the most faithful of servants, your loyalty to me has always been impressive. Just like a noble horse, even though he may be old, doesn't lack for spirit in times of trouble, but rather pricks up his ears all the more – so too do you urge us on and offer us all your support.

²⁹ I'll tell you my decision, and so I ask you to please listen to what I have to say, and if I say

something that sounds wrong, please correct me.

³² When I went to the oracle at Delphi to find out how I could get my vengeance for my father by punishing his murderers. Apollo gave me a prophecy that I'll tell you now. He said that I should come alone, without the help of armed men or an army, and that I should carry out this just murder through cleverness and trickery.

³⁸ So, since the oracle offered me this advice, I want you to go into the house, whenever you can find an opportunity, and learn everything you can, so that you can report back to me. They'll never recognize you, since you've become rather old and frail, and they certainly won't suspect you.

⁴⁴ Tell them this story – that you're a stranger and that you've come from Phanoteus, their friend in Phocis, for he's their greatest ally. And I want you to tell them – swear an oath if you need to – that Orestes has been killed in an accident. Tell them that I fell down from a chariot while I was competing in the Pythian games.

⁵¹ As for the two of us, the first thing we'll do is honour the tomb of my father, as the god commanded. We'll pour libations over his grave and I'll offer him locks from my hair.

⁵³ And then we'll come back here, and we'll carry a bronze-urn in our hands, the one that we've just hid in the bushes. And then we'll trick them with our story and we'll make them happy when they hear how I was killed and how my body was burnt to ashes, which I'll convince them that I'll be carrying in this urn.

⁵⁹ Why should it bother me if I die in fiction but remain alive in real life and thereby win glory?

It's my belief that no word that brings you gain can be considered bad.

⁶² Of course, before now I've heard about many clever men who've been reported dead in fiction but who turned out not to be dead – and when they return home the honours they receive are all the greater. And I think that when I emerge alive, in spite of this story, that my star will burn as brightly as theirs.

⁶⁷ But I ask you, O land of my father and gods of this country, please be welcoming to me and help me have good fortune on this mission. And you too, O house of my fathers, please be favourable to me, for I have come to cleanse you, as your purifier, sent by the gods to achieve justice.

⁷¹ Please don't send me away from this country dishonoured, but let me take control of my house and its riches.

⁷³ There – that's all I have to say. And now, old man, I need you to go on your way and do whatever needs to be done. Now is the right time to act, and timing is the most important thing to consider when one is setting out to do something new.

ELECTRA (FROM INSIDE): ⁷⁷ Oh no...oh no... oh no!

OLD SLAVE: I think I can hear a slave crying in there.

ORESTES: ⁸⁰ Do you think it could be my poor sister Electra? Should we stay here and listen to her laments?

OLD SLAVE: ⁸² No – we shouldn't do anything until we carry out the orders that Apollo has given us. You go out and pour your libations to your father – that is what will help bring us victory.

Exit Orestes, Pylades, and the Old Slave; Enter Electra from the palace

ELECTRA: [86] O holy light and air, how many songs of lament have you heard me sing, and how many blows have you seen me strike against my bleeding breast when the dark night has been left behind?

[92] And my hateful bed in this miserable house is a witness to my sorrows and sleepless nights, to how often I mourn for my poor father, who wasn't taken by Ares in some barbarian land, but was instead killed so savagely by my mother and her lover Aegisthus. They split his head open with a murderous axe, just like a lumberjack would cut open an oak. And, dear father, I'm the only one who sings a song of lamentation to you – it comes from nobody else, even though your death was so horrible to see!

[103] But, as for me, I'll never stop my dirges and songs of sadness as long as I still look at the stars and the bright light of day, just like the nightingale, killer of her own child, crying out and making pitiful screams in front of the door of my father.

[110] O house of Hades and Persephone, O Hermes of the underworld, O holy curse and dread Furies, you revered children of the gods who look after those who were unjustly murdered, you who look after those who dishonour their marriage bed, come help me, or bring my brother to me so that he can help me avenge the death of our father!

[119] Please do this for me, for I'm no longer strong enough to handle the weight of this grief all alone – by myself.

Enter the Chorus (young women from Argos)

CHORUS: [121] O Electra, daughter of the most horrible of mothers, why are you wasting away with this bitter lament, and with your eternal sorrow for Agamemnon, who's long since been murdered, viciously slain by the cruel hand of your treacherous mother?

[126] If it's proper for me to say so, I hope that the one who did this thing to your father receive the evil reward that she deserves!

ELECTRA: [129] O you noble women, you've come to comfort me in the midst of my sorrows. I know and understand what you say, and yet I'm not willing to stop mourning for my poor dead father.

[134] You're all such dear friends to me, so I ask that you bear with me while I wander around and show these signs of sorrow and madness. I can't help it.

CHORUS: [137] But your tears and cries of sorrow will never be able to raise your father up from the lake of fire in Hades, the place where we all must go someday.

[140] No. All this pain, all this self-torture, will only lead to your own ruin. There's no way to undo what has been done to your father, so why are you so dead-set on this horrible path of self-destruction?

ELECTRA: [145] But the one who forgets the pitiful end of his parents is foolish and worthless! Always in the back of my mind is the nightingale, who was once the woman named Procne, and now as the bird she's always calling out in mourning for her lost child Itys… Itys – always this messenger of Zeus cries out in her pain.

[150] And what about Niobe, who had to endure the worst kind of sorrow – O, poor woman, I think of you as a goddess, you who sit there forever in your rocky grave.

CHORUS: [153] But my dear child, this pain hasn't come to you alone, for you seem to show your grief much more than do your own sisters Chrysothemis and Iphianassa.

¹⁵⁹ And just take a moment to think about Orestes, who's perhaps happy somewhere, hidden out of the way and safe in his youth from all these painful things. One day this famous land of Mycenae will welcome him back, if Zeus will bless him when he returns.

ELECTRA: ¹⁶⁴ I've been waiting for him all this time... I never get tired of waiting for my dear Orestes, I stay here, childless, unmarried, always drenched with tears, trying to endure the misery that surrounds me.

¹⁶⁷ But it looks like he's forgotten what he's suffered, for what message has he sent me that doesn't end in the disappointment that he won't come back? He says that he always feels the longing to return, but in spite of all this longing he still chooses not to come.

CHORUS: ¹⁷³ Have courage, my child, and take heart! Zeus is still great in the heaven, and he still looks after all things and rules them. Confide all of your pains to him.

¹⁷⁷ Don't show too much anger to your enemies, yet don't forget it either – for time is a god that is eventually kind to us.

¹⁸⁰ Your young brother, who now lives far off on the coast, is not forgetful of his duty, and nor is the god of death, Hades, who rules down by the waters of Acheron.

ELECTRA: ¹⁸⁵ But so much of my life has already gone by without any hope, and I hardly have any strength left.

¹⁸⁷ I feel as if I'm melting away – no children, no husband to protect me. I'm just like a slave, even though I live in the house of my father, wearing such ugly and lowborn rags like these and forced to stand at the table.

CHORUS: ¹⁹³ Oh, when your father came home, the cry he let out was so horrible, so pitiful, when the blow of the bronze axe came straight at him!

¹⁹⁷ They planned it with trickery and were moved to commit murder due to their own lustful passions, and they became the shape of something so hideous... so monstrous... something between a god and a mortal.

ELECTRA: ²⁰¹ Oh, that day was the most hateful day that I have ever had to endure! And that night, it was so horrible, for that was when my father met his unspeakable punishment at the hands of those two, betrayed by his wife and her lover – a deed that also took away my life.

²⁰⁹ I pray that the gods on Olympus will make them suffer just as badly for what they did to my father, and I hope that they'll never gain any profit from their evil and cruel treachery!

CHORUS: ²¹³ Please be careful that you don't say too much. Don't you remember how your own words and actions have led to your current situation? You need to find a way to put up with this, because you can't constantly struggle against those in power. You're only bound to lose those battles.

ELECTRA: ²²¹ They did terrible things, and those terrible deeds of theirs caused me to say terrible things. I know that I'm often ruled by my passion and by my spirit. But with all of this... this... this bullshit that's going on around me, I can't keep quiet, and I won't keep quiet about it, as long as I live.

²²⁶ Does anyone really believe that there are words that can act as a form of comfort for me? No, there's nothing that can do that, and that's why you should leave me, you women who want to offer me consolation.

²²⁹ There's no cure for my pains – and so I'll never let go of this sorrow and misery.

Chorus: [233] But I just want the best for you, you know – like a mother whom you can trust, and I don't want you to create even more misery out of your current misery.

Electra: [236] How can there be a limit to my pain? How can it be considered honourable to forget about the dead? Is there any human so insensitive, so unfeeling, that he could do that?

[239] I hope that I'll never receive any honour or praise if I fail to mourn for my father properly. If the poor man is just simply to lie there dead as earth and nothingness, and if the two who did this to him aren't punished for what they did to him, then all sense of shame, justice, and piety is dead in this land.

Chorus: [251] My child, I came here both in your interest and in my own. But if I've said something wrong, then have it your way, because we'll follow you.

Electra: [254] My dear women, I feel ashamed if you think that I am showing too much grief. But since I am forced to do this, I ask you to bear with me. I mean, how could any noble woman behave when she's constantly faced with such wrongs against the house of her father?

[261] First of all, the relationship that I have with the woman who bore me has now turned into one of hatred. Next, I'm forced into living in this house with the same people who murdered my father. And, to make it even worse, they're in charge of me and it's up to them whether I get anything to eat or whether I have to go without.

[266] And then how do you imagine that I pass my days when I am forced to see Aegisthus sitting on the throne that belongs to my father, when I see him wearing the royal robes that belong to my father, and when I watch him pouring libations in the same room where he killed my father? And how do you think I feel when I have to endure the final outrage and see that murderer take my father's place and lie down in his bed with my bitch of a mother – if even I should call that slut a mother.

[275] She has no shame at all. She's so brazen, so shameless, that she'll live with this polluted creature and seems to fear no avenging Fury. It seems as if she found the whole thing funny, since on the anniversary of the day in which she so callously slaughtered my father she always holds a dancing festival and she offers sheep for sacrifice, paying her thanks to the gods who saved her.

[282] And I have to sit in that damned house and watch the accursed feast named in honour of my dead father, weeping silently, for I'm not allowed to cry or show any outward emotion.

[286] That's right – this woman, the one who's thought to be so noble, so regal, assaults me day and night, calling me hateful, and asking me: "Do you think you're the only one ever who lost a father? Can anyone else on this earth other than you have feelings? Well, I hope that gods below never release you from this pain, even after you die a miserable death!"

[293] Those are the kinds of things that she shouts at me. And if she hears anyone suggest that Orestes might return, then she really grows wild and starts screaming things like: "Are you the cause of this? Is this all a part of your scheming, you little bitch? After all, you're the one who stole Orestes from my arms and had him smuggled out of here. Well, you can be sure that you're going to pay for this."

[299] She barks out these words at me, sounding just like a dog, and her "noble" husband

stands right next to her, encouraging her – that little coward, that diseased maggot, that man who needs a woman to fight his battles.

303 But I am waiting for Orestes to come back, always waiting for him to come and put an end to all this.

305 I feel like I'm dying, constantly waiting for him to return, and he is always delaying, never actually coming back, and he is destroying my hopes.

307 When things are as they now are, my friends, it's no time to be moderate or restrained or pious. Not at all – for when evil is all around me, then it forces me to be evil as well.

Chorus: 310 Tell me – is Aegisthus near while you're saying these things now, or is he away from home?

Electra: Oh yes – he's away! If he were home, there's no way that I'd be able to wander like this outside. He's gone to visit his estate in the country.

Chorus: 314 Good. If this is the case, then I can talk to you more freely.

Electra: Then you can be assured that he's not at home. What do you want?

Chorus: I want to ask you about your brother. Is he going to come back here or not?

Electra: He says that he's going to come, but so far he's done nothing to back up his claims.

Chorus: 320 Well, a man often hesitates before he does great things.

Electra: I certainly didn't hesitate when I saved him!

Chorus: Calm down a little. You know that he's a good man and that he'll help his friends.

Electra: Of course I believe this – otherwise I wouldn't have remained alive.

Chorus: 324 Shhh....don't say anything more, for I can see your sister, Chrysothemis, born from the same father and mother as you. She's coming this way and she's carrying burial offerings that people usually make to the gods below.

Enter Chrysothemis

Chrysothemis: 328 What are these things that you've come outside to say, my sister? Haven't you learned, after all these years, not to engage so openly in such pointless anger?

332 I've learned this much about myself: that the present situation troubles me so much that I'd be willing to reveal my feelings, my hatred, if only I had the power to do so. But as things are, because I'm scared of what they might do to me, I think it's best for me to keep calm and quiet, and not to appear to be plotting to do them any harm. And I think it's best if you do the same.

338 I realize that what I suggest seems at odds with justice and that your thoughts and feelings stand hand-in-hand with justice, but if I'm to remain alive and not live as a prisoner, then I have to obey my lords in all that they tell me.

Electra: 341 It's strange and terrible that you, a daughter of your father, can manage to forget him and show such respect for your mother. I imagine that all those warnings you just gave me really come from her and that nothing of what you say is your own.

345 Now is the time for you to choose – either to be foolish or wise. You just said that if you had the strength then you'd show them how much you really hate them. But when I did all I could to honour my father, you never did a thing to help me. In fact, you tried to discourage me.

³⁵¹ So now am I not right in adding to your troubles by calling you a coward? Please tell me what great benefit I would gain if I gave up my mourning for my father. Am I not still alive? This life is a pain in itself for me, but my respect for my dead father causes them pain, and that's what gives me real pleasure.

³⁵⁷ You say that you hate them, but hate to you is just an empty word, for you still keep company with our father's murderers and show them the respect that they don't deserve. Well, as for me, I would never give in to them – not even if they brought me the kinds of gifts that you now enjoy.

³⁶¹ Go ahead and enjoy your rich table and comfortable lifestyle. My clear conscience is food enough for me, and I certainly have no desire to share in your polluted honours – and neither would you if you were thinking rightly. You know, you could have been called the daughter of the most noble of men, but instead you'll be called the daughter of your mother, which means that most people will think of you as an evil traitor, who betrayed her own father and those who honoured him.

Chorus: ³⁶⁹ I beg you – please don't say such things in anger. Both of you have said intelligent things, if only you, Electra, could listen to her advice and she could listen to yours.

Chrysothemis: ³⁷² That's ok, women, for I am used to how my sister speaks. I wouldn't have said what I said, if I hadn't heard news that there's a great evil about to come her way that will put an end to her long, loud, and clear signs of mourning.

Electra: ³⁷⁶ What is this? What have you heard? Come, tell me what this terrible thing is! If you tell me about something that's worse than my present situation, then I won't argue with you any more.

Chrysothemis: ³⁷⁸ I'll tell you everything I know. From what I've learned, if you don't give up these lamentations and displays of mourning, then the two of them are going to send you to a place where you'll no longer be able to see the light of the sun. It will be some kind of underground dungeon, and it will be far away from the city, and you'll be able to mourn all you like, since nobody will be able to hear you.

³⁸³ Please keep this in mind, and don't blame me if you suffer for it later. There – now you know it all, and so it's time to think about how to show good sense.

Electra: ³⁸⁵ Is that what they've really decided to do to me?

Chrysothemis: Yes, and they're going to carry it out as soon as Aegisthus gets home.

Electra: Well, then let him get home quickly!

Chrysothemis: But, my dear sister, why on earth would you hope for that?

Electra: I want him to come back – to see if he has the courage to do what you said.

Chrysothemis: ³⁹⁰ Don't you realize what that would mean for you? Are you crazy?

Electra: It would at least let me get away from all of you – as far away as possible.

Chrysothemis: Do you hate the life that you now have so much?

Electra: My life now? What kind of life is this? Is this really a life to be envied?

Chrysothemis: It would be, if only you could think and behave sensibly!

Electra: ³⁹⁵ Don't even think of telling me to betray my own blood!

Chrysothemis: I'm not trying to say that at all. I'm just suggesting that you learn to yield to those who are in power.

Electra: That kind of subservient behaviour is for you! This is not my way.

Chrysothemis: But it's a bad thing – and it's dishonourable – to come to grief because of your own foolishness.

Electra: If I do come to grief, then I'll do so trying to defend the honour of my dear father!

Chrysothemis: ⁴⁰⁰ I know that my father will forgive me for what I do.

Electra: Those are the kinds of words that cowards and sophists use to justify their moral failings.

Chrysothemis: So you won't listen to me at all?

Electra: Oh, I listened to you – but I'm not going to be so stupid as to do what you suggest.

Chrysothemis: Then I'll just have to keep going on this mission on which I was sent.

Electra: ⁴⁰⁵ Where is it that you're going? And to whom are you bringing these sacrifices?

Chrysothemis: My mother is sending me to my father's grave with these offerings.

Electra: What? Why? Why would she send libations to her worst enemy?

Chrysothemis: "The man she killed" is what you mean.

Electra: Who persuaded her to do this? Whose idea was it?

Chrysothemis: ⁴¹⁰ I think she was driven by some midnight terrors.

Electra: O gods of my father, now is the time for you to stand with me!

Chrysothemis: Does her fear give you some kind of confidence?

Electra: I'll only be able to answer that when you tell me about her dream.

Chrysothemis: But I can only tell you a little.

Electra: ⁴¹⁵ Tell me whatever you know. Often it takes only a little to bring disaster or success.

Chrysothemis: ⁴¹⁷ They say that she saw my father, your father and mine, and that he had come back life once more to live with her.

⁴¹⁹ He took hold of the sceptre that he used to carry, the one that Aegisthus now holds, and he placed it right next to his throne, and from this sceptre a large and luxuriant plant – no, a tree – grew, and this tree covered the whole land of Mycenae.

⁴²⁴ Anyway, that's the story I heard when from someone who overheard our mother telling the dream to the sun-god Helios. But that's all I know, other than to say that it's because of this dream, this fear, that she's sent out with these offerings.

Electra: ⁴³¹ My dear sister, don't place any of the things that you're carrying on the tomb! It's not right, and it's against the will of the gods for you to place burial offerings or pour libations to our father on behalf of his enemy.

⁴³⁵ Throw them out to the winds or, better yet, hide them somewhere deep in the ground, where none of them will be able to ever come near my father's place of rest. That way, if they're in the ground, they'll be stored down below as treasures for the day when she dies!

⁴³⁹ If she weren't such a horrible and hateful creature, then she would never have dared to place these hateful things on the grave of the man she murdered.

⁴⁴² Do you really think that the dead man, our father, will be happy to accept these offerings sent by the woman who slaughtered him? Will he be pleased with these gifts sent by the

woman who mutilated him? From the woman who previously thought that it was enough for her to wipe the bloodstains from his head? Do you really think that these things will absolve her of that murder?

⁴⁴⁶ Ha! There's no way that these gifts of hers will do anything to help her. Throw them aside, and instead cut a lock from your hair and I'll give you a lock from my poor head as well.

⁴⁵⁰ Give him these locks of our hair, and then kneel down and pray that he may come and be kind to us as we fight his enemies. And pray that our brother Orestes will come back and defeat our enemies, so that in the future we can honour our father with better gifts than the ones you're bringing now.

⁴⁵⁹ I believe that it was our father who sent these ugly dreams to her. So, my sister, you have to do this on behalf of both you and me and, most important of all, do it for the sake of our dear father, who now lives below in Hades.

Chorus: ⁴⁶⁴ The girl is giving good advice and you, Chrysothemis, you'll do what she says if you're wise.

Chrysothemis: ⁴⁶⁶ I'll do it. It's not good for us to fight about this, especially when we both know what justice requires.

⁴⁶⁸ But when I do what she asks, my dear friends, I ask you to keep silent about it, for if my mother hears about what will have done, then I'm sure that she'll make me pay for it.

Exit Chrysothemis

Chorus (lengthy ode): ⁴⁷³ Unless I'm mistaken, Justice has predicted the outcome, and your triumph will soon come, my child…

Enter Clytemnestra

Clytemnestra: ⁵¹⁶ So it looks like you're on the loose once again and raging about. This always happens whenever Aegisthus is away, for he's always the one who prevented you from running around and causing a disgrace to this family. But once he's away you pay no respect to me, even though you lie to so many people around here by saying that I treat you unjustly and that I'm brutal and violent with you.

⁵²³ I've never done any violence toward you, and the only bad things that I've done to you are in response to the abuse you so often send my way.

⁵²⁵ You always use your father – oh, your father – as your pretext, shouting at me that I killed him. Believe me, I know what I did, and I won't deny it. But understand that Justice was his killer, and that I didn't do it alone – and you would be on the side of Justice, if you had any sense at all.

⁵³⁰ It was that father of yours, the one you're always mourning, alone among all the Greeks, who was cold and callous enough to bring himself to sacrifice your sister to the gods, even though he didn't have to go through the pains of giving birth to her as I did.

⁵³⁴ So tell me this – for whose sake did he sacrifice her? Did he do it for the Greeks? For the Argives? Bah! They had no right to kill her, because she was mine.

⁵³⁷ But if your father killed my daughter for the sake of his brother Menelaus, then shouldn't Menelaus pay me the penalty? I mean, didn't Menelaus have two children, and shouldn't one of them, or even both, have died instead of mine? Wasn't it for the sake of their father and mother that the whole god-damned expedition to Troy took place?

⁵⁴² Did Hades have some special desire to feed on my children rather than on Helen's? Or did

your damn father feel some special affection for the children of Menelaus that he didn't feel for mine?

⁵⁴⁶ Wouldn't that be a clear indication that he was a bad father and lacked good judgment? This is how I see it, even though I know you don't see it that way – and I'm sure the young girl who died would agree with me, if only she had a voice to say so.

⁵⁴⁹ For my part, I have no regrets about what I did, and if you think I was wrong in my actions, you should start worrying about yourself before you even think of throwing holier-than-thou accusations about!

ELECTRA: ⁵⁵² This time you won't be able to say that I was the first one to say something abusive and that I provoked you!

⁵⁵⁴ But, if you allow me, I'll speak the truth to you on behalf of the dead man and of my sister as well.

CLYTEMNESTRA: ⁵⁵⁶ Of course I'll allow you! If you had always been willing to start our conversations in this way, then you wouldn't have been so painful to listen to.

ELECTRA: ⁵⁵⁸ Good enough – then I'll speak! You admit that you killed my father! What words could be more shameful than those, whether your act was just or not?

⁵⁶⁰ And I'll tell you that you didn't have Justice on your side when you killed him, but that you were persuaded into that action by the evil man with whom you're now living.

⁵⁶³ Ask the huntress Artemis what made her hold the winds in check way back there in Aulis. Or, better yet, I'll tell you – since we're forbidden to learn that from her.

⁵⁶⁶ My father, as I've heard, was hunting in the sacred grove of the goddess when a horned stag started up in response to the sound of his footsteps, and when he killed it with his arrow he happened to utter some boast that he shouldn't have said.

⁵⁷⁰ And in her anger at this, Artemis stopped the Greeks there in Aulis so that my father might sacrifice his daughter in response for the beast that he had killed.

⁵⁷³ That was how her sacrifice came to be, for there was no other way to release the army to either go home or to Troy. This was the reason that he sacrificed her. It's not as if he did it willingly! Far from it - he did it against his will, and he fought against it as much as he could.

⁵⁷⁵ And he didn't do it for the sake of Menelaus. But even if he did this to help his brother, as you claim, is that any reason for him to die at your hands? What law demands this? If this is some new kind of law or principle that you've established, then you should take care that you haven't established some kind of law that will eventually come back to harm you. For if the new rule states that it's just to take a life for a life, then it will be proper for you die first, for that's what you deserve. So you should take care of what you say!

⁵⁸³ I mean, please tell me why you're doing the most shameful action of all – why you're sleeping with the man who helped you kill my father. Please tell me why you're having children with this man, while you've thrown aside and driven away your previous children who were born from a proper marriage.

⁵⁹¹ Am I supposed to praise you for this? Or will you claim that you're doing these things all because of what happened to Iphigenia? If you say that, then it would be a shameful thing for you to say, since it's not honourable to marry your enemy even for the sake of your daughter!

⁵⁹⁵ But no, no one can dare question you or

give advice to you, for you'll merely reply that I spend all my time abusing my mother. Phah! I think of you more as a tyrant than as a mother, since you and your lover are always throwing such misery and suffering my way.

⁶⁰¹ And my poor brother has to lead such a sad existence. It's true that he's escaped your violent hand, but he has to live off somewhere as an exile. So many times you've accused me of trying to turn him toward murdering you – and I would have done it, if only I had the power.

⁶⁰⁶ Go ahead and call me whatever you like – announce to the world that I am a traitor to you, that I am shameless, that I won't keep my mouth shut. If that's those words apply to me, then it just proves that I am a worthy daughter of yours!

Chorus: ⁶¹⁰ It's clear that you think she's angry, my lady, but I don't think that you're considering whether she has justice in what she says.

Clytemnestra: ⁶¹² And why the hell should I show any consideration to this one who insults her own mother in such a way, and at such an age? Don't you think that she's shameless enough to do anything?

Electra: ⁶¹⁶ Oh, you can be certain that I feel shame, even though you don't think so, and I am well aware of what's causing me to act the way I do – it's due to the hatred that you've thrown my way, and it's your actions that have forced me to behave this way, for hateful deeds have taught me hateful deeds.

Clytemnestra: ⁶²² You damn creature – in truth I have let you say far too much!

Electra: It's you who are doing the talking, not me. The actions are all yours, and your actions invite my words.

Clytemnestra: I swear by the goddess Artemis that you won't get away with this insolence once Aegisthus gets home.

Electra: Don't you see? Like always, you let me say what I want, and then become outraged that I actually say what I think. Clearly you have no idea how to listen.

Clytemnestra: ⁶³⁰ Will you at least allow me to make my sacrifice now that I have let you say what you wanted to say?

Electra: Go ahead – by all means, make your sacrifice. My lips will be sealed.

Clytemnestra: ⁶³⁴ Then I'll lift up my offerings to the lord of this land here, so that he may release me from the fears that now plague me.

⁶³⁷ Hear me, O Phoebus Apollo, our protector, as I speak to you in hushed tones. I realize that I don't speak to you among friends, and it's not possible for me to tell you everything when she is standing so close to me, lest she use her evil tongue to stir up trouble for me among the people. No, my lord Apollo, please listen as I talk to you in whispers.

⁶⁴⁴ Please arrange it, my lord, that the two dreams that I had last night were favourable to me, and please allow them to happen. But if those dreams were actually hostile to me, then I beg you to send them elsewhere. And if there are people who are planning to rob me of the riches that I now have, please stop them, and allow me to always live my life free and unharmed, and to rule the house of Atreus and this kingdom, to keep living with the friends that I now have, to enjoy this wealth and prosperity with those children of mine who don't hate me or cause me pain.

⁶⁵⁵ Please hear me, O lord Apollo, and be kind of enough to make my wishes come true. As for all the rest, I think it will be best for me to remain silent, since you are a god and it's

natural that you and the other gods see and know everything already anyway.

Enter the Old Slave

OLD SLAVE: 660 Women of Mycenae, how can I be sure that this is the house of king Aegisthus?

CHORUS: This is the house, sir – your guess is correct.

OLD SLAVE: And would I be right in guessing that this lady here is his wife? She has the look of a queen.

CHORUS: 665 Yes, that's right – she's the queen of this land.

OLD SLAVE: Greetings, my queen! I have come this way from a friend with good news for both you and Aegisthus.

CLYTEMNESTRA: I welcome you and your kind words. But first I want to know who sent you here.

OLD SLAVE: 670 I was sent this way by Phanoteus the Phocian, who gave me this very serious task to accomplish.

CLYTEMNESTRA: What is it, stranger? Tell me, please. I know that you come from a friend and so therefore you must be bringing a friendly message.

OLD SLAVE: Orestes is dead. There it is, in one short sentence.

ELECTRA: O gods, this day will be the death of me!

CLYTEMNESTRA: 675 What was that you said, stranger? No, just ignore her. Tell me again.

OLD SLAVE: I said it a moment ago and I'll repeat it now – Orestes is dead.

ELECTRA: O god help me – I can't go on living!

CLYTEMNESTRA: Just leave her alone and ignore her. Tell me the truth – how did he meet his death?

OLD SLAVE: 680 I was sent here to tell you this, and I'll tell you everything I know.

681 He came into the heart of Greece, for that glorious gathering known as the Delphic games, and when he heard the loud announcement that the first contest would be a running race he entered it immediately – and he cut a brilliant picture and was admired by everyone.

686 His running was the equal of his appearance, and he finished holding the honoured prize of victory. I don't know much about the performances of the other athletes in these games, but one thing I can say for sure is that he took away the first prize in each and every contest that he entered, and men loudly praised his good fortune. He was announced to us as a citizen of Argos, Orestes by name, the son of Agamemnon who once gathered together the armies of Greece.

696 That's as far as things stood there, but when a god wants to cause mischief, not even a strong and mighty man can stop him.

698 On the next day at sunrise there was a chariot race scheduled, and so Orestes entered this along with all the other many other competitors. One was from Achaea, another was from Sparta, two were from Libya, who are masters at driving chariots, Orestes was the fifth among them, and he had Thessalian mares to drive his chariot. The sixth contestant came from Aetolia, while the seventh was from Magnesia, the eighth was from Aenea and had white horses, the ninth was from god-built Athens, and the tenth and final chariot came from Boeotia.

709 They all took their positions where the

judges placed them, and at the sound of the bronze trumpet they darted away. The drivers were shouting out to their horses, their hands flicking the reins, and the whole place was filled with the noise of the chariots. Clouds of dust rose up everywhere, and each driver was desperately hoping to pass the wheels and horses of the others – and you could feel the intensity of not only the drivers, but that horses as well.

[720] At first Orestes did well to keep his horses near the inside pillars, and each time he managed to just graze the post, which allowed him to block off his pursuers on the right. At first all the horses and drivers remained upright, but then suddenly the colts of the Aenian, as they finished their sixth lap and started on their seventh, smashed their heads against the chariot that was in front of them.

[728] That's how it all began, for one driver then crashed into another one, smashing them both to bits, and the whole racing plain suddenly seemed to be filled with the wreckage of chariots just from this one accident.

[731] But the driver from Athens was clever, for he pulled his horses away from the scene of the accident and he thus managed to avoid all the confusion as the other chariots became muddled in the middle of the wreckage.

[734] At this point Orestes was in last place, holding his horses back, confident in their ability to perform a closing sprint. When he saw the Athenian suddenly left alone at the front of the pack, he sent out a sharp command to the ears of his swift horses, and he set out after the leader.

[739] He managed to catch up to him, and the two chariots drove level for a while, with one, now the other, pushing his horses' heads in front.

[741] Throughout all the other laps Orestes managed to stay upright, for he barely grazed the turning post with his wheel, but this time he let go of a part of the reins while he was turning, and before he realized it he struck the pillar, breaking the axle of his chariot right in the middle while he himself became tangled up in the reins.

[746] The horses had no idea of what had happened to him, so they just sprinted forward, running wildly into the middle of the racetrack.

[749] When the crowd of spectators saw Orestes fall down from his chariot, they let out a shout of pity for the young man, as they watched the terrible things that resulted from the accident. At one moment the poor boy was thrown down toward the ground, then at the next moment he would be shot upward toward the sky, with his legs flailing away, until the other charioteers managed with difficulty to finally bring his horses to a stop. When they managed to untangle him from the mess he was so bloody that there was no way any of his friends could have recognized him in such a mangled and disfigured shape.

[757] Men were chosen from the Phocians to build a pyre and burn him there, and I was given the task of bringing the ashes of his once mighty form back here in a small urn bronze so that he might be buried in the home and according to the customs of his ancestors.

[761] This is the horrible event that I and all those other spectators had to witness, and I think I can safely say that it's the most horrible thing that I've ever had to witness.

CHORUS: Oh no – the whole ancient family of our masters has been brought down!

CLYTEMNESTRA: [766] Oh my gods! What should I say or think? Should I call this a stroke of good luck? Or should I say that it's terrible but beneficial?

⁷⁶⁷ I realize how horrible it is to admit this, but I have to preserve my life by means of my own disasters.

OLD SLAVE: My lady, why do you seem so down in response to our news?

CLYTEMNESTRA: ⁷⁷⁰ The relationship between a mother and a child is a strange one – for even when they are hostile to one another, a woman can never truly hate her own child.

OLD SLAVE: It seems like my trip here was pointless then.

CLYTEMNESTRA: ⁷⁷³ Pointless? How can you call your trip here pointless if you've come here with the sure proof of death of a boy who came from my womb, but turned away from my nurturing breast to a foreigner in exile?

⁷⁷⁷ After he walked away from this land he never came back to see me, but he did reproach me in all manners of ways for the death of his father, and he threatened to do all kinds of terrible things to me. It was so bad that I couldn't find any rest, any sleep at all – neither at night nor in the daylight. At every moment it looked like I was just carrying out the motions toward my inevitable death.

⁷⁸³ But now, now on this day I've been freed from the fear that I had both of this woman here and of my dead son. Yes, she was even a worse problem for me, since she lived here in the palace and spent her time draining my very life-blood. But now, thank the gods, I'll be able to have some peace from her threats. It's so good that the light of day has finally returned!

ELECTRA: ⁷⁸⁸ Oh, this is so terrible! Now I have to mourn your death, my dear Orestes, while your mother here celebrates it! Could it be any worse?

CLYTEMNESTRA: That's not true at all – but things are better for him this way.

ELECTRA: O please hear me, avenging Nemesis of the one who just died!

CLYTEMNESTRA: Nemesis has heard from everyone she should have heard and has made her proper decisions.

ELECTRA: Oh just go ahead and insult us now, for it looks like you've won.

CLYTEMNESTRA: ⁷⁹⁵ Then won't you and Orestes finally put a stop to all of this?

ELECTRA: What? Clearly we have been stopped – but we can't make you stop.

CLYTEMNESTRA: You will have brought a welcome message, sir, if you will have stopped her from all her screaming and moaning.

OLD SLAVE: Then would it be fine if I leave now, since everything is well?

CLYTEMNESTRA: ⁸⁰⁰ No, no! That would be wrong of me, and it would be an insult to the friend who sent you. Come on inside – please, I insist. Let's just leave her outside to scream out her miseries and those of her loved ones.

Exit Clytemnestra and the Old Slave into the palace

ELECTRA: ⁸⁰⁴ Do you think that this horrible woman will ever weep or mourn for her dead son? Did you see any tears, any real signs of pain and sorrow?

⁸⁰⁷ No, there weren't any at all. It was plain to see that she walked away laughing!

⁸⁰⁸ O my dear Orestes, your death is also my death! With your death you have torn away from my heart whatever small hope still remained that you would one day come back

home to seek revenge on behalf of your father and poor poor me.

⁸¹² But now where can I turn? I'm completely alone. I've lost both your and my father. Now once again I have to become a slave in the house of the people I hate the most – the murderers of my father. Is this the way it's supposed to end for me?

⁸¹⁷ No! I can't just let this happen and sit by so passively. I won't – I can't – live inside there with them anymore. No, I'll just stay here fixed at this gate, and I'll let myself waste away here, since I no longer have any friends or loved ones.

⁸²⁰ If the people who live inside have any problems with what I'm doing, well then just let one of them come out and kill me, if they have to courage. Death would be a favour to me now, since life is such a misery. I'm sick of life.

CHORUS: ⁸²³ Where are the thunderbolts of Zeus? And where is the blazing sun? How can they look down on this and just let it happen?

ELECTRA: Oh! Why why why?

CHORUS: Why are you crying, my child?

ELECTRA: Oh…ahhh….ahhh…

CHORUS: Please don't be so loud in your cries.

ELECTRA: ⁸³⁰ You're destroying me!

CHORUS: What do you mean?

ELECTRA: If you suggest that I pin my hopes on those who are now dead and in Hades, then it's like you're setting a firmer foot on top of me – trampling on me all the harder, mocking me almost.

CHORUS: ⁸³⁷ Well, I know that king Amphiaraus was killed by his wife Eriphyle, who had been bribed by a golden necklace, and now he rules the spirits below the earth…

ELECTRA: Oh gods!

CHORUS: But…I am telling you this because his killer received her just punishment.

ELECTRA: ⁸⁴⁶ I know – their son Alcmaeon came back to avenge his father and thus killed his mother…

But for me there is no one who can come back and do such a thing, for my poor brother is now gone, dead, taken so far away from me…

CHORUS: You poor girl – I feel so bad for you.

ELECTRA: ⁸⁵⁰ I know these pains too well – I've become used to them. My life has become filled with horrors and torture, and they never leave me.

CHORUS: We understand what you mean.

ELECTRA: ⁸⁵⁴ So then don't try to make me think of people who will give me help and hope, when there's nobody anywhere who can help me.

CHORUS: ⁸⁶⁰ Every man must die at some point.

ELECTRA: But did my brother have to die in the middle of a horse race? Did he have to be tangled up and so brutally mangled by the reins, the ground, and those hoofs?

CHORUS: We can't predict where or when our end will come.

ELECTRA: ⁸⁶⁵ That's true enough. But why did he have to die in a foreign land, so far away from my touch, and with no grave, no proper funeral? Why why why?

Enter Chrysothemis

CHRYSOTHEMIS: ⁸⁷¹ O my darling, I'm so glad that I found you here. I've got the kind of news that made me hurry and look for you, leaving all sense of proper decorum behind. I am bringing you some happy news, and it will bring you relief from all your sorrows.

ELECTRA: ⁸⁷⁵ And how could there be any news that would serve as a cure for my sorrows?

CHRYSOTHEMIS: Orestes is here among us. You've heard me correctly – he is here just as plainly as you see me now.

ELECTRA: What's this? Have you gone mad? Or are you making fun of me, and of yourself and all our troubles?

CHRYSOTHEMIS: ⁸⁷⁹ No – I swear by the grave of our father that I'm not speaking in mockery. He really is here somewhere among us.

ELECTRA: You foolish girl! Who told you this story that you believe so easily in your gullibility?

CHRYSOTHEMIS: ⁸⁸⁵ I believe this story because I have seen solid enough proof with my own two eyes. I didn't hear it from anyone else.

ELECTRA: And what have you seen that proves it? What is this proof that's setting your heart on fire?

CHRYSOTHEMIS: ⁸⁸⁹ Just listen for a moment and I'll tell you the story. Then, once I've finished, you can call me sane or foolish.

ELECTRA: Go ahead, if telling this gives you any pleasure.

CHRYSOTHEMIS: ⁸⁹² Good enough – let me tell you everything that I saw. When I went up the tomb of our father, on the very top of the mound I saw newly poured streams of milk flowing down, and beautiful fresh flowers had been placed inside the funeral urns that surround the tomb.

⁸⁹⁷ I wondered about all of this when I saw it, and immediately I looked around in case anyone was close by. Once I realized that I was alone, I went up close to the tomb, and on the very edge I saw a lock of hair. As soon as I saw this lock of hair, something jumped inside of me, for it was very familiar. That is, I knew that it was a token from the one we miss the most – our Orestes!

⁹⁰⁵ I took it up into my hands, not uttering a sound for fear of saying an offending word, but my eyes were filled with tears of joy. Both back then and now I am completely certain that this offering came from Orestes alone.

⁹⁰⁹ Who else could've done this, other than you and me? I know that I didn't do it, and I'm sure it wasn't you either. I mean, how could you have done it, since they won't let you leave the area of the house?

⁹¹³ As for our mother, she wouldn't do such a thing, and she wouldn't do anything like that in secret – that's for sure.

⁹¹⁵ No – these offerings must have come from Orestes himself. So, my dear, that's why you need to take courage. The same fortune doesn't always stay with the same person, and our fortune in the past was miserable, but maybe from this day forward luck will be on our side.

ELECTRA: ⁹²⁰ Oh you poor foolish naïve girl!

CHRYSOTHEMIS: What's wrong? Aren't you happy with my news?

ELECTRA: You really have no idea…no idea at all…

CHRYSOTHEMIS: But how can I be wrong about what I saw with my own eyes?

ELECTRA: ⁹²⁴ My dear sister, our brother is dead! We're not going to be rescued by him, so please don't bother looking at him for our salvation.

CHRYSOTHEMIS: Oh no! Where did you hear this news?

ELECTRA: From a man who was next to our brother when he died.

Chrysothemis: And where is this man? I'm so confused right now.

Electra: He's inside the house right now. Our mother was so happy with the news that she's thanking him.

Chrysothemis: Then where did all those offerings on our father's tomb come from?

Electra: I don't know – perhaps someone put them there as a memorial to the dead Orestes.

Chrysothemis: [934] This is terrible! And here I was, hurrying here with what I thought was such delightful news! And now it seems that I had absolutely no idea what kind of a situation we were in. But now I find not merely the same old miseries, but new and worse ones as well.

Electra: This is how things are, yes. But if you listen to me and obey, you'll be able to relieve the pain that's weighing so heavily on us.

Chrysothemis: [940] I don't understand. How am I supposed to bring the dead back to life?

Electra: That's not what I mean. C'mon – I'm not crazy.

Chrysothemis: What is it that you want me to do? What can I do?

Electra: I need you to have enough courage to do what I say.

Chrysothemis: If it brings us any help, then I'll do it gladly.

Electra: [945] Just remember that success only comes from hard work.

Chrysothemis: I'll do as much as my strength will allow.

Electra: [947] Then listen to me know and the plan that I have in mind. You know that we really have no friends left here, but that Hades has taken them and robbed us of them. So we're alone – just the two of us.

[951] While I still had word that my brother was alive and thriving, I held onto hopes that one day he'd come back here, someday, to avenge the murder of his father.

[954] But now Orestes is no more, and so now I look toward you, and ask you not to shrink from helping your sister kill the man, that Aegisthus, who murdered our father.

[957] I won't conceal anything from you anymore. How long are we going to wait doing nothing? Is there any other hope that we're looking toward? We can just sit here and feel sorry about our dead father, about being deprived of him and our rightful places within this house, and about growing older without a wedding and without the prospect of marriage. Don't hope that you're going to find a good husband now, for Aegisthus is not so stupid that he's going to let the two of us have children, since they'd only bring trouble for him in later years.

[967] But if you listen to me and do as I ask, you'll earn praise from our dead father and also from our brother. What's more, you'll once again earn your freedom, so in the future you'll be free and will be able to find a marriage that's suitable to your noble and virtuous nature.

[972] Can't you see that you'll gain a great reputation if you follow my advice? Every citizen here, even every foreigner, when they see us, will greet us and welcome us with praise. They'll say things like: "Look at those two sisters there. They saved the house of their father when it looked like their enemies had the upper hand. They didn't even think about their own lives, but they were willing to risk their lives to avenge the murder of their father. And

that's why we'll honour and revere them, and at every feast and public festival we'll honour these two girls for their courage and bravery."

^{984} Those are the kinds of things that all men will say about us, and we'll achieve an undying fame in return for our actions. Come now, my dear sister, take the side of your father and your brother, and deliver me from my miseries – and save yourself as well, and remember that it's shameful for nobles like us to live such shameful lives.

Chorus: ^{990} In matters such as these it's best for everyone to think clearly about what you plan to do before you go through with it.

Chrysothemis: ^{992} Yes, it's best to think before we speak, and to think before we act.

^{995} What gives you such confidence to arm yourself and to call on me as your helper? Don't you see that you're a woman and not a man? And your physical strength is less than that of any of your enemies. Every day their good fortune seems to grow stronger, while ours gets worse and worse.

^{1001} Who on earth then would plan to kill a man such as Aegisthus and plan to get away with it unharmed? The two of us are in a lot of trouble as things stand right now, so we should be careful that we don't make things even worse for ourselves if anyone happens to hear what we say. Nothing good will come our way if we receive a good reputation but an ugly death.

^{1009} And that's why I beg you to hold back your passion before we're killed and our entire family is destroyed. I'll leave everything that you said to me alone, as if they were never spoken, and you should be sensible enough to give way to those in power – especially when you have no power yourself.

Chorus: ^{1015} Please Electra – listen to your sister. There's no greater gift for a man than to have a sensible mind.

Electra: What you've said doesn't come as a surprise to me. I knew that you would reject what I proposed.

Fine. Then it's clear that I'll have to take care of this deed all on my own, and I'll gladly do it alone, for I won't leave it undone.

Chrysothemis: ^{1021} I only wish you had shown such energy and resolution when our father died. You would have been able to lead the whole population of Argos.

Electra: I felt the same way then that I do now, but back then my judgment was much weaker.

Chrysothemis: I think it would better if you had the same judgment now.

Electra: ^{1025} This lecture from you is a clear indication that you won't help me.

Chrysothemis: That's right, I won't help – because this attempt is bound to fail.

Electra: Maybe I should envy you for your good sense, but I think you're a coward.

Chrysothemis: I'll be just as patient with you when you praise me.

Electra: You'll never receive my praise, I can assure you of that.

Chrysothemis: ^{1030} There will be a long time in the future to help determine that.

Electra: Get out of here – you're no good to me now.

Chrysothemis: I could be good for you, but you are unwilling to learn.

Electra: Whatever – go and report all this to your darling mother.

Chrysothemis: I wouldn't do that. I won't betray you.

Electra: [1035] Maybe not, but you certainly are dishonouring me.

Chrysothemis: But this is not out of dishonour, but because I care for you!

Electra: Do I really have to agree with your idea of justice?

Chrysothemis: It will make you sensible, and then I'll let you guide me.

Electra: It's so sad when one speaks so well and yet says such terrible things.

Chrysothemis: [1040] That's a perfect description of yourself.

Electra: What? Don't you think that what I said is right?

Chrysothemis: There are times when being right can be harmful.

Electra: I refuse to live by those kinds of rules.

Chrysothemis: If you do what you say, then you'll just go ahead and confirm that I was right.

Electra: [1045] Your words will neither frighten me nor stop me.

Chrysothemis: Really? You won't even think twice about this?

Electra: Bad advice is worse than any enemy.

Chrysothemis: You don't understand anything of what I'm saying.

Electra: My mind is already made up – and this was decided long ago.

Chrysothemis: [1055] Well, if you're so sure that you're right, then just go on thinking like that. Later on, when you're in trouble, then you'll agree with my words.

Exit Chrysothemis

Chorus (lengthy ode): [1058] Above our heads we see birds, so wise and taking care...

Enter Orestes and Pylades, with two attendants – Orestes is carrying an urn

Orestes: [1098] I wonder if you women can tell us whether we're on the right path and have arrived at the place we want to go.

Chorus: [1100] What place are you looking for? And what do you want here?

Orestes: I've been looking for the place where Aegisthus lives.

Chorus: Someone gave you good directions, because you've come to the right place.

Orestes: Then which one of you could go inside and report to those inside that some welcome visitors have arrived?

Chorus: [1105] This woman over here would probably be the best one to bring your message.

Orestes: Great. Please do us this favour, my dear lady, and let those inside know that some men from Phocis are looking for Aegisthus.

Electra: Oh no – are you bringing evidence of the story that we just heard?

Orestes: [1110] I'm not sure what story you mean, but old Strophius asked us to bring news about Orestes.

Electra: What news do you have? Suddenly I've become frightened once again.

Orestes: He's dead, and we're carrying his ashes in this urn that I have here.

Electra: [1115] Oh gods – this really is the worst then! What on earth will I do?

Orestes: I'm sorry... if you really feel so badly for Orestes... then maybe you should be the one to carry his ashes.

ELECTRA: O stranger, please let me carry it and hold it in my arms. I need to weep and lament for myself and the whole miserable family.

ORESTES: ¹¹²³ Here – please take it. I realize that whoever you are, you are asking to hold this not out of hatred but rather out of love. Clearly you must be a friend or a relative of the dead man.

ELECTRA: ¹¹²⁶ Oh, this urn is the only thing left of the man who was the dearest in the world to me. My darling Orestes, I welcome you home, but this is so different from how I sent you off, and the hopes that I had for you then. Now all I hold is nothingness, but you were glorious when you left.

¹¹³¹ I wish that I had died before I could have taken you and sent you into a foreign land, saving you from murder – that way you could have died here on the same day as your father and shared in the glory of his tomb. But now you have died so pathetically, far from home, an exile in a foreign land, without your sister near you…you must have been so lonesome…so unhappy.

¹¹³⁸ And, much to my sorrow, I didn't have the chance to wash you with my loving hands, or to lift you up, the sad weight of misery, as was my right and duty, and bring you to your blazing funeral pyre. No, you received your funeral rites from the hands of strangers, and now you come home at last, nothing more than ash inside this tiny urn.

¹¹⁴³ Oh, just to think about all the times I took care of you in the olden days – all for nothing now. It gave me such joy to look after you, to love you…but now there's nothing left. You must know that you never belonged to your mother as much as you were mine, for I was the one who raised you. And the none of the women in this house was your nurse, but you always called me both nurse and sister…even sometimes mother.

¹¹⁴⁹ But now all of that that has vanished in one day, for you have died. You've gone away, just like a whirlwind, and in your departure you've carried off everything with you.

¹¹⁵¹ Our father is dead, gone; you have died, and with your death you've killed me. Our enemies now laugh at us, and our bitch of a mother – she was no mother! – is overwhelmed with joy and frenzy, that woman whom you so often said to me, in those secret messages, that you yourself would come back and punish.

¹¹⁵⁶ But your sad fate, and my sad fate, have taken this hope of vengeance away from me, and now all that's left of you is this dust that was once my brother and…nothing more.

¹¹⁶¹ You poor poor boy! Your poor miserable body! You've completed the sad journey home, but in that journey you've ended me! Yes, my dear brother, you've destroyed me! That's why I ask you to welcome me into the place where you now are, so that I may live with you from now onward – since I am nothing now, it's natural for me to become nothing – and I will join you in the eternal shade of death. When you lived here in the land above I shared your fate, and now I want to die and share your grave, so that I can be next to you, for I see that the dead can no longer feel any pain and suffering.

CHORUS: ¹¹⁷¹ Please, Electra, be more cautious in your approach. Your father and brother were both mortal, as you yourself are mortal – and so death is something that will come to all of us at the proper time.

ORESTES: ¹¹⁷⁴ Oh gods, what should I say? What words can I use? I…I don't know how to speak…I'm at a loss…

Electra: What's wrong with you? Why are you acting like this?

Orestes: Are you the glorious form of Electra before me?

Electra: Yes, I am Electra, but I am more miserable than glorious.

Orestes: Oh, this is so…so…awful!

Electra: [1180] Surely you can't be moaning like this about me, stranger.

Orestes: You've been so dishonoured…so abused!

Electra: You speak the truth, but I still don't understand…

Orestes: And a life unmarried, without the joy of having a husband and children!

Electra: Why are you looking at me like this and saying such laments, stranger?

Orestes: [1185] I knew so few of my own sorrows!

Electra: How does any of this relate to you?

Orestes: I can see all that you've had to endure.

Electra: But you only see a part of it.

Orestes: How can there be anything worse than what I see now?

Electra: [1190] Because I have to live with murderers.

Orestes: Whose murderers? Where is the evil that you speak of?

Electra: The murderers of my father, and they've forced me into a position of slavery.

Orestes: Who has done this to you? Tell me.

Electra: She calls herself my mother, but she's nothing at all like a mother.

Orestes: [1195] What does she do to you? Is she violent with you, or does she force you to lead a hard life?

Electra: Violence…hardship…she does it all.

Orestes: Is there no one around who can help you to stop her?

Electra: Of course not! You just showed me the ashes of the only one who could have done so.

Orestes: O you poor girl. I look at you and feel such pity.

Electra: [1200] Then you'll be the only one who has ever felt any pity for me.

Orestes: Yes, I alone have come here…and I feel your pain.

Electra: Does this mean that you are a relative of mine in some way?

Orestes: I'll tell you, if you in turn tell me whether we can trust the loyalty of these other women here.

Electra: They are friends, so you can speak freely.

Orestes: [1205] So then just let go of that urn and you can know everything.

Electra: Please don't take this from me, stranger – I beg you!

Orestes: Just do as I say – you won't be making a mistake.

Electra: Please, I beg you, don't rob me of what I love the most.

Orestes: I can't let you keep it.

Electra: [1209] O my poor Orestes! I'm going be cheated of the chance to give you a burial!

Orestes: Don't speak such words! You have no reason to mourn.

Electra: How can I have no reason to mourn my dead brother?

Orestes: You shouldn't refer to him that way!

Electra: Why am I refused this honour?

Orestes: ¹²¹⁵ No honour is being taken away from you – but this urn doesn't belong to you.

Electra: Wrong! It should be in my hands, if it is the body of Orestes that I hold.

Orestes: It's not Orestes in there – it's just a trick.

Electra: Then where's the tomb or ashes of my poor brother?

Orestes: There is no tomb, and no ashes. A living man has no need for such things.

Electra: ¹²²⁰ What is this you're saying? A "living man"?

Orestes: I speak the truth.

Electra: Then my brother's alive?

Orestes: Yes – if I am alive, then he is.

Electra: What? Are you … are you Orestes?

Orestes: Just take a look at this ring, which once belonged to our father, and thus discover whether I'm telling the truth.

Electra: O happiest light!

Orestes: Yes, my dear, I agree – so happy, so joyous!

Electra: ¹²²⁵ Is this really your voice?

Orestes: It's the voice of no other.

Electra: And do I really hold you in my arms?

Orestes: I hope that you'll always hold me this way!

Electra: O my dear women, my friends, here you see my Orestes, dead by trickery, and now alive once again brought to life by trickery.

Chorus: ¹²³⁰ We see him, O child, and we're starting to cry at your good fortune.

Electra: O you dearest child of my dear father, you've finally come back, you've arrived to see the one you've longed to see.

Orestes: ¹²³⁶ Yes, I'm here. But you need to keep silent for a while still.

Electra: Why? What's wrong?

Orestes: It's safest to keep quiet in case anyone inside hears us.

Electra: ¹²³⁹ No! I swear in the name of Artemis, that virgin goddess, that I'll never be afraid of the women there inside the house.

Orestes: But you need to remember that women too have a warlike spirit inside themselves. You – and that woman in there – are the very proof of that.

Electra: ¹²⁴⁵ Oh gods yes! You've just reminded me of our pain and sorrow – it will never go away, never be forgotten.

Orestes: ¹²⁵¹ Yes, it's always in my mind as well. But there will be a time when we can speak freely about it – just not quite yet.

Electra: Every time seems right for my complaints, so I can certainly hold my tongue a bit longer. My lips will be set free soon enough.

Orestes: Yes, that's true – so protect that coming freedom.

Electra: How so?

Orestes: Be quiet until the moment is right.

Electra: ¹²⁶¹ It's a good bargain to exchange my silence for your presence. You came here when I no longer had any hope, any expectation, that you'd come.

Orestes: You see me here because the gods urged me to come.

Electra: ¹²⁶⁵ You're telling me of even better news, if in truth the gods have told you to return to your rightful house. Clearly then the gods are on our side.

Orestes: I don't want to restrain your joy, but at the same time I fear that you're giving in to happiness too quickly.

Electra: Orestes, now that you've come back to me after all these years, after so much loneliness, so much pain, I beg you... don't...

Orestes: [1276] Not to do what?

Electra: Don't cheat me of the joy of seeing your face.

Orestes: Please don't worry, since I'd be angry with anyone who tried to take me from you.

Electra: [1280] Then you agree?

Orestes: Of course.

Electra: My dear brother, in you I've heard a voice that I never thought I'd hear again, but I still managed to keep calm and not scream in delight. But now that you've come, I'll never forget your face even in the midst of all this suffering.

Orestes: [1288] Let's put aside all of this needless speech, and there's no need to tell me that our mother is evil, nor that Aegisthus is destroying my father's wealth with all of his luxury and waste. If we spend too much time in conversation then we'll lose the moment for action.

[1293] Instead I need you to tell me what we need to do in the present, the now, and whether we should remain hidden or whether we can openly put a stop to the laughter of our enemies.

[1296] And please be careful that our mother doesn't discover my arrival from the happy expression on your face when we go inside the house. No – you need to groan in pain as if the news you heard of my death were still the truth.

[1299] When we win, when we defeat our enemies – then you'll be able to celebrate and laugh in total freedom.

Electra: [1301] O my brother, I'll follow your wise advice. The joy that I have right now I owe all to you, after all. And I wouldn't be able to accept any good thing for myself if it came at the cost of pains that you would suffer. If I did that... well, then I'd be working against the god who's helping us right now.

[1307] I think you know the situation inside the house already. You've heard that Aegisthus is not at home right now, but our mother is there. But you don't need to worry that she'll see some happy expression on my face and that I will accidentally give you away – the hatred I feel for her is far too strong.

[1312] And since I've seen you, I can't stop crying, but she won't realize that these are tears of joy.

[1313] How can I help but cry when I've seen you both alive and dead on the same day? For me your return is so amazing that if our father were suddenly to return today, I wouldn't consider it to be a miracle at all, but I would easily believe that it were true.

[1318] So, since your arrival here has changed everything, please lead the way. If I were here all alone, I would have had only two options – to find a way to save myself with honour or, failing that, to die with honour.

Orestes: Shush please – I think I hear someone coming out of the house.

Electra: [1324] Ok... that's right, strangers, this is the door to the house. Since you are carrying what nobody would refuse yet what nobody would be glad to have, you might as well go inside...

Enter the Old Slave from the palace

OLD SLAVE: [1326] Are you people crazy or just plain old stupid? Don't you realize how dangerous this is for you?

[1331] If I hadn't been standing next to the door right now, because I was worried that something like this might happen, then your plans would have been already known throughout the entire house by now.

[1334] Good grief – it looks like I'm the only one who's taking any precautions and thinking ahead. Anyway, it's high time that you finished all of your long speeches and your cries of delight.

[1336] It's time for you to enter the palace – so go on in. As things stand right now, any delay could bring disaster to us, so now is the perfect moment to bring it all to a fitting conclusion.

ORESTES: But how will things look when I go inside?

OLD SLAVE: [1340] Things look good for us – especially since no one recognized me.

ORESTES: And you told them that I'm dead?

OLD SLAVE: They believe that you are now in Hades.

ORESTES: Are they happy with this news, or what are they saying?

OLD SLAVE: [1344] We'll talk about that when everything's over and done with. As things stand now, they think that all is going well for them, even when that's not true at all.

ELECTRA: Orestes, who is this man? Please tell me.

ORESTES: Don't you recognize him?

ELECTRA: I don't think that I've ever seen him before.

ORESTES: Don't you recognize the man to whom you once entrusted me?

ELECTRA: What? Is this the same man?

ORESTES: [1349] By his hands and your wisdom I was led toward the plains of Phocis.

ELECTRA: Is this the only man whom I found to be loyal back when our father was murdered?

ORESTES: Yes, that's him – but there's no time for such questions.

ELECTRA: [1354] O dearest man, O savior of the house of Agamemnon, have you really come back? Are you really the same man who rescued Orestes and me from so many sorrows?

[1358] How could you have been here so long without my recognizing you? What you said at first was killing me, even though you were really brining me something delightful.

[1361] O bless you, my father, for in you I think I see a father figure. O bless you, for on this same day I have gone from hating you to loving you.

OLD SLAVE: [1364] I think that we've spoken enough about this for now. As for what happened in all those days between the day we left and today, I think there will be plenty of time to tell you all about it, Electra, in the days to come.

[1368] But I'm telling you all of you that now is the time for action. Clytemnestra is home all alone. No man at all is inside with her. If you hold back and hesitate now, then you'll soon have to fight with others who are more numerous and better skilled than the ones who are here at the moment.

ORESTES: [1372] Pylades, we don't have any time to make long speeches. We need to go inside at once and act, only stopping to quickly pay respects to the ancestral gods whose statues stand here in the entranceway.

Exit Orestes, Pylades, and the Old Slave into the palace

ELECTRA: ¹³⁷⁶ O lord Apollo, please be favourable to them, and also to me, who have so often stood before you in supplication and made you offerings, from whatever good things that I had.

¹³⁷⁹ But now, O Apollo, I fall on my knees and beg you to become an active helper in this plan of ours and show mankind how the gods reward wickedness!

Exit Electra into the palace

CHORUS: ¹³⁸⁴ Look! See how the war-god Ares approaches, breathing out his bloody vengeance. They're under the beams of the roof now, hunting down those who've committed such evil crimes.

¹³⁹¹ The clever and tricky defender of the dead man has entered the house and is now approaching the ancient throne of his father, carrying a blade that has been newly-sharpened for murder. And Maia's son, Hermes, that guide of the dead, is helping young Orestes bring this deed to its fitting conclusion.

Enter Electra from the palace

ELECTRA: ¹³⁹⁸ Dear women, the men are soon going to finish the deed, but you need to keep quiet.

CHORUS: ¹⁴⁰⁰ How do you mean? What is happening in there?

ELECTRA: The creature is preparing the urn for burial and they are standing right next to her.

CHORUS: But why did you come running out here so quickly?

ELECTRA: I need to keep watch in case Aegisthus comes this way.

CLYTEMNESTRA (INSIDE): ¹⁴⁰⁴ Oh gods, all my friends have left the house, and now it's filled with killers!

ELECTRA: Someone is shouting inside – can you hear?

CHORUS: I heard something terrible, and it's making me shudder.

CLYTEMNESTRA (INSIDE): Oh Aegisthus, where are you?

ELECTRA: ¹⁴¹⁰ There it is again – that scream.

CLYTEMNESTRA (INSIDE): O my son, my son – please show some pity for your mother!

ELECTRA: You had none at all for him, nor did you have any for his father.

CHORUS: O you poor city, you poor family, you cursed house – you are losing your battle with fate…

CLYTEMNESTRA (INSIDE): ¹⁴¹⁵ Ah! You've struck me!

ELECTRA: Do it again, if you have the strength!

CLYTEMNESTRA (INSIDE): Oh no – again!

ELECTRA: I wish that Aegisthus were there with you!

CHORUS: ¹⁴¹⁸ The curse of this house is being fulfilled. Those who live under the ground are alive, for the blood of the murderers is now flowing, drained by those who died such a long time ago.

¹⁴²² And look! Here they come. Their bloody hands drip with their sacrifice to Ares, and I can't blame them for it.

Enter Orestes and Pylades from the palace

ELECTRA: Orestes, how did it go?

ORESTES: ¹⁴²⁴ Everything's fine in the house, if the oracle of Apollo is true.

ELECTRA: Is the horrible woman dead?

Orestes: You don't have to worry that your arrogant mother will dishonour you ever again.

Chorus: Hold on a moment! I can see Aegisthus coming this way.

Electra: ¹⁴³⁰ Boys, get back into the house!

Orestes: Wait – where do you see him?

Electra: He's coming toward us from the gates of the city, and it looks like he has a smirk on his face.

Chorus: You boys need to get back inside the house as quickly as possible. You've finished one part of this matter, now you have to settle this one as well.

Orestes: ¹⁴³⁵ Have some courage – he's ours for the taking.

Electra: Then please hurry and go where you need to go.

Orestes: We're on our way.

Electra: I'll take care of everything here on the outside.

Exit Orestes and Pylades into the palace

Chorus: ¹⁴³⁸ Try to say a few nice things into his ear, so that he'll head into the house to face Justice completely unaware.

Enter Aegisthus

Aegisthus: ¹⁴⁴² Which one of you knows where the strangers from Phocis are? I hear that they've come here to announce that Orestes has died in a chariot race.

¹⁴⁴⁵ You there! Yes, you Electra – I am talking to you. You were always so bold, so brazen, to me before, and so I think this news will affect you the most – and that's why you should be the one to tell me where these visitors are.

Electra: That's right – I know where you can find them. The news they brought concerns those I love the most, after all.

Aegisthus: ¹⁴⁵⁰ Then where are these strangers? Tell me that.

Electra: They're inside. They've found a kind hostess who already invited them in.

Aegisthus: Did they really come here to announce the death of Orestes?

Electra: More than that – they even brought evidence.

Aegisthus: Will I be able to see this with my own eyes?

Electra: ¹⁴⁵⁵ Yes you can – and it's a very ugly sight.

Aegisthus: What you are telling me makes me very happy – which is very unusual.

Electra: Go ahead and enjoy this, if you can find pleasure in this news.

Aegisthus: ¹⁴⁵⁸ I tell all of you now, you slaves, to open the doors and reveal the sight to all people of Mycenae and Argos to see. I want it to be made clear that if anyone had placed their empty hopes in this young Orestes, then they'll now witness his corpse and accept that I am the tyrant of this land, and from this day forward I won't have to use the threat of violent punishment to teach men to have common sense and accept my rule.

Electra: ¹⁴⁶⁴ I've done everything that I was asked to do, so I suppose you can say that I've learned to have this "common sense" you mentioned.

The door of the palace are opened, and Orestes and Pylades stand above a shrouded corpse

Aegisthus: O Zeus, I see an image of something that even the gods would envy, if I may say it like that. If Nemesis forbids such a declaration, then I take it back.

Take all the coverings away from the boy's face so that I too can mourn for my poor relative.

Orestes: [1470] Remove the covering yourself. It's not my place to touch the body of this boy. No – you are his family, so you should be the one to look on him and touch him with loving words.

Aegisthus: That's very good advice. But one of you go in and call Clytemnestra, if she's in the house.

Orestes: But she's already here – you don't need to go looking for her.

Aegisthus lifts the shroud

Aegisthus: [1475] Ah! What the hell is this that I'm looking at?

Orestes: Are you afraid of something? Don't you recognize that face?

Aegisthus: Who are you that have lured me into this trap?

Orestes: Can't you put two and two together? Don't you see that you've been talking with someone you thought was dead?

Aegisthus: [1479] Ah, I understand. And so you must be Orestes.

Orestes: You're good at guessing. It's strange that you've been deceived for so long.

Aegisthus: This is the end of me, but let me say one final word.

Electra: [1483] No! My brother, I beg you, don't let him say anything. Just kill him as quickly as you can, and then hand his body over to anyone who wants to give him a proper burial – as long as it is away from our sight.

As far as I'm concerned, this is the only thing that can bring us release from our past sufferings.

Orestes: [1491] Then it's time for you to go inside now – at once! I'm not interested in talk, but rather your life.

Aegisthus: Why are you forcing me to go into the house? If you think that you're doing something honourable, then why are you doing this in darkness? Why aren't you willing to kill me in the light of day?

Orestes: [1495] Shut up! You don't give the orders here. You're going to die in the very same spot where you killed my father.

Aegisthus: Does this house need to see more sufferings of the children of Pelops?

Orestes: It's going to witness your suffering, at any rate. In this one case I'm an excellent prophet.

Aegisthus: [1500] It's a pity your father didn't have your knack for such prophecy.

Orestes: Fuck you! Enough with this talk – go on in!

Aegisthus: You lead the way.

Orestes: No – you go first.

Aegisthus: Are you scared that I'll make an escape?

Orestes: [1503] No, but I won't let you choose your place of death. It's important for me that your death be as bitter as possible for you. It necessary that anyone who breaks the law should receive justice – and a just punishment for their crimes. This way, there will be less crime and fewer criminals.

Exit Aegisthus, followed by Orestes and Pylades

Chorus: [1507] O house of Atreus, after so many sufferings you've finally emerged into freedom, brought to fulfillment by this day's actions!

Translated from the Greek by Stephen Russell, PhD

Chapter 16
Euripides
Electra

THE STORY: When king Agamemnon of Argos sets sail for the Trojan War, he sacrifices his oldest daughter Iphigenia in order to persuade the goddess Artemis to send him a fair wind. Agamemnon's wife, Clytemnestra, swears that she will avenge her child and, while her husband is away at war, begins an affair with Aegisthus, the cousin and enemy of her husband.

When he returns from war, Clytemnestra and Aegisthus kill Agamemnon in his bath and seize the throne. Clytemnestra's young son Orestes is spirited away from the murderers and out of Argos to seek refuge in a neighbouring city. Clytemnestra's daughter Electra, mourning interminably for her dead father, is forced by Aegisthus to marry a failed noble who ekes out a shabby living on a farm outside the city limits of Argos, and it is there that our story begins...

CHARACTERS

FARMER
ELECTRA, DAUGHTER OF AGAMEMNON
ORESTES, SON OF AGAMEMNON
PYLADES, FRIEND OF ORESTES
CHORUS (OF ARGIVE PEASANT WOMEN)
OLD MAN
MESSENGER

AEGISTHUS, A CORPSE
CLYTEMNESTRA, WIFE OF AGAMEMNON AND AEGISTHUS
ATTENDANTS OF CLYTEMNESTRA, SLAVE GIRLS FROM TROY
CASTOR AND POLYDEUCES (THE DIOSCURI – GODS)

SCENE: A depressing dirt farm on the outskirts of Argos, complete with altar.

Enter the Farmer who, arrested by the sight of the altar, bows guiltily and proceeds to explain himself to the gods.

FARMER: Ancient land of Argos, where the waters of the river Inachus flow: from here King Agamemnon set sail for Troy with a thousand ships of war, and there killed Priam, its ruler, and took control. Returned to Argos, he set the spoils taken from the barbarians upon the towers of our lofty temples. In Troy he found success, but back in the bosom of family his wife Clytemnestra plotted his demise, abetted by Aegisthus, son of Thyestes. Agamemnon is dead, relinquishing the ancient sceptre of his great-grandfather Tantalus, and Aegisthus is king in this land, which he rules with Clytemnestra.

[14] As for the children Agamemnon left behind when he sailed for Troy, the boy Orestes was spirited away to Phocis by his father's old tutor before Aegisthus could slay him, and placed in the care of Strophius, who has seen him safely to manhood.

[19] But Electra remained in her father's home, and when she blossomed, suitors came seeking her hand – the leading men of Greece. But Aegisthus feared noble offspring who might be capable of avenging her father, and so kept her locked up and forbade her to marry any of them. Yet even then he dreaded she might secretly bear the child of some noble, and determined to kill her. However, her mother – cruel and savage though she is – saved Electra from that fate, for you see, Agamemnon sacrificing one of her children had justified her killing her husband, and killing one of them herself might just stir up bitter resentment here in Argos...

[31] So Aegisthus worked things this way – he promised gold to whoever killed Orestes, and he gave Electra to me as my wife. My ancestors are from Mycenae, so I bear no shame insofar as the place of my birth, but I lack possessions. Settling her on a lowly man like me, Aegisthus thinks that he'll have fewer reasons to fear reprisal, for a nobler husband than I might rouse the spectre of foul murder from its sleep, and introduce Aegisthus to justice.

[43] As Aphrodite is my witness, though, Electra is untouched. I am not so shameless that I would inflict myself on the daughter of a blessed family when I am unworthy of her. And, also, I prefer to be blameless when my 'brother-in-law', poor Orestes, returns to Argos and sees the unlucky marriage that his sister has made. Anyone who mocks me for never having laid a finger on my virgin bride simply hasn't thought the thing through...

Enter Electra, carrying a water-jug on her head

[50] Unhappy woman, why do you insist on working so hard? You were raised to live better than this, so why do you not stop when I ask it?

ELECTRA: [54] O black Night, nurse of the golden stars, beneath which I carry this pitcher to the stream to get water: know that no one forces me, I choose to do this, so that despite my isolation at least the gods can look down and see how thoroughly Aegisthus, in his hubris, has ruined me. Even my mother, deadly daughter of Tyndareus, has cast me out in favour of her new husband, for since she gave him new children my brother and I are robbed of our status in that house.

[67] Husband, I regard you as true a friend as any of the gods, for you have not seen fit to take advantage of my difficulties, as clearly you might, but instead balm my wounds like the most tender of medics – which is just the way I think of you.

[71] So though you don't demand it of me, I share your load to the extent that my strength allows. You have so much to do on the farm, and it is my job to keep the house in order, for when a man comes home from the fields, he likes to find things just so.

FARMER: [77] Well, if that's the way you feel about it, I won't fight you. I suppose, after all, the stream is not so very far from the house. And, for my part of the bargain, at dawn I will take the oxen and begin the planting. None may live without some manner of toil: pray to the gods, but sow your fields, I always say...

Exit both the Farmer and Electra; Enter Orestes and Pylades from the opposite side

ORESTES: [82] Pylades, I regard you as the first and dearest among friends. You alone of those whom I loved have stayed with me, reduced though my circumstances have been by the man who, with the help of my bitch of a mother, killed my father.

[87] I have returned in secret to Argos by way of Apollo's shrine at Delphi, in order that I might

fulfill the oracle that I received there and pay the murderers of my father in kind. This night we visited the family tomb, where I offered tears and a lock of hair for my poor father, and over the altar sacrificed a sheep, all unseen, unknown to the tyrants now ruling this land.

94 We won't set foot inside the city just yet, but linger on the outskirts to seek my sister. They say she is no longer a girl, now married, yet I would make her my partner, in murder, and learn what really goes on within the city walls. So, since dawn is just now lifting her bright white eye, let us move from the thoroughfare and wait our chance. Perhaps some peasant will pass by, and then we might ask directions to my sister's abode.

106 Here comes one now, with a pitcher of water balanced on her shaved head. Hunker down and listen sharp, Pylades, and perhaps we may hear something pertinent to our mission...

Orestes and Pylades hide; Enter Electra, with the water-jug on her head

ELECTRA (SINGING):
111 *Move your feet, now's the time –*
Keep on in sadness: me oh my!
Born to Agamemnon,
Mother Clytemnestra
– Daughter of Tyndareus –
Call me poor Electra,
For I sing of work and pain,
Lamenting both this hateful life
And Agamemnon dispatched below,
By Aegisthus, and an evil wife.
125 *It feels so good to sing along,*
The bitter pleasure of a sad, sad song!
Move your feet, now's the time:
Keep on in sadness – me oh my!
In what far city,
And what strange home,
Brother do you shelter,
Brother do you roam?
For crowned now by a ceramic cistern
Your sad, forlorn, forsaken sister
Dreads and yet anticipates
The next disaster, or next blister.
Come and free her from suspense,
And this desperate life of endless woe –
Avenger find your wandering way
And wander back to old Argos!
140 *Take the pitcher from my head*
And lay it down upon the ground,
And I will raise chin to the sky
And make a mournful crying sound
For you, my father, my father, for you,
'Neath earth directing my desolate cry,
Daily unending bitter lamenting
For the dreadful way it was fated you die.
Ever I grieve at the thought of the axe
And its surgical use in the ploy
That descended unexpected when you traveled
Unmolested and home arrived safely from Troy.
159 *She did not receive you with garland or wreath,*
Nor ribbon of victory,
But upon you bestowed a double-edged sword:
New husband for her, and for you treachery.

Enter the Chorus

CHORUS: 167 Child of Agamemnon, we have come to pay a visit. We just had a visitor ourselves, a man from Mycenae, bred on the milk of the mountains, and he told us they proclaim a sacrifice in Argos two days from now. All the girls will pass in procession to the temple of Hera.

ELECTRA: 175 No, my friends. No beautiful garments or golden necklaces for me, for no such finery could move my sad heart. I won't dance along with the girls of Argos and twinkle my toes. In tears I'll pass my nights, for in tears is the way I spend my days. Look at my filthy hair, the dirty rags I wear – is this fitting attire for the daughter of a king, or suitable tribute from Troy, which surely cannot have forgotten my conquering father?

CHORUS: [190] Great is the goddess! You must borrow from us thick-woven party garments of wool, and gold to decorate them! But do you think that lamentation alone will bring victory over your enemies? Only prayers and reverence for the gods bring about better days.

ELECTRA: [198] Clearly none of the gods is with us or they'd have been watching over my father, murdered all those years ago. All we can do is cry for the dead man and his wandering son somewhere in another country, trudging miserably through empty days, though noble born. And here I languish in the home of a farmer, rotting away up here in the mountains, exiled from my home while mother revels in her murderous marriage with a stranger.

CHORUS: [212] Your mother has become just like her sister, Helen – she who is most to blame for so many evils visited upon the Greeks and on your house.

Enter Orestes and Pylades

ELECTRA: [215] What's this? Strangers approach who lay in ambush behind our altar! Fly, women: run down the path and I'll take my refuge in the house!

ORESTES: [220] Wait, girl! You need fear no violence from me!

ELECTRA: Apollo save me! I beg you, please sir, do not kill me!

ORESTES: There are a good many others I'd kill before you, believe me.

ELECTRA: Keep back! You have no right to lay a finger on me!

ORESTES: On the contrary, there is no person yet living that I have a greater right to touch.

ELECTRA: [225] Why do you lie in wait outside my home with sword in hand?

ORESTES: Well, if you'd quiet yourself a moment you might find out...

ELECTRA: Well, then, I'm not going anywhere, am I? For I could hardly resist if you should decide to take me against my will...

ORESTES: Good gods, woman, I have come with word of your brother!

ELECTRA: Orestes? Is he alive then?

ORESTES: [230] Alive and well. I see you prefer your good news first, then.

ELECTRA: You have already given me the best news! But where in the world does he bear his terrible burden of exile?

ORESTES: From city to city, calling none of them home.

ELECTRA: [235] Does he eat well? And keep a roof over his head?

ORESTES: As far as that goes he is fine, but then again there is more to life than bodily comfort.

ELECTRA: But what word do you bring from him?

ORESTES: I bear not a message so much as a mission, to see if you live, and if so, just what manner of existence you lead.

ELECTRA: Well, as to that, just look at me!

ORESTES: [240] Yes, you certainly appear eaten away with grief and toil.

ELECTRA: And my beautiful hair has all been shorn away.

ORESTES: Separation from your father and brother still preys upon you, then?

ELECTRA: Of course. Who in this life was dearer to me than they are?

ORESTES: And do you imagine anyone dearer to your brother than yourself?

ELECTRA: [245] He may love me, but he isn't here, is he?

ORESTES: ...Why are you living up here, so far from the city?

ELECTRA: Because I have been given in marriage to an ignominious fate, stranger.

ORESTES: Which man of Mycenae is your husband?

ELECTRA: None to whom my father would ever have allowed me to go.

ORESTES: [250] Then give me his name so that I may tell your brother.

ELECTRA: This is his house here, where I live quite isolated from the city.

ORESTES: Is he a worker then, or a shepherd, that he must reside in a hovel such as this?

ELECTRA: He is a poor man, yet still a noble one, and treats me well.

ORESTES: Well? How does this husband of yours treat you well?

ELECTRA: [255] He has never yet come to my bed.

ORESTES: What, has he made some vow of chastity, then, or are you not good enough for him?

ELECTRA: No, he simply thinks it beneath him, for he thinks me above him.

ORESTES: But he should be over the moon at having made such a marriage!

ELECTRA: And yet he understands that the man who gave me to him had no right.

ORESTES: [260] Ah, I see: he's afraid of what would happen to him should Orestes return...

ELECTRA: That too, but nevertheless he is a good man.

ORESTES: A truly noble man, then, to be esteemed rather than punished?

ELECTRA: Yes, if the one who would esteem him should ever come home.

ORESTES: But what of your mother? Did she approve this marriage?

ELECTRA: [265] Sadly, stranger, it has been my experience that mothers prefer their men to their children.

ORESTES: Just what did Aegisthus have in mind when he shamed you this way?

ELECTRA: I think he hoped a powerless man would give me similarly powerless children who he need not fear.

ORESTES: He though to deprive you of sons of quality enough to revenge you and father? That was his plan?

ELECTRA: Yes, and I hope, with the passage of time, to make him rue the day he ever thought of it.

ORESTES: [270] Does he know you are still a virgin?

ELECTRA: No, we have kept this to ourselves.

ORESTES: And, uh, these eavesdropping women? They are friends of yours, I trust?

ELECTRA: Oh, they won't tell anyone.

ORESTES: And what should I tell Orestes he must do about all this?

ELECTRA: [275] You need to ask? What a question! Surely he must come home!

ORESTES: And...?

ELECTRA: And do to his enemies what they dared do to our father.

ORESTES: Would you be bold enough to join with him in murdering your own mother?

ELECTRA: Yes, and with the same axe used to kill Father.

ORESTES: [280] Can I tell him this? Are you absolutely certain you're ready to take that step?

Electra: I would die happy.

Orestes: If only Orestes could hear this...

Electra: Sadly, stranger, I don't think I'd recognize my brother if he stood before me right now.

Orestes: Well, you were very young when you were separated.

Electra: [285] Yes, and I have only one friend who might still recognize him.

Orestes: Ah, the one they say took him out of harm's way?

Electra: Yes, our childhood servant, now very old.

Orestes: And... your father... I trust he found his way into the family tomb?

Electra: The only grave he found was the dusty street in front of our house, where they cast his body like so much garbage!

Orestes: [290] What! This news is painful even to one who is not part of the family, but do not spare me! Tell me all, so I may take your words, hard as they are, to your brother, who must certainly hear them. Ignorance may be bliss, but it is suitable only for slaves, so educate me, however much it hurts.

Chorus: [297] Our desire is the same as the stranger's, for living so far away from the city we know little of what happens there.

Electra: [300] If you insist, for we are all friends here, are we not? I will tell you all about the fate that befell our family, and then, stranger, I beg you to relate every word just as you hear it to Orestes, for these are his troubles as well.

[304] First, tell him how you found me, the rags I am forced to wear, penned here like any other animal relegated to this farm. Tell him of the filth that coats my body, and the shack that I have to call home in lieu of the palace. Here I must make my own clothes on the loom like a common slave or go naked and, as you have seen, I am reduced to lugging my own water from the river. Nor am I allowed to attend holy festivals, or take part in dances, and even so, lonely as I am, I keep my distance from the other women, for I am still a virgin, still blush like a girl to think of Castor, my uncle, who was my suitor before he ascended to the ranks of the gods.

[314] In the meantime, my mother sits upon her throne, which is balanced atop all the spoils of Troy, and at her hand cluster the Trojan women my father won when he plundered the city. Clad in robes woven from the wool of Troy's snow-covered Mount Ida and fastened with golden brooches, they are her servants now. And all the while the blood of my father still stains the floor black where he fell, and the man who murdered him gads about town with the reins of the dead man's chariot in one hand and, in the other, the scepter with which our father commanded the army of the Greeks.

[323] Agamemnon's tomb goes without honours, never yet having enjoyed holy libation nor received the green branches of the myrtle. The altar before it has never seen a single offering, though they do say that mother's new husband visits when he's in his cups so that he might dance upon the empty grave, chuck stones and gob upon the marble, asking, "So where is Orestes now, when he should be here protecting his father's tomb?"

[333] So please, stranger, tell Orestes that many people call for him to come home and take his rightful place. I am only their spokesman – my hands, my tongue, my miserable thoughts, my head shaved in mourning – and his father's blood cries out to him to return as well. It would be shameful beyond reason if the son

of he who sacked Troy could not find the courage to kill one insignificant man.

Chorus: [339] Look! Your husband, finished with his work for the day, returns home.

Enter the Farmer

Farmer: [341] What is all this? Who are all these strangers at my door? Why have they come to the gates of my farmhouse? To see me? For it is a shameful thing, I tell you, for a woman to be keeping company with young men.

Electra: [345] Dearest husband, there's no call for suspicion. The truth is that these strangers are here as messengers with news of Orestes! Strangers, please forgive my husband's rudeness, he meant no offense.

Farmer: Then does you brother still walk in the light of the living?

Electra: [350] So they say, and I pray they are not untrustworthy.

Farmer: And does he still think of you?

Electra: I hope so, but what can a man in far off exile do about it?

Farmer: Well then, what news have they brought of Orestes?

Electra: He sent them here to find out my troubles.

Farmer: [355] Well, they can plainly see some of them. Did you tell them about the rest?

Electra: Yes, I left out nothing of my shame.

Farmer: [357] Oh, good. Well, then we might as well invite them in! Please, friends, do step inside, and in return for your good news let us give you what meager hospitality we can. Allow me to get your baggage and spears – no, I insist, any friend of Orestes', after all… We may not have much, but let no one say we're ill-bred.

Orestes (to Electra): [364] This is the man who shams marriage with you so as not to disgrace Orestes?

Electra: Yes, he is called husband to the poor woman before you.

Orestes: [367] You see! It just goes to show, virtue is a tricky thing, isn't it? You just never can tell when it comes to men. It often happens that the sons of the noble turn out worthless, while excellent children regularly spring from the loins of men who are themselves of no perceptible value. I have seen wealthy men with heads full of air and poor men of enormous character. How then can we test to divide the good from the bad? What scale can we use? Not wealth, certainly. Lack of wealth, then? But poverty can drive men to evil out of basic necessity. Perhaps we should judge a man according to his prowess in battle?

[380] This man here is neither great nor noble by the standards of the Greeks, nor does he lay claim to a great family name. He is an ordinary man. Yet we have found him to be truly noble. When will we learn to distinguish nobility by the company a man keeps and the way he behaves? For it is men of this kind who rule our cities best, not to mention our homes, while the well-bred stud, with muscle and no brains, is only good if you want a model for a statue to decorate the park. Even in battle great size is no guarantee of valour – it all boils down to a question of nature and courage.

[391] Well, then, since by a more proper standard this must certainly be a noble house – as is the house of Agamemnon, whose son we represent – let us gladly accept its hospitality. I'd much sooner be welcome in the home of a poor, generous man than one who is merely rich. Still, I cannot help but wish it were your brother returned and leading us inside his reclaimed palace.

³⁹⁸ But perhaps he will come, for the oracles of Apollo do not err, though men are prone to misinterpreting them.

Exit Orestes and Pylades into the hut

CHORUS: We have a good feeling about this, Electra. Perhaps a change in your fortune slouches toward home even now.

ELECTRA: ⁴⁰⁴ How could you, husband? You know that the cupboards are bare! Don't you see they're better off than we?

FARMER: ⁴⁰⁶ Well, what of it? If they are as well-bred as they seem, they will be as content among the humble as they would the wealthy.

ELECTRA: ⁴⁰⁸ Since it's apparently slipped your mind that we're destitute, you'd best cut along to the home of my father's old tutor. He's lived and tended his flock by the Tanaus river, right at the point where it crosses out of Argos into Sparta, since he was driven from the city. Tell him of our visitors and ask him to fetch along some fit food. He will thank the gods to do it, I am sure, when he hears that the child he once rescued still lives. Of course, the news wouldn't be received nearly so well at the palace...

FARMER: ⁴²⁰ If that is what seems best to you, I'll go, but in the meantime you should hurry inside and see to our guests. A woman can always scratch together a decent meal when she has to, and as a matter of fact there's more than enough in the house to fill these men's bellies for one day, maybe two...

Exit Electra into the hut

⁴²⁶ It never ceases to amaze me, the stock people place in money. Yes, it allows you to treat guests lavishly, and, too, gold attracts the doctor when you need him, but the price of good, simple food enough for a day isn't so very much, and whether he is rich or poor, a man's stomach holds just about the same amount...

Exit the Farmer

CHORUS: ⁴³² Famous ships once sailed for Troy, propelled by countless oars, escorted by the dancing sea-nymphs and the dolphin, who loves the flute – he leapt and jumped among the dark-nosed boats as he led Achilles the swift runner and Agamemnon to the banks of the river Simois, near Troy.

⁴⁴² It was the sea-nymphs from the banks of the Euboea that bore the heavy golden shield and armor up along Mount Pelion, along the sacred woodland slopes of Mount Ossa, and through the rocks where they kept watch for the horse-man, Chiron. For he had raised Achilles the swift runner, the son of Thetis – herself a nymph – to be a light for Greece and a help to the sons of Atreus. We heard it in the harbour of Nauplia, from a man returned from Troy, that on Achilles' shield were engraved emblems – terrors to the Trojans. On the outer rim was Perseus flying over the sea with the head of Medusa in his hand, and beside him Hermes, great messenger of Zeus and son of Maia who enjoys the flocks and fields. On the shield's bowl blazed the chariot of the sun, driven by winged horses, and the stars danced in the heavens – the Pleiades, the Hyads. On the helmet were Sphinxes, the human prey they had trapped with their song in their talons. On the bit that covered Achilles' ribs was the clawed Chimaera, breathing fire and running, affrighted at the sight of winged Pegasus. Truly here were scenes that dimmed with fear the eyes of even mighty Hector! Such was the armor worn by the fearless leader of that legion that evil-minded Helen's base lust decimated, for which the gods in heaven will one day exact just retribution upon her and

we will see the red blood jet from her slender neck.

Enter the Old Man

OLD MAN: [487] Where is she? Where is my princess, the daughter of Agamemnon, whom I once raised and love so dearly? How steep is this path up to her house, especially for a withered old man. But when friends call, you must make your way as best you can despite your weak back and weaker knees...

Enter Electra from the hut

[493] O my daughter, there you are! As you asked I've brought you this young lamb, best of my flock, and also flowers for garlands, and cheeses fresh from the churn, and this deliciously odorous vintage, a gift of Dionysus – just a bit at once, mind you, but good to mix with weaker drink. In a moment we will take it to your guests, but first let me dry my eyes on these filthy rags I am reduced to wearing.

ELECTRA: [502] But why are you crying, old man? Not because my situation reopens wounds long since healed, I hope? Or do you still weep after all these years over Orestes' exile and the fate of my father, both of whom you helped raise. Much good though it did you, poor soul...

OLD MAN: [508] I received little enough reward for that, it is true. But there was one thing the bastards could not prevent me doing: I stopped by his tomb on my way here, and wept at the graveside. I poured a small libation for your father from this very wineskin I brought for your guests, and put down some myrtle.

[513] But right on the altar I saw a black-fleeced sheep, with its throat cut and its blood still warm! It was only recently slaughtered! And I also saw trimmed locks of golden hair made as an offering to Agamemnon!

[516] My child, who in the world would have had the courage to pay homage to that tomb? No one from Argos, surely. Could it somehow have been your brother, come here in secret to pay his respects to your father? Take a close look at this hair – place it beside your own and see if it is not the very same shade...

ELECTRA: [524] Oh, do stop prattling! Surely you don't really think that my brother, if he returned to the land of Aegisthus, would come fearfully and undercover? And what similarity could you hope to find between the locks of a great man trained in rugged games and the cropped tresses of a veritable slave girl like me? There is no match, because it is an impossibility that he could be here. I'm sure you could find a great many people you could match that hair to, old man, even some who aren't blood relations to Orestes.

OLD MAN: [532] Well, then go there and stand in the footprints left about the tomb – see if they match your own!

ELECTRA: Even if there were a footprint left in that rocky ground, what on earth makes you think the foot of brother and sister would be the same size?

OLD MAN: [538] But if your brother has come back to Argos, mightn't there be some scrap of clothing, woven by you and worn by him when I helped him escape, by which you might recognize him?

ELECTRA: [541] I was a child when Orestes fled Argos, and even if I had made some garments for him, they would hardly fit him now... Stop this. Either some stranger or some kind citizen of Argos took pity and left his locks on father's grave, despite the watchful eyes of Aegisthus' spies.

Old Man: Yes, mistress. Then introduce me to these guests of yours, if you would, for I should like to ask after your brother.

Electra: They'll be joining us presently.

Enter Orestes and Pylades from the hut

Old Man: 550 Well, they look noble enough, but none know better than we how apparently noble people may turn out evil. All the same, greetings to you, strangers.

Orestes: And to you, old man. Electra, where, or to which of your friends, does this ancient relic belong?

Electra: 555 This is the man who raised my father, stranger.

Orestes: What's this? The man who spirited your brother away and saved his life?

Electra: The very same – if, indeed, Orestes is still alive.

Orestes: Why does he peer at me so strangely, as if he's searching for marks on a silver coin?

Electra: 560 For pity's sake, old man! My apologies, stranger: I suspect he is just happy to meet a friend of Orestes, and perhaps hopes to divine an echo of him in you.

Orestes: Yes, well, Orestes is dear to me... But what is the old man doing now? Why does he circle round me this way?

Electra: I'm wondering that myself – for the gods' sakes, old man, what are you doing?

Old Man: O my lady, my daughter Electra, pray to the gods!

Electra: What would you have me pray about, then, something I have or something I lack?

Old Man: 565 That you may have the sense to grasp the gift, within your reach at this very moment, that some kind god has sent you!

Electra: Fine! I'm praying, I'm praying, all right? Now will you calm down, old one?

Old Man: My dear child, open your eyes and look upon this man!

Electra: Are you out of your mind? I've been looking at him!

Old Man: Perhaps I have indeed relinquished my senses, for it seems to me that I see your brother before me!

Electra: 570 How can you make such a cruel jest, and to me of all people!

Old Man: I tell you that I see the son of Agamemnon in this man!

Electra: How so? Persuade me!

Old Man: The scar that runs along his eyebrow! Orestes once fell and cut open his head, in the yard in front of your father's house, while you and he were chasing a fawn.

Electra: 575 It seems to me I do detect the mark of a fall...?

Old Man: Then what are you waiting for? Embrace him!

Electra: Orestes, could it be? Have you returned to me at long last? Come, let me hold you, as I never dared hope I would again have the chance to do!

Orestes: Nor did I, sister, after all this time!

Electra: 580 I never thought it would happen!

Orestes: I, too, gave up hope, if only for a while!

Electra: Is it really you, Orestes?

Orestes: 582 Yes, I am he, your best friend and hunting companion of old. Now if only we can catch up with our new prey... I know we will, for if we should fail, and evil were to escape justice for all time, we'd have no choice but to conclude that the gods no longer exist.

Chorus: ⁵⁸⁵ Finally the long awaited day has arrived! You have shone out bright and made a beacon of the city, calling home the miserable exile who wandered so far from his ancestral land. Now a god – a god! – brings about our victory, dear friend. Raise hands, raise voices, send up prayers to the gods so that good fortune accompanies your brother as he sets foot within the city.

Orestes: ⁵⁹⁶ Well then, I have had the sweet pleasure of your embrace, sister, and I will repay that warm welcome again and again in years to come. But you, old man, have arrived just in time to advise me: please tell us, what would you recommend as an adequate gift for the man who murdered my father, and my sweet mother who helped him do it? Do I have any friends in Argos? Am I alone, as bereft of allies as I am of means, or is there someone I should meet?

Old Man: ⁶⁰⁵ My child, you have no friends anymore: they left your side when your luck deserted you. It's rare that you find a man who will share your portion both good and bad, and as you are regarded as utterly ruined, with no hope of return, you must take heed of what I tell you now: everything depends on you, and you alone. Your own courage and your good fortune will dictate whether or not you are to take back your city.

Orestes: ⁶¹² Then by night or by day, what approach should I take toward my enemies?

Old Man: You'll have to kill them both.

Orestes: This is the goal and the crown I have set myself, but how can I take this victory?

Old Man: ⁶¹⁵ You won't do it by going inside the walls, however much you might wish it.

Orestes: Many watchmen and bodyguards, then?

Old Man: Oh, yes, for Aegisthus sleeps badly at night, awaiting your return.

Orestes: That is a pity – perhaps you might suggest a way I might better attempt to release the poor man from his agony?

Old Man: An idea does occur to me.

Orestes: ⁶²⁰ I hope it's good, and that I am its equal.

Old Man: It just so happens that I saw Aegisthus on my way here.

Orestes: That does sound promising – where?

Old Man: He was in the royal pastures, not so very far from these fields.

Orestes: You interest me strangely. What was he about?

Old Man: ⁶²⁵ He appeared to be preparing a feast for the goddess Nymphs.

Orestes: This offering, was it on behalf of the children he's got or one that's on the way?

Old Man: I only know one thing, he was armed only for ox-killing.

Orestes: How many were in his party?

Old Man: Just a couple of palace servants.

Orestes: ⁶³⁰ Were there any among them who would know me?

Old Man: They are all slaves imported from his former household, and as such would never have had occasion to see you.

Orestes: And how do you think that these household slaves would react if I were to kill him?

Old Man: The way slaves typically react in such a situation – which is an advantage to you.

Orestes: What would be the best way to get close to him?

Old Man: [635] Simply let him see you pass while he is the performing his sacrifice –

Orestes: I take it his fields are right beside the road then?

Old Man: Yes, and when he sees you he'll invite you to join in the feast.

Orestes: He'll find me an unpleasant dinner-guest, gods willing!

Old Man: After that you're on your own.

Orestes: [640] But where is my mother while all of this is happening?

Old Man: In Argos. She will join her husband when it is time for the feast.

Orestes: Why didn't she accompany him?

Old Man: Presumably she dreads the reproachful looks that would be directed at her and wishes to delay them as long as possible.

Orestes: The people are against her, then?

Old Man: [645] The people hate a promiscuous woman.

Orestes: How then will I get at her?

Electra: Leave our mother to me.

Orestes: Fine, but fortune has lent a hand in the murder of Aegisthus; who will aid you in your attempt?

Electra: Our friend here will help out.

Orestes: [650] Right then. How do you propose to kill mother?

Electra: Old man, you will go to Clytemnestra and tell her I've given birth to a son.

Old Man: And should I say when?

Electra: It's been nine days – that's how long a woman must stay ritually clean after childbirth.

Old Man: [655] But how will this facilitate your project?

Electra: I am confident she'll come as soon as she hears that I am confined to bed.

Old Man: But why? Do you really think she still cares for you, child?

Electra: Yes, I do, and she will be feeling bad about my child's low birth.

Old Man: Perhaps. Then what happens, when she arrives?

Electra: [660] Well, then she dies.

Old Man: Yes, yes, but she makes the journey to the doors of your house, and then...?

Electra: And then she'll only have to go a bit further to get to Hades.

Old Man: ...To be allowed to see that I would happily die myself.

Electra: You can't die just yet, old man, you still have to point the way for Orestes.

Old Man: [665] To the place where Aegisthus is sacrificing to the gods...

Electra: Yes, and then take my message to mother.

Old Man: I'll make it sound as if the words were coming right out of your mouth.

Electra: Now it is up to you, Orestes – you have drawn the first lot.

Orestes: I'm ready if my guide is.

Old Man: [670] It will be a pleasure.

Orestes: O Zeus, god of our fathers and defeater of my enemies...

Electra: ...have pity on us, for our suffering is worthy of your pity.

Old Man: Yes, pity them, for these children are your descendants.

Orestes: [674] O Hera, you who rule over the altars of Mycenae...

Electra: ...help us achieve victory, if you deem our intention just.

Old Man: Yes, grant vengeance to these children for the murder of their father.

Orestes: [678] And you, father, wrongly ensconced below the earth...

Electra: ...and Earth, my queen, on whom I beat my hands...

Old Man: ...defend, defend these children, so dearly loved by you.

Orestes: ...come, father, and bring an army of the dead to fight with us...

Electra: ...the men who helped you lay waste to Troy...

Old Man: ...and bring along, besides, all others in Hades who find adultery an offense to the gods.

Orestes: Do you hear, father, who suffered such horrible things at the hands of my mother?

Old Man: [682] Your father hears, believe me. But now it's time to go.

Electra: [684] I know it. Be a man like he was, Orestes, and see to Aegisthus. For if you are taken, then I too am dead, for I will spit my head on a double-edged sword. I retire now to make ready. When I hear happy news, the whole house will ring out in celebration. But if you die things will turn out very differently, that is my word to you.

Exit Orestes, Pylades, and the Old Man

[694] As for you ladies, be prepared to signal the results of this encounter. I will be standing at the ready with sword in hand, either way. Even if I am defeated, they will have to be content to take their vengeance on my corpse.

Exit Electra into the hut

Chorus: [699] There is an ancient tale told of a golden lamb, stolen from beneath its tender mother in the hills of Argos – pilfered by Pan, guardian of the fields who plays sweet music with his wondrous reed pipes. A messenger stood on a platform of stones and cried: "Go to the assembly, people of Mycenae, see this marvel, this fearful portent." And choruses cheered on the house of Atreus.

[713] Altars of hammered gold were built and a sacrificial fire burned round the town of Argos. The lotus flute, servant of the Muses, sent up a beauteous melody in praise of Thyestes, for he it was that had secretly wooed the wife of Atreus and with her help carried off the remarkable lamb, and told the people that the golden beast, was at his house, fleece and horn.

[726] It was then that Zeus changed the course of the blazing stars, reversed the shining sun and the gleaming face of dawn, and afflicted the western sky with the heat of his divine flame. The clouds flew northward and the land of Africa dried up, parched, thereafter denied the bounty that Zeus's sweet rain provides.

[737] That, at any rate, is what they say, though we don't give much credence to them: that, to the sorrow of the entire world, the sun turned its back and changed its position in the sky, all to punish one man. But such frightful stories bring profit to men and further worship to the gods. You would have done well to have remembered it, Clytemnestra, before you killed your husband – you who are a sister of glorious brothers.

[747] Wait! Listen, friends, do you detect shouting? Or have we been tricked by anxiety into hearing things, such as happens when someone claims to hear the thunder from Zeus?

No, there it is again! The breath of the wind rising from the city brings a message. Princess, come out of the house! Electra, come quickly!

Enter Electra from the hut

ELECTRA: ⁷⁵¹ Friends, what is happening? Have you heard something?

CHORUS: We know only that we heard a sound that contains some manner of death in it.

ELECTRA: I hear it, also, quite far off...

CHORUS: Very far, but growing nearer...

ELECTRA: ⁷⁵⁵ Is it the people of Argos who groan, or my people?

CHORUS: There is a great welter of voices, all confused...

ELECTRA: What you are saying bodes ill for me. Why do I hesitate to do what is inevitable for me?

CHORUS: Wait! Wait until we know for certain!

ELECTRA: It is over. We are lost. Otherwise where are our messengers?

CHORUS: ⁷⁶⁰ They will come. It's no small matter to kill a king.

Enter a Messenger

MESSENGER: Women of Mycenae, I bring the glad tidings that Orestes has triumphed. Aegisthus, killer of Agamemnon, lies dead, praise the gods!

ELECTRA: ⁷⁶⁵ But who are you? How can I trust that you speak the truth?

MESSENGER: What? Don't you recognize me?

ELECTRA: Uh...

MESSENGER: I was just here. The servant of your brother?

ELECTRA: Oh, yes, dear, dear... uh, servant! Yes, yes, it was only my great fear that prevented me recognizing your face, but I remember you now.

Could you repeat what you just said? Is the hated destroyer of my father finally dead?

MESSENGER: ⁷⁷⁰ Yes, he's dead – it's news so nice I give it to you twice...

ELECTRA: Oh gods, all-seeing Justice, at long last you have come! How did he die? Tell me everything, leave nothing out!

MESSENGER: ⁷⁷⁴ When we set out on our way from this house, we soon came to a wagon-path that led us to the pasture where the new king of Mycenae was. As we approached he was walking about a lush orchard, plucking sprigs of tender myrtle to put in his hair, and when he caught sight of us he called out, "Hello strangers! Who are you and from where do you hail?"

⁷⁸¹ Orestes replied, "We are from Thessaly, and headed for the Alpheus river to offer sacrifices to Zeus."

⁷⁸³ When he heard this, Aegisthus declared, "But today you stop here and share our feast as our guests, for as it happens I am sacrificing an ox to the Nymphs. In the morning you can be on your way, but for the time being accompany us to the shrine." And, so saying, he took us each by the arm and led us off the road – "I won't take no for an answer."

⁷⁹⁰ When we reached the garden he called out, "Someone fetch purifying water, that our guests may join us at the altar."

⁷⁹³ But Orestes told him, "There is no need, we only just left the pure waters of a flowing stream that we used to purify ourselves. If strangers may join with citizens in the sacrifice, my lord Aegisthus, then we are ready."

⁷⁹⁷ They were speaking thusly in the midst of the crowd when the slaves set aside the

spears they used to protect their master and set themselves to new duties, some bringing a bowl to catch the blood, others carrying baskets, still others lighting the fire, placing basins round the cauldrons round the base of the fire...

^{803} Then your stepfather took up the barley in his hands and threw it upon the altar with the words, "Nymphs of the rocks, bless me so that we may make many sacrifices to you in the future, both me and my wife who is at home, the daughter of Tyndareus. May we continue to fare as we now fare, and our enemies not so well." By which he meant Orestes and you. And as Aegisthus said these things, my master prayed for the exact opposite, though not aloud – that he would regain his family house.

^{810} Next Aegisthus took a straight-blade sacrificial knife from the basket, cut some hair from the calf and with his right hand placed it on the fire. Then he cut the throat of the calf as the servants lifted it on their shoulders, and once again he addressed your brother – "I have heard boast that the men of Thessaly are best at butchering bulls and also in breaking horses. Please, stranger, take the knife in your hand and prove whether what they say is true."

^{819} Orestes took the Dorian knife in his hands, shrugged his cloak from off his shoulders, and chose Pylades to help him in his task, waving away the slaves offering to assist. Taking hold of the calf's hoof, he skinned the hide faster than a runner can twice lap the horse-track, then opened up its sides.

^{826} Aegisthus took the sacred portions of the beast in his hands and examined them. On the liver was no hanging lobe, and the portal-vein and the gall bladder said plainly to him that some evil was imminent. His face darkened so that my master asked what was bothering him?

^{830} Aegisthus responded, "I fear some manner of ambush crouched at my door. The greatest enemy of my house, the son of Agamemnon, yet lives."

^{833} Orestes said, "How is it you live in fear of one exile when you rule an entire city? Come now, please – won't someone help us feast on the insides of this beast? Fetch me a Phthian knife instead of this Dorian one here, so that I can smash open the breast bone."

^{838} When they handed him the requested blade he turned to Aegisthus, who was leaned over, taking up the entrails one by one and examining each in turn, and raising himself on the tips of his toes Orestes struck the king square through the backbone. Aegisthus' body convulsed, twisting and jerking as he shrieked his agony, and he then fell dead in his own grimy blood.

^{844} When the servants saw this, they moved quickly for their spears – it was to be an army of men against two. But we, spurred on by courage, stood our ground, and Orestes shouted, "I have not come to this city to oppose my own people, but to exact deserved vengeance on the murderer of my father! I am Orestes, son of Agamemnon! Will you kill me now, you men who used to serve my father?"

^{851} When they heard him speak these words, they lowered their spears, and one old man who used to serve his family recognized him. Right-away they put a crown of flowing leaves on your brother's head, and shouted in celebration. And now he's on his way here to give you a gift. It isn't Medusa's head he brings, oh no, but that which belonged to the man you hated, who has now paid a bitter and bloody price for the bloodshed he caused.

Exit the Messenger

Chorus: ⁸⁶⁰ Set your feet to dancing, dear girl! Skip like a fawn! Your brother has won the contest for the crown, a far greater glory than any awarded at the Olympics! Come, sing a song of victory, and give us something to dance to!

Electra: ⁸⁶⁶ O bright light, chariot-mounted fire of the Sun, O Earth and Night on which I gazed so many years past: finally I am free to open my eyes and heart to you again, for the murderer of my happiness is at long last himself dead. Come, friends, let us bring from the house whatever I have kept hidden as adornment for the hair, so that I may wreath the head of my victorious brother when he arrives.

Exit Electra into the hut

Chorus: ⁸⁷⁴ That's okay. You dig out your brother's new crown, we'll delight the Muses and keep dancing, for once again our former, beloved rulers will be masters in this country – with justice on their side they have defeated the unjust! Come, let us sing and dance!

Enter Electra from the hut; Enter Orestes and Pylades with the body of Aegisthus

Electra: ⁸⁸⁰ Orestes, truly you are your father's son! Please accept these twisted garlands that I settle upon your brow with my own hands, for you return home not from some worthless sporting competition, but having dispatched the one who slaughtered our father.

⁸⁸⁶ And you, Pylades, my brother's companion in arms, most loyal of men, please accept a wreath from my hand as well, for you carry an equal share of glory in this victory. May both of you be blessed always!

Orestes: ⁸⁹⁰ Electra, we must credit the gods first and foremost as the ones responsible for all that has transpired today, and praise them first. Only then should you praise me, as their agent.

⁸⁹³ I return as the killer of Aegisthus, it is true, but to remove all possible doubt and anxiety from your mind I bring you the body that you may look at it. Set him out for the beasts to gnaw, or impale him high on a stake for the children of the air if it pleases you. Whatever you decide, he who was once your master is now your slave. You might even give him a piece of your mind.

Electra: ⁹⁰⁰ I... I am too ashamed to speak what is in my heart aloud, and yet, and yet...

Orestes: Why ashamed? Of what? Tell me your mind, at least, for there's nothing to fear any longer.

Electra: I am fearful of insulting the dead, for fear of repercussions.

Orestes: No one here would blame you, that is certain.

Electra: Ah, but the city is quick to criticize, and loves slander.

Orestes: ⁹⁰⁵ Get if off your chest, sister. We owe the man nothing but bile.

Electra (to the corpse of Aegisthus): Well, then... where to begin? And where end?

⁹⁰⁹ I fantasized for a long time about what I would say to you, Aegisthus, if I no longer had reason to fear you. I went over my speech last thing at night, first thing in the morning, every day. Now I am finally free I no longer feel a burning need to say much of anything, but I will try...

⁹¹⁴ You destroyed us, me and my brother, though we'd never done you any harm. You formed a shameful alliance with our mother to kill our father, the man who commanded

the whole Greek army – you, who never went to Troy yourself.

⁹¹⁶ Were you really so fond as to believe that mother would make a faithful wife? Did you somehow fail to notice she was already married when she took up with you? Anyone would think that a man who seduces another man's wife would be in a position to know just what he is getting, but not you, apparently.

⁹²⁵ Sure enough, your life together was torture, though you presented as if everything were fine to the world outside your house. Because, in the end, you could not ignore the fact that you had made an unholy marriage, and your bride had first hand knowledge that she had married a weak and evil man. As married people do, you helped one another carry your burdens, but, rotten to the core, all that meant was that she got a share of your evil, while you took a share of hers. Zero sum.

⁹³⁰ All of Argos whispered, "There goes the man who belongs to a woman who doesn't belong to him." It's a disgrace when a woman has all the power in the house, and the children are known in the city by the name of their mother and not their father. For when a man marries a woman of greater status than he, no one pays him any mind – they speak only of her, except to disparage him.

⁹³⁸ But what marked you as a truly quintessential fool was that you never knew it, because you were wealthy, and thought that was enough. Worldly riches are nothing and fade away – strength of nature, strength of character, is eternal, and determines whether or not we may survive the loss of riches, to live to see riches again. A fool and his money are soon parted, leaving only... a fool.

⁹⁴⁵ It would be indelicate for me, as a virgin, to discuss in detail your dealings with women, and decorum dictates I only hint as to my knowledge, but I witnessed disgraceful things in the short time we resided under the same roof. You thought you could get away with it because of your power and your physical charms, but I tell you frankly that your effeminate looks always turned my stomach. Personally, I prefer a man who looks like a man, and plays at war, rather than a boy who plays at dancing.

⁹⁵² Enough of this. You have consumed enough of my life and I'll waste no more of it upon you. So go ahead and rot, damn you, never knowing how time has found you out and meted out fit punishment. Be an example to other criminals that they can't outrun Justice, even if they happen to get a good head start – show them what awaits them at the finish line...

CHORUS: He did terrible things, and now has paid a terrible price. Justice may be slow, but it is sure, and inescapable.

ORESTES: ⁹⁵⁹ Take his body into the house and hide it in the shadows. I wouldn't want to spoil the surprise when mother comes calling.

Pylades carries the corpse of Aegisthus into the hut

ORESTES: On that subject, look who approaches...

ELECTRA: ⁹⁶⁵ Good. Here she comes. See how regal she looks, in her chariot and fine robes, riding blithely into our trap!

ORESTES: Are we really going to do this?

ELECTRA: Surely you feel no pity for her?

ORESTES: O god, how can I bring myself to kill the woman who bore me?

ELECTRA: ⁹⁷⁰ The same way she killed our father!

ORESTES: Forgive me, Apollo, but there was much in your pronouncement that seems unwise!

Electra: If Apollo is a fool, what man can then be called wise?

Orestes: He tells me to kill my mother!

Electra: Don't think of it as killing your mother, but avenging your father.

Orestes: ⁹⁷⁵ That I have already done, and no dishonour could attach to me: now I will be a matricide, when previously I was without stain.

Electra: You'll hardly be unstained if you fail to carry out the instructions of the oracle!

Orestes: I know! But could it be worse? These instructions I've been given are so awful I can't help but wonder if a demon impersonated Apollo?

Electra: ⁹⁸⁰ A demon? Throned and sitting on the holy altar in Delphi? I think not!

Orestes: But how can this be right?

Electra: Don't be a weakling! Go inside and prepare the same welcome for her that she and Aegisthus gave our father!

Orestes: ⁹⁸⁵ ...I'll go. But it is an awful place I go to, and a terrible thing I am about to do. If this is the will of the gods, then so be it. But it is a bitter game for children to be playing with their mother...

Exit Orestes into the hut; Enter Clytemnestra on her carriage, attended by several Trojan slave girls

Chorus: ⁹⁸⁸ Greetings, O queen of Argos, sister of the Dioscuri, Zeus' sons, Castor and Polydeuces, twin patron gods of sailors who breathe in the fiery heaven between the stars! Revered you are, for your great wealth and blessed life, and on this blessed day may you get the rest of what's coming to you.

Clytemnestra: ⁹⁹⁸ Step lightly from the chariot, women of Troy, and help me down. Good day ladies. We gave most of the spoils of Troy to the religious houses, you know, but I decided to keep these, the flowers of Troy, to decorate my home. They are but paltry compensation, and no substitute for Iphigenia, my beloved daughter, but I think them rather nice ornaments all the same.

Electra: ¹⁰⁰⁴ Very pretty. I would offer you my hand to assist you from your chariot, but fine as they are I fear that I would be no substitute, considering my reduced circumstances.

Clytemnestra: They have me, you needn't put yourself out on my account.

Electra: ¹⁰⁰⁸ No. After all, I am but prisoner, who like your pet women here has lived to see my home captured.

Clytemnestra: ¹⁰¹¹ Well, you can blame your father for that, for he brought it about when he betrayed those who deserved only his deepest love and devotion. It is time you heard the story from someone who knows, child, and I'll tell it gladly, for when bad reputation begins to take hold of a woman, she can become rather bitter about it. I am bitter. I have reason to be. If you will insist on slandering me, daughter, learn the facts first so you can do it right – if you can still find it in your heart to hate me.

¹⁰¹⁸ When my father bestowed me on your father, it was no part of his plan nor mine that my children should die as a result of it. But your father tricked Iphigenia – your sister – into believing she was going to marry Achilles, lured her from our home and spirited her away to Aulis where his ships were stuck.

¹⁰²¹ And there he stretched her above an altar and slashed her pale white throat. Now, if he had done this to prevent the capture of Argos, or to help our house in some way by sacrificing one child to save the other two, perhaps I could have forgiven him. But my daughter

died because Agamemnon's brother Menelaus couldn't control his slut!

1030 Even then I had no notion of killing your father, richly though he deserved it. But then he dared come back from Troy with a raving mad prophetess, and brought her into our bed! He tried to keep two wives beneath the same roof! Now, women can be foolish, too, why deny it? And when a husband desecrates the marriage bed, the woman may very well follow his lead and find a new partner of her own. She is criticized for this, while the man who made it happen receives no blame at all.

1041 Just imagine that it was Menelaus who had been spirited away to Troy as some trophy. Should I then have killed your brother so that I could sail off and save my sister's husband? How would your father have liked that? What would he have done to me?

1046 Yes, I killed him, and I did it in the only way open to me – I turned to his enemies.

1049 Now you can speak if you wish, and tell me why it was wrong for your father to die.

Chorus: 1051 There is some justice in what you have said, but it is shameful nonetheless. A sensible woman goes along with her husband in everything, and anyone who thinks differently is beneath contempt.

Electra: 1055 Bear in mind, mother, what you just said at the end – you told me that I had the freedom to say exactly what I wanted against you.

Clytemnestra: Yes, and I say it again, and won't retract it, child.

Electra: And you won't hear me out and hurt me after?

Clytemnestra: I won't do that. I want to know what you think.

Electra: 1060 Fine, then: let's get started. Above all, I really wish that you had more sense, mother. You and your sister Helen are equally beautiful; you are also equally vicious, and wholly unworthy of Castor, your brother. Helen went willingly to her own ruin, and you, mother, destroyed the most noble man in Greece. You claim to have done it for the sake of your lost daughter, but other people don't know you as I do, and I know better. Even before your Iphigenia was sacrificed to free the ships – the very second your husband had set out for war – you were sitting in front of your mirror, preening and fixing your hair. Any woman who goes out of her way to make herself beautiful while her husband is away is a dirty whore: there's simply no need for her to show her pretty face in public unless she's looking for trouble.

1076 I was there with you, mother! I know only too well that you alone, of all the Greek women, were happy as a lark when reports were that things went well for the Trojans, but when the tide turned and it began to look again as if you might have to face Agamemnon, returned from Troy, your mood became black as a stormy sky. It would have been so easy for you to have behaved properly! Agamemnon was not inferior to Aegisthus – you were married to the man that the whole of Greece had chosen as its commander! And seeing that your sister had behaved so disgracefully, this was your great opportunity to prove your virtue and gain your own glory and have it stand out in stark relief, for virtue fairly pops against so black a backdrop as the one Helen provided.

1086 But for a moment let's forget all of that, and tell me one thing – Agamemnon killed your Iphigenia; fine; but tell me, what wrong did I or Orestes ever do you? Are we not your children, too? How is it possible that once you'd killed our father you then proceeded to drive us from his house and used it as a dowry to buy yourself a lover? How is it this new husband of yours is not in exile himself for having sent one of the children you love so very dearly away? Why haven't you killed him in retribution for making my life more painful than my sister's death?

1093 If murder demands another murder in return I should kill you myself on behalf of our father, and then Orestes can kill me for killing you, and we can all be dead together. How would it be any less just than what you have done?

1097 Any man who marries for wealth or status is a fool, for he will find that a humble home and respectable marriage would have been preferable to his great one.

CHORUS: 1100 It's always a gamble when one marries a woman. Some marriages are good, others not so much: this I have seen.

CLYTEMNESTRA: 1102 Electra, you always preferred your father to me. I always knew, and I've learned to live with it. And I forgive you for what you have said. For you see, child, I regret the things I have done. You will never know how I suffer for all that I plotted! I allowed the anger that I had for my husband to push me much further than ever I should have!

ELECTRA: 1111 The time for mourning is long past: father is dead and nothing can change that. But why don't you seek to bring home your son now, who is wandering around from place-to-place in exile?

CLYTEMNESTRA: 1114 Because I am afraid. They say he is bitterly angry about his father.

ELECTRA: And what of me? How can you stand to see me treated so?

CLYTEMNESTRA: What can I do? You and Aegisthus are equally prone to anger and equally immoveable!

ELECTRA: The difference between us is that I am in pain! But my anger will eventually cease...

CLYTEMNESTRA: At which point he'll stop persecuting you, I know he will!

ELECTRA: 1120 That would be most magnanimous behaviour on the part of the stranger who lives in my house instead of me.

CLYTEMNESTRA: You see? There you go again!

ELECTRA: I'll keep silent, then, since I fear him...

CLYTEMNESTRA: Oh, enough of this circular talk – why did you summon me here, child?

ELECTRA: 1124 I think you know that I've given birth. I wanted you to make the appropriate sacrifice on my behalf... the one that is supposed to be made on the baby's tenth night in the air, according to custom. I have no experience of such matters, this being my first child, and don't know the appropriate thing.

CLYTEMNESTRA: But this is the proper work of the woman who delivered your child.

ELECTRA: I was my own doctor. I gave birth alone.

CLYTEMNESTRA: 1130 What? Is your house so distant from friends and neighbours?

ELECTRA: No one wants people as poor as we are for friends.

CLYTEMNESTRA: And look at you now. You've just given birth and yet you stand here so filthy and clad in rags. Of course I will sacrifice for the child!

1135 Come, girls, take the chariot and lead the horses to the feed stall. Find me here when adequate time has passed for a sacrifice to the gods, after which I go to meet my husband.

Exit Attendants of Clytemnestra

ELECTRA: ¹¹³⁹ Please, step into our poor home, mother, but take care not to let the soot that covers the walls get on your fine clothes.

...I just know you'll make the appropriate sacrifice to the gods.

Exit Clytemnestra into the hut

> The basket of grain is ready and the sacrificial knife already sharpened – the one that was already used to kill the bull, next to whom you will soon lie, cow, and thereafter you can marry him again in Hades... That is my favour to you, and all I ask in return is that you finally give father the justice he deserves.

Exit Electra into the hut

CHORUS: ¹¹⁴⁶ The evils are being repaid. The winds of the house's fortune change direction. Then it was our ruler, killed while he bathed – the very foundations groaned in sorrow, the stones on high echoed throughout the palace as the poor man shouted: "Cruel woman, why do you murder me who has finally returned after ten long years to my dear homeland?" Her luckless husband had returned after many years to his high stone walls, built by the hands of the Cyclopes, and she lay in wait for him, the sharp axe in her hands. O poor tormented husband – whatever madness made of that woman a mountain-lioness that prowled your oak-covered home, the tide of justice has finally reversed and now she is repaid for her shameful union.

CLYTEMNESTRA (FROM INSIDE): ¹¹⁶⁵ My children, in the name of the gods, do not slay your mother!

CHORUS: Do you hear the shouting?

CLYTEMNESTRA (FROM INSIDE): I am murdered!

CHORUS: ¹¹⁷¹ We shudder to hear you slaughtered at the hands of your children. God always hands out justice, be it sooner or later. You suffered greatly, but the things you did, hard-hearted woman, were unholy.

Enter Orestes, Electra, and Pylades from the hut; The corpses of Clytemnestra and Aegisthus can be seen behind them

¹¹⁷³ Here they are, splattered all over with the blood of their mother... Look, there lies their trophy – their act of sacrifice.

¹¹⁷⁵ There is no house, nor has there ever been, that has endured more suffering than the one that belongs to the family of Tantalus and Atreus.

ORESTES: ¹¹⁷⁵ Gods who see everything men do, look upon these bloody deeds, these bodies lying side by side, struck dead by my hand in payment for the wrongs done me.

ELECTRA: ¹¹⁸² Cry for me, brother, and what I have done. The hatred I bore for our mother burned so strong within me, and this is the sad result...

CHORUS: ¹¹⁸⁵ Cry for the fate of a mother whose unfathomable pain gave birth to unforgiving anger, for all her children brought her such sorrow it would have been better for her if she'd been barren. But she has paid her just debt now for the murder of their father.

ORESTES: ¹¹⁹⁰ Phoebus Apollo, the purity of the justice you directed I obtain remains a mystery to me, but the pain you've given me is crystal clear. Now my destiny will be that of a matricide, doomed once again to wander in exile, far from the land of Greece.

¹¹⁹⁴ But where can I go? What city will have me, what host will embrace me, the child who slew his own mother?

Electra: [1198] And what of my fate? Where will I go, who will ask me to dance, what marriage could I possibly make now?

Chorus: [1201] Their thoughts have shifted just like the wind now that the deed is done. They speak like the pious again, when only moments ago sister egged brother on to dreadful things, dear girl, when he was reluctant.

Orestes: [1206] You all saw her agony, how she revealed to us the pale breasts upon which we were suckled — and I answered by plunging in the blade! Oh god! When she crumpled to the ground all my strength left me, too!

Chorus: [1210] We know this only too well, for how could you not be agonized at the miserable cry of she who gave you birth...

Orestes: [1214] She reached her hand up to my face and cried, "My child, I beg you!" And the sword drooped in my hand...

Chorus: Poor woman! How could you bear to look at her as she took her final breath?

Orestes: [1221] I didn't look, but covered my eyes with my cloak like a frightened child, and blindly drove the blade through her throat...

Electra: [1224] And I urged you to it... I held the sword as surely as you, just not in my hand...

Orestes: Take it! Take my cloak and cover our mother's limbs! Clean her wounds and close them up!

O mother, you gave birth to your own death!

Electra: [1230] Look, mother: we who loved and hated you, cover you lovingly now... bringing a close to this family's great sorrows...

Enter Castor and Polydeuces from the sky above

Chorus: [1233] Look! Up in the sky! Over the top of the house something divine comes into view — for human beings don't travel through like that! What could compel gods to make themselves visible to the eyes of men?

Castor: [1238] Listen, son of Agamemnon, and see who is calling you! We are the twins of Zeus, brothers of your mother! I am Castor and beside me is Polydeuces, come from calming a storm at sea that was threatening the ships — for we saw from afar the murder of our sister!

[1244] Her punishment is just — but it was not just that you be the one to mete it out! Apollo is our lord, so we say nothing against him except that, wise though he is, what he told you to do was not wise, though we have to accept it — what Fate and Zeus ordered you to do.

[1249] Give your sister Electra to Pylades to be a wife for his house — and you yourself, Orestes, must leave Argos, never to return. Having killed your mother, the dreadful Furies — beast-faced goddesses — will hound you to and fro across the earth, so get you to Athens and embrace the knees of the sacred statue of Athena you find there. For though the foul creatures hiss round you like terrible serpents, she will keep you from their reach.

[1254] In Athens there is a hill dedicated to the war god Ares, where the gods first sat jury in a trial of murder, on account of Ares having killed Halirrothius, the son of Poseidon, ruler of the sea. He'd done it in vengeance for Halirrothius having taken his daughter in impious marriage. From that time onward they have argued cases there, and been commendably honest and scrupulous in their judgment. There it is you must stand your trial for murder.

[1264] But I'll call it now and predict that the voting pebbles will come up an even number on each side and deadlock will save you from death. If I know Apollo, he will take the blame for what you did upon himself — with some justification, since he was the one who ordered the matricide. And ever after the law will be that a hung jury means victory for the accused.

¹²⁷⁰ The dreadful Furies will shake with grief and rage at the decision, and go down into a crack in the earth alongside the hill of Athena, which will thus become a holy oracle for men to venerate them.

¹²⁷³ As for you, Orestes, you are tasked with founding a city in Arcadia, close by the streams of Alpheus and the Lycaean sanctuary, and this city will receive its name from you.

¹²⁷⁶ As to the body of Aegisthus – it will receive burial here from the citizens of Argos. Clytemnestra's brother-in-law, Menelaus, has only just returned to Greece after his long journey back from Troy, so he and Helen will bury her. Helen, by the way, has come from the land of Proetus in Egypt. Proteus, you ask? Yes, Proteus! She never went to Troy! Zeus, feeling impish, sent an image of her to Troy and the real Helen to Egypt! So there's that...

¹²⁸⁴ So then let Pylades marry your sister Electra, his virgin-wife, and let him take her out of the land of Achaea to his homeland. He can drop Orestes' other brother-in-law, that farmer fellow, off in the land of Phocis, where they will heap riches upon him.

¹²⁹⁰ Well, Orestes, it's a long trip, so you might as well get started. Make your way now – on foot, mind – across the narrow isthmus, and from there to that blessed hill in Athens. But don't be too downcast, for when you have fulfilled your latest destiny, you'll then have happiness and rest from your troubles.

Chorus: O sons of Zeus, might we have a word?

Castor: Of course: none of you are defiled by this murder.

Chorus: We were just wondering, if you are gods as well as brothers to the deceased woman, why don't you just speed the process along and refuse the Furies entry to this house?

Castor: Look, everything has happened the way it had to. Fate and necessity, dear ladies, fate and necessity. Well, that and the unwise proclamations of Phoebus Apollo.

Electra: ¹²⁹⁵ Might I ask a question as well, uncles?

Castor: Well... Oh, why not? Let's be honest: we place the blame for this murder entirely at the feet of Apollo, anyway. What is your question, child?

Electra: Just this: what oracle said that I had to murderer my mother?

Castor: ¹³⁰⁵ Your actions have been done as one. Your destinies are shared. The single doom of your house has afflicted you both.

Orestes: Well, sister, no sooner do I get to see you after so many years apart, than I am again robbed of your love. We are doomed to be apart, it seems.

Castor: ¹³¹¹ You just worry about yourself, young Orestes. She'll have a husband and a house. She hasn't suffered so badly and needs no pity, except that she has to leave Argos.

Electra: Oh yes? And what grief is greater than to be forced to leave the land of your birth?

Orestes: ¹³¹⁶ Leaving the land of your birth to be judged by foreigners in the murder of your mother, perhaps?

Castor: It won't be so bad: you'll get to see the holy city of Athena, after all.

Electra: ¹³²¹ O dear brother, hold me tight! Once again the curse of our mother separates us from our family home!

Orestes: [1325] Come to my arms, sister... Sing a lament for me, sometime.

Castor: Oh... oh... these words of yours are terrible even for the gods to hear. The gods above still feel pity and pain for the sufferings and toils of mortals.

Orestes: [1331] I'll never see your face again, dear sister...

Electra: And I shall never again feel your presence, or visit your grave...

Orestes: These are the final words we will ever speak to one another.

Electra: [1334] O my city – farewell! And a fond farewell to all of you, my fellow citizens!

Orestes: My sister, my most loyal love, must you leave so soon?

Electra: I cannot bear to remain, for my eyes well up with tears!

Orestes: [1340] Farewell Pylades. Go forward, and be good to your new wife...

Castor: [1342] Well, Polydeuces, off they go to be married, like we told them. And if you squint, Orestes, you can just now see the Furies approaching! If I were you I'd hurry for Athens while you can! They have snakes for hands and their skin is black, and they are on track to collect their terrible reward from you...

[1347] As for us, we're off to the Sicilian seas! For as you know, we are forbidden to offer safe harbour to the impious or the polluted, and there are some boats out there that require our attention.

[1354] So remember – always sail a straight course, and never ship out with those the gods have reason to hunt. It's good advice, nephew, and the most we can do for you.

Chorus: [1357] Farewell. It just goes to show you: the man who does no evil avoids troubles and leads a blessed life.

Exit all

Translated from the Greek by Stephen Russell, PhD

English by Jonathan Allen and Stephen Russell

Chapter 17
Euripides
The Bacchae

THE STORY: *The Bacchae* is a revenge tragedy that tells the tale of the return of the god Dionysus to his native city of Thebes. Cadmus founded Thebes when his father Agenor forced him to leave his city of Tyre. Agenor ordered his son to go out and search for his sister Europa, whom Zeus had taken off to Crete on his back when he disguised himself as a bull.

CHARACTERS

DIONYSUS
CHORUS (OF BACCHAE – FEMALE WORSHIPPERS OF DIONYSUS)
TIRESIAS
CADMUS
PENTHEUS
AGAVE
SOLDIER
MESSENGER #1
MESSENGER #2

SCENE: Thebes – before the palace of King Pentheus

Enter Dionysus

DIONYSUS: I have come, Dionysus, the son of Zeus, to the land of Thebes. I was born when the daughter of Cadmus, Semele, produced me, helped as she was by the lightning blast of fire.

⁵ Here I stand at the stream of Dirce and the waters of the Ismenus river – I have taken the form of a mortal instead of my normal appearance as a god. I see over there in front of the palace a memorial to my lightning-struck mother – it's her grave. I can also see the ruins of her shattered home and household, where it seems that the living fire of Zeus still keeps its smoky blaze – forever affirming the deathless anger that Hera held against my mother.

¹⁰ I praise Cadmus – he made this tomb of my mother into a sacred shrine, and I was the one who surrounded her grave with the green cluster of the grapevine.

¹³ I've left the gold-rich lands of Lydia and Phrygia far behind, made my way through the sun-burnt plains of Persia, the troublesome lands of the Medes, the walled towns of Bactria, and all the way through prosperous Arabia and all of Asia – where cities with their beautiful and inspiring towers lie along the salty sea, populated by Greeks and barbarians alike.

¹⁹ I have come here, the first Greek city that I've entered, only after I started the dances in those other places and established my rites of worship there, so that I would be clearly revealed to everyone on earth for what I truly am – a god.

²³ Of all the places in Greece I decided that the first one which I would stir up the women with

cries and shouts would be Thebes. It's here that I attached the skin of a fawn to the flesh of my Maenads and put a thyrsus in their hands – that spear of ivory. I did this here because the sisters of my mother – who should have known better, of all people – had the hubris to say the Dionysus was not born the son of Zeus. Instead they said that my mother Semele was seduced by some foreigner and that Cadmus cleverly told her to deflect the shame by pretending that she had been seduced by Zeus. These same people say that she was killed by Zeus because he grew angry at the lie she told, and so he blasted her with a bolt of lightning.

[32] Because of this offence, I have stirred the women of Thebes into a frenzy and have driven them out of their homes and into the mountain. They are no longer in their right minds, but I've compelled them to wear the clothing of my cult – they are now my Maenads. Every woman from the race of Cadmus, all the women I could find in Thebes – I sent them out of their home in an insane rage. Even the daughters of the former king Cadmus, the sisters of my mother, are there – they are all mixed up together over there on the mountain, running wild under the green fir trees, or some of them are sitting on the exposed rocks.

[39] This city is going to have to learn its lesson. Since it doesn't yet recognize or acknowledge my cult and its rites, I'm going to teach it the Bacchic revelry, and I'll get revenge for the way they impugned my mother Semele. They'll soon come to see that I am a god, and that I am the son of Zeus.

[43] Cadmus is no longer the king – he has handed over the title and rule to Pentheus, the son of his daughter Agave. He's now waging the fiercest war against recognizing me as a god. He won't allow anyone to pour libations to me, and he purposefully leaves out my name in his prayers. Thus, I am going to give ample proof to him, and to every man in Thebes, that I am very much a god.

[45] When my worship is finally established here in Thebes, then I'll turn my foot and make my way to reveal myself to men in other lands and other cities. But if this city of Thebes decides that it's going to rise up in anger, gather an army, and try to forcibly drive my Bacchae from the mountain, then I'll turn into a fierce warrior and will unite my Maenads into an even more powerful army than these people could even imagine. Because of all these things, I've decided to put my divine form aside as I walk hereabouts in the disguise of a mortal man.

[55] Now come, my women, my Bacchae, my worshippers – I led you out of the battlements of Lydia, from Mount Tmolus and its rampart. I collected you as my companions when I journeyed from those barbarian lands. You are my assistants and companions. Now lift up those drums – the ones that are native to Phrygia, the one that I discovered along with the one that belongs to mother Rhea – and beat those drums for all they are worth at the gates of the royal house of Pentheus. Make everything in the area resound with the noise of your drums, so that the whole city of Cadmus will take notice.

[62] For the moment I'll take my leave and join my Bacchae on the side of Mount Cithaeron, and I'll take my turn in their dances up there.

Exit Dionysus; Enter the Chorus

CHORUS: [64] From the land of Asia, having left sacred Mount Tmolus, I hurry with my sweet labour for the Thunderer – I hurry to do the work of the god, no work at all, shouting the praises of Bacchus.

⁶⁸ Who is out there on the road? Who is out there on the streets? You there – you! Get away from your homes, come out and join us! Let's all together devote our good-omened voice to the god, and I'll sing the praise, a song for Dionysus, singing things that are always recognized as belonging to the god.

⁷³ O blessed are they whoever in their happiness can know the rituals of the gods. They keep their minds and lives pure, and their souls are turned to mountains and the Bacchic dancing, cleansing everything with Bacchus.

⁷⁸ They are also celebrating the rites of the great mother goddess – Cybele – shaking the thyrsus high and all about, above their heads that are crowned in ivy. Blessed are they, for they serve the god Dionysus.

⁸³ Go Bacchae! Go Bacchae! Bring down the Thunderer, Dionysus, the god, the son of a god – bring him down from the mountains of Phrygia into the broad open streets of Greece. Bring down the Thunderer!

⁸⁸ His mother gave birth to him through labour pains that were brought on my force. He was cast out of her womb when the lightning bolt of Zeus struck her, leaving her to die because of the thunderous blow.

⁹⁴ Right away Zeus the son of Cronus took him up and saved his son. He found a way to give him a birth, found a safe place to house him until birth, so he bound the boy in his upper thigh and he set him firmly in there, holding it all together with golden pins, keeping him hidden from Hera.

⁹⁹ He was born when the Fates said that his time was right – a god with the horns of a bull and covered with the crown of a snake. This is the reason that his Maenads cover themselves with wild serpents in their hair.

¹⁰⁵ O Thebes, nurse of Semele, let your hair be crowned with ivy! And I hope you are teeming all over with the creeping green vine, and that the berries turn red everywhere. O Thebes, join with the Bacchantes, grab branches of pine or oak, cover yourselves with the skins of spotted fawns and with the locks of wool from the white lamb. And take care to respect the holy and proud thyrsus of the god.

¹¹⁴ Straightaway let the whole land dance, to wherever the Thunderer leads his worshipping revelers. To the mountain! To the mountain! There a crowd of women is waiting, having left their looms and spindles, driven mad, possessed by the power of Dionysus.

¹²⁰ And I praise the holy places in Crete, the caves there that served as shelter to give birth to young Zeus. Inside the caves, the Corybantes found this drum for me, three times covered in circles of stretched cowhide. And they supplied the beat for the swift intense Bacchic dance and added the sweet sounding tune of the Phrygian lyre.

¹²⁵ This was the gift of the Corybantes, the warriors who sheltered the baby Zeus, to his mother Rhea – they gave her the holy drum to be used by Bacchantes. Then the satyrs, maddened with happiness, brought if from the goddess mother and they set it down to be used in the dances that we celebrate every third year – a joyful tribute to Dionysus.

¹³⁵ On-hey-Dionysus! He is welcomed in the mountains, whenever he falls toward the earth and joins the festive gatherings. He runs around clothed in his holy garments of fawnskins; he hunts after the blood of slaughtered goats, with raw uncontrolled flesh-eating joy; he hurries toward the mountains of Phrygia,

to the mountains of Lydia – he is the Thunderer, Dionysus, who leads us all. On-hey!

¹⁴¹ The earth is flowing with milk, it's flowing all around with wine, and everywhere I look I can see the nectar of bees.

¹⁴⁴ Just like the smoke that streams from incense in Syria, Bacchus holds up and waves his bright-burning torchwood in motion. He is running, he moves quickly, he lights the stragglers on fire, he sets their cries in motion, throwing out his soft hair into the air, and to their Bacchic screams he adds these words –

¹⁵² "O run my Bacchae, O run my Bacchae – rich with the ornaments from golden Tmolus, celebrate Dionysus in song and dance. Do it to the sound of thundering drums – on-hey! – praising and exalting the god of the shout, your god Dionysus, with Phrygian cries and shouts of battle!"

¹⁶⁰ Whenever the melodious and sacred flute roars out a sacred song, then there's a gathering together – run wildly to the mountain, to the mountain! It's then and there that she takes pleasure – just like a foal with her grazing mother, she leaps about on swift feet: she is a Bacchant.

Enter Tiresias

TIRESIAS: ¹⁷⁰ Hey there – who is guarding the gates? Someone call Cadmus to come out! Yes, get Cadmus, the son of Agenor, who was forced to leave city of Sidon in Tyre and came here to build these towers and walls in Thebes.

¹⁷³ Go, someone, get him! Tell him that Tiresias wants to see him. He knows why I'm here. He and I made an agreement, even though we are both old, to place a thyrsus in our hands and to cover ourselves in fawn skins and to crown our heads in ivy.

Enter Cadmus, dressed as if he were a Bacchant

CADMUS: ¹⁷⁸ My old friend, I could hear your voice from inside the house – for you have a wisdom that is apparent whenever you speak. I've come out to join you, wearing the costume that is required to celebrate the god. And it's only right that I should do this. After all, he is the son of my daughter Semele, and he has been revealed to mortals as the god Dionysus, so it's our task to praise him as much as we can.

¹⁸⁴ Where should we go to dance? Where do we put our feet and shake our old and grey heads? Please tell me Tiresias, one old man to another old man, for in matters such as these you are wise.

¹⁸⁷ I hope that I'll never grow tired of beating the ground with my thyrsus , night and day. It's such a sweet thing to forget that we are old.

TIRESIAS: ¹⁹¹ I feel just the same as you – I feel like a young man again and long to put my feet into the dances.

CADMUS: And so should we grab a chariot to bring us to the mountain?

TIRESIAS: I think it would be better to walk – that's the best way to do proper honour to the god.

CADMUS: That sounds fine – so even though I am old, let me guide you as we walk.

TIRESIAS: I think that the god will guide us there quite easily – we don't need to worry too much about that.

CADMUS: ¹⁹⁵ Are we the only men in the city who are going to dance for Bacchus?

TIRESIAS: Yes, we're the only ones who are in our right minds, the only ones who can see straight. The others are all blind.

CADMUS: But we're spending too much time delaying here – here, take my arm.

TIRESIAS: Here – place your hand on mine.

CADMUS: I'm a man, born a mortal – and I'm not one who scorns the gods.

TIRESIAS: [200] That's right. Nor do we try to use cleverness in dealing with the gods. No, we have inherited the speech, customs, and traditions of our ancestors – they're old and have passed the test of time. No trickiness of thinking of sophistry can knock down our traditions, our thought – not even the smartest fellows in the room could do it. Perhaps people will say – "Aren't you ashamed, as old as you are, to dance around here like this with your head all decked out in ivory?" The answer is no – I am not ashamed. The god doesn't care who's young and who's old. It's the obligation for all of us to dance – the god wants to receive the same honour from all of us alike. He's not going to exclude anyone from his worship.

CADMUS: [210] Because you're blind and can't see the light, Tiresias, let me act as a type of prophet for you in this once instance, as I tell you what I see happening at the moment. Pentheus is on his way here right now, crossing through the palace in a hurry. Pentheus, the son of Echion – this is the boy that I decided to leave my throne. Oh my – he's really in quite a state of excitement! What on earth is he going to say?

Enter Pentheus, who doesn't notice the others at first

PENTHEUS: [215] I happened to be away, out of the city, but I nevertheless heard reports that that are all kinds of new troubles in Thebes. I hear that the women have all left their homes and have all run off to the dark mountains, dressed up as if they are Bacchantes. They're rushing about up there, acting all wild and out of control, dancing praises to this new god, Dionysus, whoever he is.

[221] So now the women are all out there, and right in the middle of them sit giant bowls filled to the brim with wine and then one by one the women sneak off into the dark places of the forests, where they do all kinds of favours to men, serving their lusts and satisfying them sexually.

[226] They actually call themselves priestesses – these Maenads! Ha! They're hardly priestesses of this god Dionysus that they claim to worship. No – rather, they are slaves of Aphrodite. I've already taken quite a few of them – my guards have led them back in chains and placed them in jail for their own safe-keeping. As for the others, all of them out there – whoever is running about madly near the mountains and behaving like wild animals – I'm going to take them and trap them in nets just as if they were wild animals. Yes, I'll even do this to my own mother, who gave birth to me with my father Echion. And I'll also do this to my aunts Ino and Autonoe, the latter of whom gave birth to Actaeon. It won't take me any time at all to trap them in my iron nets, and then I'll quickly finally put an end to all of this disgusting behaviour of these Bacchantes.

[234] There's a story out there that some foreigner has come to Thebes from Lydia. He's apparently some kind of wizard who really knows how to use his charms. I hear that he's got these flowing locks of golden hair, and that it's filled with delightful perfume, that his eyes are filled to the brim with the charms and wine-induced spells of Aphrodite. He spends all his nights and days in the mountains, out there with our women and girls, showing off his foreign rituals, his mysteries, his perversions.

²³⁹ Just let me bring him here and place him under the roof of my house - that will stop him rattling his thyrsus about and shaking his hair around. I'll cut his damn head off – that's what I'll do!

²⁴¹ I mean, the fellow claims that he's the god Dionysus, and says that he was stitched up into the upper thigh of Zeus just after he was burnt to ashes along with his mother by the bright flash of lightning because she lied and told that tale that she had slept with Zeus. Don't all of these terrible things make him deserving of a hanging? Isn't it right to answer hubris with hubris, whoever it is that this stranger claims to be?

²⁴⁸ But what's this? O god! I can't believe this – right before my very eyes I see the prophet Tiresias all decked out in a fawn-skin! And right there next to him is my grandfather Cadmus – the father of my mother. I can't believe the sight of you there, walking around with that cane and pretending that you are a Bacchant. You look so ridiculous! O gods, it makes me so ashamed, dear grandfather, to see you behaving this way in your old age. Have you gone senile? Come on now and cut all of this nonsense out – just get rid of that ivy and drop that thyrsus of yours. Come on, grandfather, please let go of that stuff.

²⁵⁵ Tiresias, you must have been the one who convinced him to do this. You're in favour of having a new god for the people of Thebes so that you can take in the profits for predicting all of the burnt offerings that will have to be made, and for reading the omens for the citizens. Good grief, if you weren't an old man then I wouldn't hesitate to chain you up with the other Bacchantes there who are trying to bring in their foreign rituals to Thebes. It's like I always say – if there's wine at any ceremony in which women are present, then you can be sure that the whole thing is rotten and that the people there are up to no good.

CHORUS: ²⁶³ That's blasphemy! O stranger, don't you have any respect for the gods? And don't you have any respect for Cadmus, your grandfather who planted the dragon's teeth that brought up those earthborn men in Thebes? Are you, the son of Echion, going to act in such a disgraceful way to your own house?

TIRESIAS: ²⁶⁶ If you give a wise man the opportunity to state his case, his eloquence and intelligence will come to the front quickly and it won't seem like such an amazing accomplishment. But you are quite shallow in what you say and, even though your words pour out of mouth so smoothly that you appear to be rather wise, you're actually quite foolish. Any man who speaks rashly without thinking first is revealing who he really is – that is, a useless, foolish, and stupid citizen.

²⁷² This new god, the one you are mocking so strongly, I can predict will one day have a level of greatness and honour throughout the whole of Greece. For, young man, human beings have found two supreme blessings. The first one is the goddess Demeter, who is the Earth – or you can call her whatever name you like. She is the one who raises mortals from the soil, both in giving birth to them and in providing them with grain.

²⁷⁸ But after her there came the son of Semele in opposition, or perhaps even as a complement, for he is the one who invented the wet drink of the grape and gave it to mortals. For this gift from him – this wine – helps mortals who are feeling pains be able to withstand their grief. And whenever men are filled with the juice of the grape, then it helps them fall asleep easier, and it also helps them forget all

of the evils that they might have encountered during the course of the day. It's the only effective cure for misery, toil, and pain. And when we make our offerings to the gods, it's the gift of this god – wine – that we pour out in our libations, hoping that the other gods may grant us the good returns that we seek.

286 Are you making fun of the idea that Dionysus came to full term and was born from the thigh of Zeus? Well then, let me tell you how to read this story and what it all means. When Zeus saved his son from the bolt of lightning that he sent at Semele, he brought him right away up back to Olympus with him. But Hera was upset about this and so she made plans to destroy this child if she could and hurl him down from heaven.

291 So Zeus came up with a plan – the kind of device that only a god could come up with – and he countered Hera by breaking off a bit of the ether, the sky, and then formed it into the shape of the young Dionysus. He then showed this piece of the sky to Hera, but in time people eventually messed up the story and started to confuse the word sky with thigh and argue that Dionysus was sown into the thigh of Zeus. Many of them still insist that Zeus sewed the god into his thigh when in reality the god of gods just showed the image of the young god to Hera, an image that was fashioned out of the sky, so that she would no longer pursue the young boy.

298 What is more, this child has the gift of prophecy and his followers, his Bacchantes and Maenads, also have the gift of prophecy. For whenever the god enters the body of a man he fills that man with the gift of prophecy.

300 And he even lays claim to the same realm that is usually reserved for the war-god Ares. Sometimes you might look at an army all gathered up in proper array and ready for battle. But then you look at them and note how they are filled with a combination of panic, fear, and insanity. It's Dionysus who brings this madness upon them.

306 And you might even have the chance to see him at the rocks near Delphi, leaping across the mountaintops with his torches, moving quickly and shaking his Bacchic branch, and bounding his way through the whole of great Greece.

309 But, Pentheus, just listen to me and obey my words. Don't start thinking that you have any special divine-like power over men, and don't start thinking that whatever springs from your mistaken and sick mind is wise. No, you're delusional, and you need to welcome this god to Thebes. Put some ivy on top of your head. Pour some libations with us and come do the dance with us and praise the god.

314 Dionysus is not going to force a woman to fornicate. In every circumstance it is her character and nature that keeps her chaste and from acting improperly. But even during the rites of Dionysus, a good woman will not be corrupted – she'll still act as properly as always.

319 You see, you are happy whenever people might stand before you outside your gates and when the city praises the name of Pentheus. And it's just the same with the god – he likes to hear people praise him and his name.

322 And this is why Cadmus and I – whom you mock – have decked ourselves in ivy and are going to join the dances to honour the god. The two of us may be old, and we may look silly, but we must dance to honour the god.

326 There's no way that I'm going to wage

war against the gods, nor are you going to persuade me at all by your words, for you are mad, really really mad right now. And there's no drugs that are available that might be able to cure you, for you are already suffering from the drug of madness.

Chorus: ³²⁸ O old man, Phoebus Apollo would be pleased with your words. You are very wise to honour the Thunderer, for he is a great god.

Cadmus: ³³⁰ My boy, Tiresias has given you some good advice. Your home right now is right here with us – and don't close the doors on the laws that belong to the gods. You're not thinking clearly at all right now – your thoughts are all mixed-up and are rushing in all kinds of different directions. You're hurrying this way and that, and even though you believe that you are thinking you're not thinking at all.

³³³ Even if this Dionysus is not a god, as you claim, just let himself be called a god and go along with it. Even if it's not true, it's a really nice fiction, for this will mean that Semele will then become the mother of a god, and this birth will give all kinds of honour to our family.

³³⁷ I mean, you saw what happened to your poor cousin Actaeon and how he died. He was torn apart by those dogs of his – those man-eating dogs that he himself raised from pups. They attacked him and ripped him into shreds because he foolishly said that he was better at hunting than Artemis.

³⁴¹ Keep in mind what happened to him when he angered a god – and don't let what happened to him happen to you. Come here now, let me put this crown of ivy on your head, and come join us as we go to the mountain to celebrate and pay tribute to the god.

Pentheus: ³⁴³ Get your hands off me! You can go and worship your Bacchus, but don't pollute me with your foolishness. I'm going to catch that fellow who has taught you all of this silliness, and I'm going to make him pay for what he's doing.

³⁴⁶ I've just ordered some of my attendants, as many as I could find, to go to the places where this so-called prophet is doing his thing. I've told them to lift the whole place up with crowbars and overturn it from the top to the bottom – breaking everything that they see. I told them to throw his garlands out to the winds – this will be sure to make him angry.

³⁵² And then I ordered all of the others to go and search the city and look for that foreigner, the one who looks so much like a woman and is bringing his pollution to the women here and destroying the marriages in Thebes. And when they take him, they're going to tie him up in chains and bring him to me immediately. He's going to die in the way that he deserves – from a stoning. He'll learn to regret the day that he brought his Bacchantes here to Thebes.

Tiresias: ³⁵⁸ O, you fool! You have no idea how reckless your words are and that you'll learn to regret them. Before I called you mad, but now you're talking in a way that is even more insane.

³⁶⁰ Cadmus, let's go and pray on behalf of this madman and on behalf of the city. We'll pray to the god that he won't do any harm to Thebes.

³⁶³ Follow me with your ivory staff. Lead me with your hands and I'll do my best to hold you upright. It would be a shame for two old men like us to stumble as we make our way to the mountain.

³⁶⁵ But we have to go there all the same. For it's important that we go and pay our service to Bacchus, the son of Zeus.

³⁶⁸ And Cadmus, we have to see to it that Pentheus will not bring misery to your house. I'm not speaking this as a prophecy, but rather as a fact. For a fool like Pentheus always says foolish things.

Exit Cadmus and Tiresias, and Pentheus goes back into the palace

CHORUS: ³⁷⁰ O Reverence, queen of the gods, O Reverence, you who cover the golden earth with your wings – have you heard what Pentheus is saying? Do you hear the unholy hubris that he is shouting against the Thunderer? That he is shouting against the son of Semele – the god who is the first god of all the blessed gods at the festivals – do you hear what Pentheus is saying against him?

³⁷⁹ The god gave these gifts and holds these domains – he is in charge of sacred revelry in the dances, laughter to the tune of the flute, and the suspension of cares. Whenever the brightness of grapes may come into the feasts of the gods or the bowls of wine cause those who are in the middle of the ivy-crowned festivals to fall down in sleep – the god has caused all of this to happen.

³⁸⁷ Any tongue that runs unchecked – defiant, lawless, foolish, and unwise – brings only disaster to the speaker. But a life of leisure and calm, tranquil thoughts – that kind of good sense can keep a family together and prevent a house from being destroyed. Those who live in the heavens, the gods in the sky, may be far away from us, but they still see all that mortals do. And what often passes for wisdom is nothing but foolishness. It's foolish for people to lift our thoughts so high as if we are gods ourselves. Our lives are short and have an end – and men who aim at great things may often lose the things that are right in front of them now. Men who do such things are ill advised, mad, insane.

⁴⁰³ O let me come to Cyprus, the land and home of Aphrodite, where the delightful and charming hearts of Desires and Loves live and keep themselves ready to cast their spells on mortals, and the place where the hundred-mouthed barbarian river brings ripe fruit to Paphos even though it receives hardly any rain. O let me come to lovely Pieria, the most beautiful home of the Muses, and to the holy slope of Mount Olympus. O lead me there, O Thunderer, O Thunderer, O you, O great god of joy and pleasure, O Dionysus, god of ecstasy! That is the place that the lovely Graces go, and there we can find Desire. This is the place where it is right for the Bacchantes to celebrate and experience our joy.

⁴¹⁷ The god, the son of Zeus, rejoices in the festivities and the feasting. He loves the goddess Peace, a goddess so generous in her gifts and a protector of the young. The god gives his wine to both the rich and poor alike – the joy of this grape he begrudges to nobody. But he hates the man who scorns these rites and doesn't give them their due, and he hates the man who mocks his birth and life.

⁴²⁵ Those who find happiness in the day will find double that happiness at night, thanks to the god, for those men pass through life happy and they keep their thoughts simple and avoid the kind of hubris in their thinking that can cause men to try to stand above others and try to become equal to the gods in wisdom. But that which is ordinary, what the common people do, and the things that the

simple people think and believe – that is good enough for me.

Enter Pentheus from the palace; Enter several Soldiers from the other side, leading the captive Dionysus

SOLDIER: 434 Pentheus, here we are – we caught the prey that you sent us out to catch. We went off eagerly to find this wild thing, but we found that the beast was altogether tame when we approached him. He didn't bother trying to run away from us or hide, but he instead held his hands right out for us, not afraid of us at all and completely willing to go along with us.

434 He didn't turn pale at the sight of us or lose the blush of wine that was obvious in his cheeks, and he just stood there, smiling, even laughing at us, agreeing all the while that it was necessary for us to lead him away in chains. He was patient, waited for us to tie him up, and he even helped us in places, which made me feel rather ashamed of what I was doing. I became embarrassed, so I said to him – "Listen stranger, please don't blame me for leading you back like this. I'm just obeying the orders of Pentheus, who told me to go out and bring you back to him in chains."

443 But, my king, as for those women, those Bacchantes, whom you ordered us to tie up and then carry off and place in the dungeon of the prison – they've somehow been freed of their chains and have escaped. They're gone, run off, and running and leaping away toward the mountain, calling up to their god the Thunderer. The chains that were on their legs broke right off all on their own, and the bars and doors to the prison came right off without any mortal placing a hand upon them.

449 My lord, this man here has come to Thebes and he has brought with him many amazing things – there are all kinds of miracles taking place. I can't say anything more than that, so I'll have to leave the rest of it to you.

PENTHEUS: 451 Good work, soldier – you can untie his hands. We have him in our net now. He may be speedy and tricky, but I think there's no way that he'll be able to escape us now.

453 So now, as for you, stranger… well, you do appear to be quite the attractive fellow… at least women would find you to be attractive. Of course, that's the reason that you came to Thebes.

455 Hmmm…your long flowing hair – you're not much of a wrestler, are you? – the way your curls stream down along your cheeks, all-full of desire. Your complexion is very pale, your skin is very white and soft. You must work quite hard to get it to such a shape – you must stay out of the sun but instead do your business in the shade. Yes, I think that you must be doing your work at night, when you hunt for the joys of Aphrodite, that life of sex, bringing that beautiful body of yours wherever you want, to satisfy your desires.

460 So then, tell me first of all who you are, who your parents were, and where you are from.

DIONYSUS: There is nothing to boast about. It's quite easy to say in fact. I'm sure you've heard of Mount Tmolus and the flowers that grow there?

PENTHEUS: I know the place – it forms a ring around the city of Sardis.

DIONYSUS: I come from there. My fatherland is Lydia.

PENTHEUS: 465 What god and what rituals are you trying to bring into Greece?

Dionysus: Dionysus made us come here – he's the son of Zeus.

Pentheus: Is this some other Zeus than the one we have here? One that breeds new gods?

Dionysus: No – it's the same god, and it was here in Thebes that he married Semele.

Pentheus: Did this god visit you in a dream or did you see him face-to-face?

Dionysus: ⁴⁷⁰ Oh, I saw him right in front of me – that's how he initiated me in the rites of his worship.

Pentheus: And what form do these rituals take, the ones you perform for your god Dionysus?

Dionysus: It's against the law to tell them to those mortals who haven't become Bacchantes.

Pentheus: Ok – then what are the benefits that the people who practice these rituals receive?

Dionysus: This is also not right for you to hear – but the thing is worthy to see, to be sure.

Pentheus: ⁴⁷⁵ It looks like your answers are contrived in such a way to make me curious.

Dionysus: Not at all – these rituals of the god detest those people who don't respect them. They hate the unholy and the unwashed.

Pentheus: And you say that you saw the god – in what form did he take before you?

Dionysus: He took whatever form he wanted. The choice was his to make, not mine.

Pentheus: Once again you are avoiding my question, saying nothing.

Dionysus: ⁴⁸⁰ If you talk intelligently to a fool then he'll call you foolish.

Pentheus: Have you introduced these rites into other cities, or is Thebes the first city?

Dionysus: All of the barbarians – everywhere outside of Greece – they all dance for the god Dionysus.

Pentheus: Yes, well they're all more foolish and more gullible than the Greeks.

Dionysus: In this matter they are wiser. Customs are always different.

Pentheus: ⁴⁸⁵ Do you perform these rituals in the day or at night?

Dionysus: They're mostly done at night – the darkness helps with the solemnity.

Pentheus: Night is better suited for trapping women and seducing them – and destroying their virtue.

Dionysus: People can find plenty of ways to act shamefully in the daytime as well.

Pentheus: You're going to be punished for answering in such a smart-alecky fashion.

Dionysus: ⁴⁹⁰ And you'll be punished for showing such ignorance and hubris to the god.

Pentheus: Oh my – how brazen this Bacchant is! You seem like quite the fighter – but only when it comes to words.

Dionysus: Then tell me – what punishment do you think I should suffer?

Pentheus: First of all, I'm going to cut off those little pansy locks of yours.

Dionysus: The locks of my hair are sacred – I've grown them this way to honour the god.

Pentheus: ⁴⁹⁵ Next, you'll hand over your thyrsus from your hands into mine.

Dionysus: Go ahead then – take it away. The one that I carry is sacred to Dionysus.

Pentheus: Good. And then finally I'm going to place you in prison right here in my palace, where we are going to guard you and keep you from escaping.

Dionysus: Whatever – the god himself will free me whenever I wish.

Pentheus: But whenever you call him you'll be sitting with your Bacchae in prison.

Dionysus: ⁵⁰⁰ He's here right now, and he sees what I have to suffer from you.

Pentheus: Where is he then? I can't see him anywhere – he's not before my eyes.

Dionysus: Oh, he's very close to me, rest assured. You can't see him because your impiety makes you blind.

Pentheus: That's it. Men, take hold of him! He is mocking both Thebes and me.

Dionysus: ⁵⁰⁵ I'm warning you. Don't place any chains on me. I'm the one who has a sound mind, but none of you are thinking properly.

Pentheus: But I say – tie him up in chains! You see, I have lots more power than you, stranger.

Dionysus: Ha! You poor fellow. You don't know where you live, what you are doing, nor who you are!

Pentheus: I am Pentheus, the son of Agave, and my father was Echion.

Dionysus: Pentheus – it's just like your Greek word "penthos," which means grief and misery. You'll soon regret having that name.

Pentheus: ⁵⁰⁹ That's it – take this fellow off. I'm sick of him. Tie up his hands and lock him up near the stables, so that he might be close to the darkness that he enjoys so much. Let him dance down there alone in the dark.

⁵¹¹ As for these women here – this group of Bacchantes singing your chorus, your helpers in making all of this trouble here – I'm going to have all of them sold off as slaves or I'll put them to work on my looms. That will shut up their incessant drumming and singing!

Exit Pentheus

Dionysus: ⁵¹⁵ I'll go, but I won't suffer anything, since I can't suffer anything. But you, little man, Dionysus is going to pay you back for all of your hubris. You say that Dionysus is not a god, but he'll soon strike you down for what you've said and done. By putting these chains on me, you're attempting to place chains on the god.

Exit Dionysus, led away in chains by the Soldiers

Chorus: ⁵¹⁹ O daughter of the Achelos river, holy river Dirce, your waters once took the young god, child of Zeus, when his father Zeus placed his son into his upper thigh, snatching him from that deathless fire, and he said these things – "Come, Bacchus, step into my male womb. I call you this name, O Bacchus, and to all Thebes I proclaim that this is your name."

⁵³⁰ But you, O blessed Dirce, you turn me away when I come to your banks in a procession and holding a crown of ivy in my hair and bringing the rites along with me. Why do you reject me? Why do you flee me? I swear, by the grape-clustered charm and power of Dionysus, that someday soon you'll pay attention to the name of the Thunderer!

⁵³⁶ He is filled with such a rage, with such a rage, the proclamations from that earthborn offspring race that came from the serpent – I mean Pentheus, the son of that earthborn Echion. This king is a wild-faced monster and not a mortal man – he is just like those giants who tried to rise up in opposition to the gods. He is trying to defy the children of heaven. He has threatened to tie me up in chains, although I belong to the Thunderer. Already

he holds my comrade in this sacred dance imprisoned and caged up in the darkness of the stables.

⁵⁵⁰ O son of Zeus, O Dionysus, do you see? Do you see how those who are speaking on your behalf are chained up and held by force? O lord Thunderer, come down now from Olympus, swinging your golden thyrsus with you as you make your way here, and put an end to the hubris of this bloody man!

⁵⁵⁶ O lord, where are you now waving your thyrsus among your running and leaping followers? Are you over there on Nysa now, O Dionysus, on the mountains that nourish the wild beasts? Or are you over there on the peaks of Corycia? Perhaps you are in the forests of Olympus, the place where Orpheus once played his lyre and gathered together the trees with his songs, and gathered together the wild beasts as well.

⁵⁶⁵ O blessed Piera, you are honoured by the god of hey-ho! He comes here to lead his dance, bringing his Bacchantes to help you worship him. He steps over the swift flowing Axion river, and he'll lead his Maenads as they twist and whirl about in the dance. They'll dance over Lydias, the father of waters, the one who gives wealth and happiness to mortals from its most beautiful and well-famed waters – waters that I have heard enrich this land of good horses so wonderfully.

⁵⁷⁴ *There is thunder and lightning, and we can hear Dionysus from offstage*

DIONYSUS (OFFSTAGE): ⁵⁷⁶ Hey-ho! Hear me, hear my voice! Hey-ho, my Bacchae! Hear my shout!

CHORUS: Who is this? What is this noise that is calling me with the sound of "hey-ho"? Where are you, O my lord Thunderer?

DIONYSUS (OFFSTAGE): Hey-ho, hey-ho, I shout it again – I am the son of Semele, I am the son of Zeus.

CHORUS: ⁵⁸² Hey-ho, hey-ho master, O master. Come now to us, your followers, O master, O Thunderer, O Thunderer!

DIONYSUS (OFFSTAGE): O queen of earthquakes, move the whole of the earth!

CHORUS: ⁵⁸⁶ Oh oh – look! Soon the roofs of Pentheus will be all knocked down, ripped asunder from their heights.

⁵⁸⁸ Look! Dionysus is within those walls – worship him everyone!

Oh, we worship him indeed!

And look over there! Do you see how the marble crashes and falls from the columns, rushing headlong to the ground?

⁵⁹² It's the Thunderer who is inside – he is shouting his war cry.

DIONYSUS (OFFSTAGE): ⁵⁹⁴ O blazing bolts of the god, come on – strike at this house, bring it to its knees! Burn this house of Pentheus until there's nothing left but ashes!

CHORUS: ⁵⁹⁶ Ah! Ooh! Just look, just stare in awe, at how the fire is jumping all about the holy tomb of Semele. It's the flame of Zeus, the one who thunders so strongly, and his lightning and fire are burning there still, in the same spot where they once fell all those years ago.

⁶⁰⁰ Oh oh, Maenads, it's time for us to fall to the ground in awe of what we are seeing. Down, down, down to the ground – for our lord has come here, and he has flattened this house to the ground. He is the son of Zeus!

Enter Dionysus, while the chorus remains on the ground out of respect for him

Dionysus: ⁶⁰⁴ O foreign women, O barbarian women from Asia, what is this? Why have you fallen to the ground? Were you somehow so scared that you were forced to place yourselves there? Or did you notice, as I suppose, just how your Bacchus knocked down the wall of Pentheus? But come on now, you can lift yourselves from the ground now – there's no need to be afraid.

Chorus: ⁶⁰⁸ O greatest light to all of us, the one who brings joy to all your Bacchae, how happy I am to see you here, to see you alive – without you I felt so alone, so deserted.

Dionysus: ⁶¹⁰ What? Did you lose courage when I was sent down into the darkness of those stables, sent down into the prison below the palace of Pentheus?

Chorus: How could I help but worry? Who would then help me and lead me if something bad happened to you? But how did you manage to break free from that unholy man?

Dionysus: ⁶¹⁴ It was easy to do. I saved myself without any toil whatsoever.

Chorus: But didn't he tie your hands together with chains and ropes?

Dionysus: ⁶¹⁶ And this is both where and why I made a fool of him. I returned his insult on me with an even bigger assault on him. He thought that he had me bound up securely, but neither he nor his people ever once laid a hand on me. He fed himself on his hopes, but he failed at that.

⁶¹⁸ In the stable that he wanted to use for my prison he found a bull instead of me, and he tried to throw ropes around the legs of this bull. He was desperate to tie it up – so much so that he was breathing out fiercely while he attacked this bull, grinding his teeth, biting his lips, and sweat was pouring down from his body onto the ground everywhere around him.

⁶²¹ Oh, I was there, standing right beside him while he did all of this and watching him quietly and laughing at his foolishness. But that was when Bacchus came and shook the house left and right, and the god then lit up the grave of his mother.

⁶²⁴ When Pentheus saw what was happening, he thought that his palace was on fire, so he started running about in a frenzy, this way and then that way, shouting to his slaves to bring a river of water to put out all the fires. He ordered every slave to set themselves to this task – what a complete waste of time!

⁶²⁶ Then he suddenly stopped worrying about the fires, for he became afraid that I might escape, so he rushed back to the place in the palace, bringing his black sword with him.

⁶²⁸ Well, it seems that the Thunderer, as he appeared to me, made a shape in the courtyard that looked just like me. Pentheus rushed right up to this image of me and started violently stabbing at the thin air just as if he were stabbing at me.

⁶³² And the god wasn't finished – he added still another outrage to humiliate him even more. The god shattered his house, his palace, and brought it tumbling down to the ground. And there his palace lies right now – a fitting punishment for having placed me in chains.

⁶³⁴ When he saw what had happened to his palace, Pentheus dropped his sword at the horrible sight, completely worn out and exhausted by the fight. Here was this man, this man – nothing more than a small little man – and he thought that he could wage a war against a god!

⁶³⁶ As for me, I stepped out of the ruins of the house rather quietly and I've come out to see you. I don't care at all about Pentheus. But, if I can judge correctly from the commotion that I hear inside those ruins – and the sound of feet moving this way and that – I suspect that the man will soon show his face before us out here. Whatever will he have to say when he gets here? What will he do now?

⁶⁴⁰ Let him go on and on. Even if he explodes into a rage, he won't get a reaction out of me. I'll bear whatever he says calmly, and I won't be moved to rage. Wise men know how to control their rage and anger – we know constraint.

Enter Pentheus, from the ruins of the palace

Pentheus: ⁶⁴² I've suffered a terrible thing. The stranger has fled, escaped me – the one I held so recently in my clutches, whom I had tied up in shackles.

Whoa! What? Hey! This is the man right here! What's going on? How can you just appear like this in front of my house? How did you escape?

Dionysus: ⁶⁴⁷ Relax – your anger treads a bit too heavily here. It would be better for you if you calmed down a bit now, I assure you.

Pentheus: But how did you manage to escape from those bonds and escape?

Dionysus: Didn't I tell you – or did you just not listen – that someone would be there who would set me free?

Pentheus: ⁶⁵⁰ Who is this someone? You're always saying new and strange words.

Dionysus: I told you that already as well – it was he who brings the clustering grapes to mankind. In fact, the only one you can blame for this good deed is none other than Dionysus himself.

Pentheus: That's it – I'm locking the gates! Everyone – I order that the entire city be shut down right now and that every tower in this city's circle be locked up tight.

Dionysus: What on earth are you doing? Do you think that a god couldn't leap over the walls of a city?

Pentheus: ⁶⁵⁵ You're such a smart-ass – wise in everything except in the places where it's important to be wise.

Dionysus: Well, in all of the ways that count the most, I was born wise.

Enter a Messenger

But wait just one moment. You might want to hear the news that this messenger here brings from the mountain. It looks like he has something to tell you. We'll wait here where we are. You needn't worry – we won't try to run away.

Messenger: ⁶⁶⁰ O Pentheus, king of Thebes, I've just arrived here from the side of Mount Cithaeron, where pure-white flakes of snow gleam on, forever shining…

Pentheus: Ok…ok, get to the point. What news are you bringing that made you hurry back to me?

Messenger: ⁶⁶⁴ I have taken a good look at the screaming Bacchae, who with their white limbs shooting out like arrows have fled the city and now run about on the mountain. I've come to tell you and the city about all of the amazing thing that I've seen – they do the kinds of things that look like miracles and are even beyond miracles.

⁶⁶⁸ But first I want to know whether you want to hear openly about all the things that I've

seen up there, or whether I should hold back and censor my report before I speak. For I fear that you have an excessively sharp mind and tongue, and I know that you are easily driven to anger – like all kings, you can often be impatient.

PENTHEUS: [672] Go on – you can speak freely in front of me, and I assure you that you won't be punished for anything that you say to me. It's wrong for anyone to get angry with and cause harm to someone who is speaking the truth.

[674] At the same time, the worse your stories about these Bacchae get, that means the worse the punishment will be for this fellow here, since he is the one who polluted our women with his vile magic and spells.

MESSENGER: [677] Just at the time when the sun was starting to warm the earth with its rays, our herds of cattle were just about to climb that part of the path that sets out along the mountain ridge.

[680] All of a sudden I saw large groups of women dancers up there, those Bacchae. One of them appeared to be led by Autonoe, another was led by your mother Agave, and a third group was led by Ino. They were all sound asleep, with their bodies completely relaxed. Some of them were lying down with their heads resting on a bed of pine, while others seemed to just have fallen asleep wherever they placed their bodies on the ground – they were randomly scattered among the oak leaves that were all over the ground.

[685] But this had all been done in a way that was quite sensible and modest. They may have let themselves go, but it didn't appear, as you say, that they were all drunk with wine, nor did it look like that they were intoxicated by the beat of the drum or the sound of the flute, and I couldn't see any evidence that anyone had been rushing off to the woods to fornicate and commit adultery.

[689] Then it was your mother who was the first one to wake up, since she heard the mooing of the cattle. She stood right up in the middle of the Bacchants, while the others were striking the sleep away from their eyes and getting up slowly, then standing up straight and proper. It was an amazing sight to witness – there were young girls and old women, married and unmarried alike.

[695] First they let their hair sink down loose as far as their shoulders, and those of them whose straps had fallen loose tied up their fawn-skins once again using the slithering snakes that kissed their cheeks. The new mothers who were there, since their breasts were swollen with milk and they had left their babies behind at home, grabbed animals to suck at their breasts. Some of them held onto deer, some of them grabbed the fierce cubs of wolves, giving them all their white milk to suckle.

[699] They put ivy all over their hair, making it look like a crown – they also added oak leaves and leaves from the yew tree. One of them took her thyrsus and struck a rock with it – and immediately a stream of cool and fresh water came shooting up. Another woman sent her thyrsus down into the ground – and from there the god shot forth a fountain of wine. Those women who wanted to drink milk scratched at the soil with their sharp fingers and then streams of milk appeared. And sweet streams of pure honey came dripping out of their ivy-covered staffs.

[712] If you were there and had seen these things, you would definitely drop to the

ground and pray to the god whom you now disparage so much.

⁷¹⁴ Then all of us gathered together, the herdsmen and shepherds from the mountain area, and we all talked to one another and compared stories about the amazing events we had all just seen on the mountain – those terrible and awesome deeds that the women had just done. Then some wanderer, a fellow who seemed to be quite good at speaking well – an art that he must have learned in the city – spoke up. He said, "All of you here, you who live and work on the sacred peak of these mountains – what do you say? Do you want to go and hunt down Agave, the mother of Pentheus, and then tear her out of these Bacchic rituals? This might earn us quite the reward from the king."

⁷²¹ To us he seemed to be saying something clever and to have spoken well, so we hid ourselves in the bushes and we prepared ourselves to make an ambush. The women there, at the regular time for their dance, they shook their thyrsus and moved about in their Bacchic fashion. Altogether in one voice they raised a voice, shouting "O Bacchus, O son of Zeus, O Thunderer!" And the entire mountain, even the wild beasts, was dancing with them. And the women were running about, and everyone and everything was running along with them.

⁷²⁸ It just so happened that Agave was leaping and running right next to me, and so I jumped out, hoping that I could grab hold of her, bind her, and then we could take her away. But when I jumped out, she gave a cry, and I realized that I had revealed our hiding place to all the women on the mountain. She screamed, "O my dogs, all of you who are running with me – men are chasing after us! We are being hunted down by men! But just follow me! Follow! The thyrsus in your hands will serve as weapons!"

⁷³⁴ As soon as she said this we fled from the scene, just barely avoiding having been torn to pieces by the throng of women. But they didn't stop after we left, for they threw themselves toward our cattle that were grazing in the meadow. They had nothing other than their bare hands, and if you had been there, then you would have seen a woman with her own hands rip a fat cow in two pieces, and while the cow screamed its udder filled up with milk, spraying its contents all over the place. Others took part in the sparagmos by tearing apart more mature heifers. You'd see ribs and legs thrown all over the place, and some things were hanging off of the trees and the pines were dripping all over with blood.

⁷⁴³ Bulls that once raged and were proud from birth were now having their bodies thrown down on the ground while they were torn apart by the hands of a thousand young girls. And those girls stripped the flesh off those bulls faster than a king could wink an eye. Then they took off from there, flying away just as if they were a flock of birds, racing to the fields below, down to where the Asopus river flows, and they tore to shreds all of the fruitful crops of Thebes.

⁷⁵⁰ There are two villages down there – Husiae and Erythrae – both of which are just at the foot of Mount Cithaeron. And the Bacchae tore through these two just like they were enemies on a rampage, knocking everything down and destroying whatever they touched. They devastated the towns, then they even took the children from their homes, packing as much loot as they could upon their shoulders. Even though they didn't bother to

tie down what they stole, nothing fell to the earth – nothing, no bronze or iron, fell from their backs down to the black earth. What is more, the fire that they were carrying in their hair didn't burn them at all.

⁷⁵⁸ Then the men of those villages, completely enraged at what these Bacchantes had done, went back to get weapons so they could stand up to them. But then, my lord, then there was a sight most horrible to see. The men couldn't find a way to harm the women with their sharp javelins and spears. They couldn't make them bleed at all. But the women used their thyrsus to inflict all kinds of bloody wounds on the men. It was so bad that the men ran off in fright. Men, defeated by women! The only way this could happen would be for a god to have been helping them.

⁷⁶⁵ And then the Bacchae went back to where they had once been moving their feet in their dances. They went back to the streams that the god had made for them and they washed the blood from their hands while the snakes licked whatever blood was still resting on their cheeks.

⁷⁶⁹ O master, whoever this god may be, please accept him into Thebes, into this city. He has all kinds of great powers, as is clear. But, above all, as I have heard, he's the one who gives the wine to mortals, the wine that helps end our pains.

⁷⁷³ And if you take wine away there can be no more love and desire – and soon every other joy for men will quickly die after that.

Exit the Messenger

CHORUS: ⁷⁷⁵ I am nervous about speaking too freely to a king, but nevertheless it must be said – there is no god who is greater than Dionysus.

PENTHEUS: ⁷⁷⁸ Already the hubris of the Bacchae is increasing, coming too close, and their violent behavior is soon to spread throughout the whole of Greece. I can't turn away from this.

⁷⁸⁰ You there – go down quickly to the Electran Gates and gather all the warriors and swift horses and mounted archers. Make sure that they are ready. We're going to wage a war against these Bacchae. There is nothing worse than this – that all of our affairs are placed in disarray, and that so much trouble has been caused by a group of women.

DIONYSUS: ⁷⁸⁷ Pentheus, you've heard my words, but you clearly don't understand my warning. You've treated me badly, and yet I still give you this advice – that you shouldn't take up weapons against a god. Instead it would be better for you to just keep quiet. The Thunderer is not going to let you move his women from their celebrations and rites on the mountain.

PENTHEUS: ⁷⁹² You're certainly not going to lecture me. You barely managed to get out of your chains – or did you forget? Should I have my men lock you up again?

DIONYSUS: It would be better for you to offer a sacrifice to this god and not let your anger push so violently against what is necessary. This god will not respond kindly to being mistreated.

PENTHEUS: ⁷⁹⁶ Oh, I'll give this god of yours a sacrifice all right. I'll give him a massacre of his female worshippers up there. For all the trouble they are causing up there on Mount Cithaeron, they deserve to die.

DIONYSUS: If you try it, then you'll be forced to flee, shamefully defeated by this group of Bacchantes who use their thyrsus to turn back your shields of bronze.

Pentheus: [800] It's impossible to wrestle and argue with this foreigner here. Whether he is in jail or not, he just keeps on yapping.

Dionysus: You know, there's still a way to make this all turn out fine for you.

Pentheus: How? By making me a slave to my own slaves?

Dionysus: I'll lead the women back here without any weapons.

Pentheus: [805] Oh no – that sounds to me like some kind of trap.

Dionysus: How would this be a trap, if I want to use my abilities and skills to save you?

Pentheus: But you gathered all of these women together, so that they would always celebrate those dances.

Dionysus: That's true. I have done this – but I did it for the god.

Pentheus: Enough of this – someone bring out my weapons. And as for you, buddy –please shut up.

Dionysus: [810] Wait – would you perhaps like to have a look at them out there on the mountain?

Pentheus: What? Of course – I'd give a whole pot of gold to see them there.

Dionysus: Oh really... why has this great passion to see them come over you all of a sudden?

Pentheus: Well... I really don't want to see anyone drunk...

Dionysus: [815] But all the same you really want to have a peek at them, don't you?

Pentheus: Yes, absolutely – I could sit down quietly under the pines and watch them from there.

Dionysus: But they'll find you out, even if you come there secretly and in silence.

Pentheus: That's a good point. Then I'll go there out in the open.

Dionysus: Will I be the one to lead you there? Are you ready to go?

Pentheus: [820] Oh yes! Let's not waste time by talking – lead me on!

Dionysus: Just a moment – before we leave we'll have to change your clothing, and put this dress on you.

Pentheus: What's this? Am I going to have to dress up as a woman? Really? I'm a man and I have to dress up as a woman?

Dionysus: If they saw you standing there as a man, then they'd kill you immediately.

Pentheus: That's another good point you make. You're quite good at planning for this kind of thing, as I can see.

Dionysus: [825] Dionysus has taught me well.

Pentheus: This is all fine – but what do I do at this point?

Dionysus: Let's just go back into the remains of your house and I'll prepare you.

Pentheus: Prepare me how? As a woman? But that would be shameful.

Dionysus: So you don't want to go and see the Maenads anymore?

Pentheus: [830] Wait – of course I do. What's this clothing that you say I need to put all over my body?

Dionysus: I'll have to start with your head. I'll have to put a wig on you – with long, curly, flowing hair.

Pentheus: And what's next after that?

Dionysus: Then I'm going to have to put you into a dress – one that goes all the way down to your feet. And I'll put a headband around your temples.

Pentheus: And is there anything else that you'll add after that?

Dionysus: ⁸³⁵ I'll have to put a thyrsus in your hand, and we'll find a spotted fawn-skin for you to wear.

Pentheus: I shouldn't put on women's clothing…

Dionysus: But you'll cause so much bloodshed, if you decide to attack the Bacchae directly.

Pentheus: That's right. We'll have to go there first and take a look around.

Dionysus: It's wiser to hunt evil than to be hunted by evil.

Pentheus: ⁸⁴⁰ But how will I even be able to make it through the streets of Cadmus' city here without anyone noticing me?

Dionysus: We'll go through the empty and deserted backstreets – and I'll lead.

Pentheus: It's just important that the Bacchae don't laugh at me. I'll think over everything you say – let's go in the house now and make the preparations.

Dionysus: As you like. My plan will succeed no matter what you choose.

Pentheus: ⁸⁴⁵ Yes – I'll set out to the mountain. Either I'll go there leading an army or I'll follow your advice and go there alone.

Exit Pentheus into the palace

Dionysus: ⁸⁴⁸ Women, that man is now standing in the middle of the net, in the middle of the trap. He's going to make his way to the mountain to visit the Bacchae – and he'll pay the price once he's there. O Dionysus, the work is now yours. You're not far away from here – punish this man!

⁸⁵⁰ First drive him out of his wits, make him all confused with a type of madness. If this man were sane he'd never put on women's clothing – but if he is driven out of his senses then he'll do just as you like.

⁸⁵⁴ Because of all those threats he made, in which he tried to make himself sound tough and frightening – I will make him become the laughingstock of Thebes when he walks throughout this city dressed as a woman.

⁸⁵⁷ Now I'm going to go and help Pentheus pick out his clothing – the clothes that he's going to have to take to Hades with him, after he is murdered by the hands of his own mother.

⁸⁵⁹ He'll come to know who Dionysus is – that he is the son of Zeus, that he was born a god, and that he can be both terrible and gentle to mankind.

Exit Dionysus into the palace

Chorus: ⁸⁶² When will I throw my white feet, roused up to Bacchic frenzy, in the all-night dances? When will I toss out my dewy neck into the air, just like a young fawn who runs about in the green delights of the meadow? She has just run away from the fearful hunt, away from the spies and guards, away from the nets and the hunters shouting out to their fierce-running dogs. She is pressed on hard by them, so she leaps and runs with the speed of the wind, over meadows that are next to rivers, delighted that no men are around, and joyously celebrating the dances in the forest, in their shady leaves and the tender shoots of the deep wide woods.

⁸⁷⁷ What is wisdom? Is there another gift of the gods that we can hold in greater honour

than this, than to hold a firm and strong hand over the heads of your enemies? This honour is special and is always something to treasure.

⁸⁸² The power of the gods may be slow, but it moves forward unmistakably – it goes forward and punishes mortals who honour ignorance and those who in their madness and hubris do not revere the things of the gods. The gods are clever and cunning – they are prepared to lie in ambush for a long stretch of time just so that they may punish the wicked and hunt out the men who don't show them respect. It's important that no one should think of himself as above the laws – nobody should try to place himself above ancient customs.

⁸⁹³ The cost of believing in all these things is small – to believe that everything that comes from a god is strong, and whatever that the length of time has shown true throughout the ages is a law forever, and the laws are always brought forth by nature.

⁸⁹⁷ What is wisdom? Is there another gift of the gods that we can hold in greater honour than this, than to hold a firm and strong hand over the heads of your enemies? This honour is special and is always something to treasure.

⁹⁰² The man is blessed who has escaped from the storms at sea and has finally reached the shore. The man is blessed who has overcome all misery and suffering. The way that one man can be more blessed than another, more blessed in wealth and power, are many and diverse. There are thousands of hopes and there are thousands more still – so many of them bring riches to men, while many of them lead to nothing. But I respect the man for whom each day brings the best part of life – for he is the blessed one.

Enter Dionysus

DIONYSUS: ⁹¹² Hey you, that's right you – you're the one who is so eager to see the things that are forbidden to see, and to reach after the things that must not be sought. Yes, I mean you, Pentheus – come out here right now, in front of the house. Let me have a look at you, dressed as you are in women's clothing, looking like a Maenad of Bacchus so that you can go spy on your mother and her group.

⁹¹⁷ Hmmm...you look just like one of Cadmus' daughters!

Enter Pentheus, dressed like a Bacchant

PENTHEUS: ⁹¹⁸ Oh my, I think that I can see two suns right in front of my eyes. I'm seeing double – I see two cities of Thebes and two seven-mouthed fortresses...everything is double.

⁹²⁰ And you, you seem to me to look just like a bull, leading me in your parade, and horns are growing on top of your head. Have you ever been an animal? For you look just like a bull to me.

DIONYSUS: ⁹²³ It's the god that you see. Before he was angry, but he has made his peace with us – and now you're seeing things the things that you are supposed to see.

PENTHEUS: ⁹²⁵ But how do I look to you? Is this the way that Ino looks? Or do I look like my mother Agave?

DIONYSUS: Wow – looking at you I think I am looking at one of them, or both of them. Hmmm...but this one little lock of your hair has fallen out of place – it's not where it was when I placed the headband on your hair.

PENTHEUS: ⁹³⁰ It must have come out when I was inside and dancing round like the Bacchae. That's when it came out of place.

Dionysus: It's ok – let me be your nurse and put it back in place for you. That's right, just hold yourself still – I'll fix you up really well.

Pentheus: Yes, please fix it up for me. I'm totally in your hands.

Dionysus: ⁹³⁵ And just look at that – now your belts and straps have slipped, and your dress has fallen down to your ankles.

Pentheus: I think you're right. But it's only done so on this side – on the other side everything is still in the right condition.

Dionysus: ⁹³⁹ Here, let me fix that as well. You are going to be so impressed with me, you'll think of me as your best friend, when you see how chaste and modest the Bacchae dress and behave.

Pentheus: Should I hold my thyrsus like this, in my right hand? Is that how the real Bacchae do it? Or do they hold it in their other hand?

Dionysus: No – it should go in your right hand, and raise it in the air at the same time that you lift your right foot. I'm pleased to see your change of heart.

Pentheus: ⁹⁴⁵ Do you think that I'll be strong enough to lift up the whole of Mount Cithaeron? Could I lift the whole place up and then put it all on my shoulders, Bacchae and all?

Dionysus: You can if you want to. Before now you didn't have the proper mind, and you weren't thinking correctly – but now things are exactly as they should be for you.

Pentheus: ⁹⁴⁹ Should we bring crowbars along with us? Or should I just use my hands to rip up the mountain, by thrusting my own arms underneath the peak of the mountain?

Dionysus: What? Are you still planning on destroying the temples of the Nymphs and those places where Pan loves to play his pipes?

Pentheus: Oh, you're right. It's not right to conquer women by force. I'll take care to hide myself among the fir trees.

Dionysus: ⁹⁵⁵ And you'll find the kind of hiding place that's appropriate for a man who has come to be a crafty spy on the Maenads.

Pentheus: Just think about it. I can already imagine them out there like birds in a thicket, holding themselves up in the tangles of lust and love.

Dionysus: ⁹⁵⁹ And so this is why you've been assigned to be a guard. You might even catch them in the act, unless you yourself get caught first.

Pentheus: Then lead me immediately right through the middle of Thebes, since I alone am man enough, I alone am daring enough, to do this.

Dionysus: And you alone will be the one to suffer for this city – you alone. The battle ahead must be waged and it's waiting for you. Follow me then – I am your guide and protection. I'll take you there, but someone else will bring you back.

Pentheus: ⁹⁶⁶ Yes – the woman who gave birth to me.

Dionysus: You'll be an example for all of mankind…

Pentheus: That's the reason I am doing this.

Dionysus: You'll be carried back…

Pentheus: You're talking about my immortality!

Dionysus: …carried back in the arms of your mother.

Pentheus: You're going to make me feel spoiled.

Dionysus: That's exactly what I aim to do…

Pentheus: ⁹⁷⁰ That's it then – let me go and receive my reward.

Dionysus: You've suffered wonderful and terrible things, and you're going to endure still more wonderful and terrible things. You'll win fame that reaches the heights of heaven.

Exit Pentheus

⁹⁷³ Now Agave, stretch out your hands! All you daughters of Cadmus stretch out your hands! I am leading this boy into a great contest. And I will be the winner, for I am the Thunderer, the god Dionysus. What is about to happen will prove it.

Exit Dionysus

Chorus: ⁹⁷⁷ Go quickly, dogs of fury – go out into the mountains! Go out to where the daughters of Cadmus are holding the thyrsus. Urge them to show anger against that man who is dressed up in women's clothing, that raging madman who is so set to spy upon the Maenads.

⁹⁸¹ The first one to see him will be his mother, when he is watching from behind a smooth rock or from the heights of a tree. She'll be the one to notice him, and she'll cry aloud to the other Bacchae, shouting – "Who is this spy that has come out here to the mountain to peek at the celebrations of the women on Thebes? O my fellow Bacchae, who is the one that gave birth to this one? Surely this man wasn't born from any woman – he must have been born from lioness, or perhaps even from one of those gorgons in Libya!"

⁹⁹¹ Let justice and punishment show themselves and be clear! Reveal yourselves with your sword in hand, stabbing the throat of that godless man, that man who mocks us, who hates our traditions, and who holds no respect for our customs and laws – that earthborn son of Echion.

⁹⁹⁶ That man, that unbeliever, is out of control, and he rushes about in a lawless rage against you, O Bacchus. With his mania and frantic resolve, he tries to bring down the rituals of your mother Semele, and in his madness he tries to use force to bring down those who can't be defeated.

¹⁰⁰¹ He's rushing straight toward his own death. Death is something that the gods can bring about, showing that they're more powerful than the mouths and words of men. Through death they teach us to be humble, to remind us that we are not gods but mere mortals. We are all moving toward death, and to this I say that it's necessary for us to accept it all. Those who are humble are wise – they are blessed.

¹⁰⁰⁵ But I don't want what the rest of the world considers wisdom. I hunt after something else indeed – the things that are great, manifest, the things we can do to make our lives feel blessed. These things will be the things that I hunt – to be pure, humble, and accepting of all that the gods bring us. Let me go the normal path, the customary route of those who follow the timeless and well-worn road of serving the sons of heaven with reverence and awe.

¹⁰¹¹ Let justice and punishment show themselves and be clear! Reveal yourselves with your sword in hand, stabbing the throat of that godless man, that man who mocks us, who hates our traditions, and who holds no respect for our customs and laws – that earthborn son of Echion.

¹⁰¹⁷ O Dionysus, reveal yourself as a bull!

Show yourself as a many-headed snake, or let yourself be seen as a fire-breathing lion. Go on, Bacchus, go on! Go on with your laughing face. Throw your deadly noose around this man who goes out to hunt your Bacchae as if they were beasts. Strike him down, and let him be trampled under the feet of your Maenads!

Enter another Messenger

Messenger: [1024] O house that was once so prosperous and happy in Greece. O house once founded by Cadmus, the man who came from Sidon and who planted the earthborn crop from the teeth of that serpent. O house of Cadmus, I mourn for you. I may be only a slave, but good and respectful slaves also mourn the misfortunes of their masters.

Chorus: What's this? Do you have some news of the Bacchae?

Messenger: [1030] Yes – my news is that Pentheus, the son of Echion, is dead.

Chorus: Bravo! Praise the god, the great Thunderer! You are proved to be a great god indeed!

Messenger: O my god – what are you saying? How can you say such a thing? How can you women feel such joy at the downfall of my master?

Chorus: [1034] I am a foreigner – I am no Greek. So I praise my god, my Bacchus, with my own foreign songs, in my own foreign way. And I'm no longer standing here in fear of your prisons or chains.

Messenger: If you think that Thebes is so short of men...

Chorus: It's Dionysus, it's Dionysus, and not Thebes, that has power over me.

Messenger: [1039] Your feelings may be forgiven, but, O women, it's not right to show such joy and celebration about an evil deed.

Chorus: But tell me how the conniving bugger died. Was the unjust man killed while he was in the middle of doing unjust things?

Messenger: [1043] When we left the buildings and homes in the city of Thebes, we then came to the waters of the Asopus, which we crossed, and then we pushed forward toward the rocky heights of Mount Cithaeron. There were three of us in total – there was Pentheus and I, for I was following my master, and there was also that foreigner, who acted as our guide on our mission to spy on the Maenads.

[1048] The first place we occupied was a grassy hollow – and we stayed there silent, not saying a word, so that we could observe everything without being noticed. From that place we had a pretty good vantage point. It was a little valley with cliffs all around, moist from the streams that were flowing through, and the place was covered in pines that provided lots of shade.

[1052] From there we had a good look at the Maenads, who were sitting there quite happily, with their hands busy at their work. Some of them were taking fresh ivy and bending it around their thyrsus, which had become undone and needed repairs; others we just like young horses that had been just released from the reins and were allowed to run around freely. That's how they ran, altogether liberated, shouting out their Bacchic songs to one another.

[1053] But Pentheus, that fool, couldn't quite see the group of women from where he was, and so he said – "Stranger, from where we are right now, I can't really see what these phony

Maenads are up to. But over there on that hill, if I climbed up one of those towering pines, I'm sure that I could see the shameful acts of these Maenads more clearly."

[1063] Then the stranger did something that was truly amazing. He reached for the highest branch of a massive fir tree, and he bent it down, led it down, down, down, until its peak reached the black earth where we were hiding. It was curved down to us, and it looked just the way a bow appears, or perhaps even like the curved wheel of a compass, the one you use as it turns the round course in drawing the circle. Then, in a split second, the stranger was able to lead the top of that heavenly tree down with his bare hands, and bent it down toward the ground. This was not the action of a mortal.

[1070] The stranger made Pentheus sit on the highest branch and then he slowly let the trunk of the tree bend back to its proper upright position, keeping a calm hand on it all the while, so that the tree would not throw its passenger from his position. Then finally the tree was back to normal, towering to the heavens and straight in the air, with my master sitting on its branches.

[1075] But it turns out that he was seen by the Maenads better than he could see them. As soon as he was sitting there like that, on top of the branches, the stranger disappeared from sight and then out of the sky came some voice. If I were to make a guess, I'd say that this was the voice of Dionysus – and this voice shouted, "O young women! I lead you to the one who mocked me and my rituals. You are going to enact vengeance on him. Avenge me!"

[1084] That voice in the sky was saying these things and then a light of sacred fire shot forth, linking the heavens and the earth as one. And then all of a sudden the air was silent and still. The leaves didn't move where we were, and you couldn't hear any sounds from the wild beasts.

[1086] The Bacchae must not have heard the words of the voice so clearly in their ears, for they stood up and then started turning their eyes in all directions. And so again the voice thundered at them a second time. Then the daughters of Cadmus recognized this as a clear command from the god Bacchus and so they got up and started moving quickly, with the speed of doves. They ran and ran and ran, on an intense course – his mother Agave and all his married aunts and all the other Bacchae behind them. They moved through the swollen ravines, over jagged rocks, leaping through thickets, maddened as they were by the breath of the god.

[1095] When they finally saw my master, sitting up there in the tree, at first they aimed boulders at him, throwing them up at him with savage violence. And some of them climbed on top of a huge stone that was next to the tree he was on and from there they hurled fir trees at him as if they were javelins or spears. Others threw their thyrsus at Pentheus – up through the air went their cruel attempt, but they failed to meet the mark.

[1101] The poor man was perched up there and was higher than any of their volleys could reach. He was caught in a state of confusion, unsure what he should do, and without any defenses. Finally the Bacchae down below broke off some branches of oak and used them to dig up the roots of that tree just as if they were using iron crowbars.

[1105] But every effort at this also ended in failure. So Agave said, "Come, Maenads, let's all stand around in a circle and take hold of the trunk and grip it with all your might. If we don't take hold of this beast and destroy him, he'll go off and reveal the secret mysteries and rites of the god!"

¹¹⁰⁹ At her command, it seemed like thousands of hands were placed on the fir tree and together they tore it up and out of the earth. Pentheus fell down from where he had been sitting at the top. He fell headlong to the ground, wailing and crying as he dropped, because he was very aware that his end was near.

¹¹¹⁴ The first one to fall upon him was his own mother, just like a priestess falls upon a sacrificial victim. In this case she was the priestess of her son's murder. He immediately tore away the wig and headband that were covering his face, so that his poor and reckless mother Agave might recognize him and not kill him. And he reached out to touch her cheek and said, "Mother, it's me here. I am your son, Pentheus, the son you gave birth to in the house of Echion! O my mother, please have pity on me! Please spare me! O my mother, I have done something wrong, but please don't kill your own son because of his mistakes."

¹¹²² But Agave was foaming at the mouth, and he eyes were crazed and moving around in a frenzy – she was out of her mind, not thinking they was she should have been thinking. She was under the grip of Bacchus, and she didn't believe what her son was telling her. She took his left arm at the elbow, ignoring all his cries for pity, she then placed her foot against the ribs of the poor man, and she wrenched it away, tearing off the shoulder of her poor son – what a horrible sight to see!

¹¹²⁷ But she didn't accomplish this on her own – no, it wan't because of her own power. Rather, it was the god who was helping her in this, giving her the strength to make it happen.

And on the other side was Ino, who was tearing apart his flesh, breaking it up as if it were bits of meat. Autonoe and all the other group of Bacchae also turned their attention to him, and there was screaming everywhere. We could hear the screams and moans of Pentheus as long as he was still alive to wail – and the others filled the air with their joyful and triumphant ululations.

¹¹³³ One of them tore off his arm, another one took off his foot that was still in his boot. His ribs were all stripped down, clawed away to his very core, and tore him to pieces in the sparagmos. They were all turned bloody – at least their hands were made bloody – and then they tossed around the pieces of Pentheus' body as if it were a ball and they were playing a game.

¹¹³⁷ As for now, his body lies up there, all ripped apart, with one piece under the jagged rocks and another piece resting in the deep and frightful woods – so far out of the way that it won't be found so easily. And his poor head – well, his mother happened to take this in her hands, and she planted it on the top of her thyrsus, imagining that it's the head of some wild mountain lion. She's parading it through midst of Cithaeron now. She's left her sisters – those Maenads – back on the mountain, and she's currently making her way back to Thebes, so delighted and pleased with the results of her hunt – unaware of how horrible it really is.

¹¹⁴⁴ She is calling on Bacchus, referring to him as her partner in the hunt, her comrade in the chase, the one who led her to her glorious victory. But, of course, all that she'll really gain from this are misery and tears.

¹¹⁴⁸ But I'm going to leave now, to get away from this disaster, before Agave returns to her

home here in in Thebes. It's best to be moderate and to honour the things that belong to the gods – I think that this is the wisest way for mortals to live.

Exit the Messenger

Chorus: [1153] Let's dance to the glory of Bacchus, let's dance to the death of Pentheus – that fellow who was the spawn of a serpent, who took up and put on the clothing of women, he took up the staff, the beautiful thyrsus, the thyrsus that led him down to Hades. Following a bull up to the mountain he now goes down to death and Hades.

[1160] O Bacchae! O women of Cadmus! O women of Thebes! The beautiful victory is yours, your song of victory turns into a cry of mourning, into a cry of tears. It's a beautiful contest, to end up with blood flowing everywhere and a hand dripping with from the death of a child.

Enter Agave with Pentheus' head on her thyrsus

[1165] But look! I see Agave rushing here, toward her home, the mother of Pentheus. Her eyes are running wild in all directions. Let's welcome her – let's welcome her to us, since we're all a part of Dionysus' Bacchae!

Agave: Bacchantes from Asia!

Chorus: Yes? What are you so excited about? Tell us!

Agave: [1169] I'm just returning from the mountains; and I'm bringing with me this freshly cut down prey. The hunting was a success!

Chorus: I see that you're right. And I welcome you – you are truly one of us.

Agave: I caught hold of, trapped, and killed this young child of a wild mountain lion. I did it all without ropes, traps, or anything – as you can see.

Chorus: [1176] And where did you catch him?

Agave: Cithaeron.

Chorus: Cithaeron?

Agave: Yes – slaughtered him!

Chorus: And who is the one that killed him?

Agave: I was the one who held the honour of striking first. The other Bacchae gave me the title of "Agave the blessed."

Chorus: [1181] Who else was involved?

Agave: Cadmus'...

Chorus: What do you mean by "Cadmus'"?

Agave: The daughters of Cadmus were there with me and, once I was finished, then they took hold of the beast. This was a good hunt!

Chorus: Yes – it was very happy indeed.

Agave: Now all of you join me in the feast and celebration. Share my joy!

Chorus: What feast do you mean? And share? Do you mean in your misery?

Agave: [1185] This young animal here is just beginning to bloom, and beneath his soft mane of hair, you can see that he was only just beginning to grow hair on his cheeks.

Chorus: With his hair he looks like a mountain beast, at any rate.

Agave: [1189] O Bacchus, O dog-driving Bacchus, wise Bacchus – you were so wise and cunning in setting your Maenads against this beast.

Chorus: Yes, our lord is a hunter.

Agave: Are you saying that in praise?

Chorus: Yes – I am praising.

Agave: And soon all the people of Thebes...

Chorus: [1195] And your son Pentheus too...

AGAVE: He'll be sure to praise his mother, when he sees what I've caught from the hunt – this lion's cub.

CHORUS: It's an unbelievable catch!

AGAVE: Absolutely unbelievable!

CHORUS: Are you proud of this?

AGAVE: Oh yes – both proud and happy. I won the great prize of the hunt, and now my trophy is here for everyone to see.

CHORUS: 1200 Now then, poor woman, show the people of Thebes what you accomplished in your victory. Show them the prize that you've won in the hunt.

AGAVE: 1202 Yes – come here then, all of you who live in this walled city of Thebes. Yes, men of Thebes, come on out here now to see the trophy, the great catch, which we women of Thebes took in the hunt when we killed this beast.

1205 We didn't take this beast down with spears nor with any hunting nets – rather, we did it with our own bare hands and our own fingers. Our work has made the use of your weapons and tools to seem useless and obsolete, since we've proved ourselves so effective. I mean, we took him with these very hands of ours – and with our own limbs we tore the limbs off of this beast!

1211 But where is my aged father? Where is Cadmus? He should be here to see what I've done. And where is my son Pentheus? Someone go and find him. He should get a solid and sturdy ladder and then lean it up against our house so that there, right on the main beam, he can nail this head right there above the entranceway. Yes, this lion should be nailed right there for everyone to see – the symbol of my triumph in the hunt.

Enter Cadmus, followed by various attendants carrying the other remains of Pentheus

CADMUS: 1216 Follow me, all of you slaves. Bring along this horrible burden – follow me toward the house so we can set it down there right in front of the palace.

1218 This is what remains of Pentheus. I am bringing his body back here, having become weary of the endless searching for all of the pieces that had been strewn all over Cithaeron – no two pieces were in the same spot, and so many of them made it as far as the thick woods.

1222 I only heard about the adventures of my daughter back on the mountain when old Tiresias and I returned to Thebes from the celebrations and dancing back there. As soon as I heard what had happened, I rushed back to the mountain, and now with me I am bringing back the pieces of that boy who was ripped apart by Maenads.

1227 While I was up there I saw Autonoe, the wife of Aristaeus and mother of Actaeon. I also saw Ino up there, and both of them were still infected by the madness that had poisoned them on that mountain. But someone told me that Agave was on her way back to Thebes, that she was dancing her way back here in the way that only a Bacchant can. And now I can see that what I heard was correct, for I can see her right now in front of me – what a horrible sight it is!

AGAVE: 1233 Father! Now you can boast to the world that you've produced by far the best mortal daughters that the world has ever seen! All of your daughters are incredibly brave, but I am the bravest one of them. I left behind my sewing instruments – those shuttles and looms – and I lifted my sights to loftier goals: to hunt wild animals with my own bare hands.

[1238] And do you see what I've brought you? This prize here I killed with my own hands. I brought it back here quickly so we can hang it as a trophy above the entrance to your home. Here, father, take it – it's yours. And celebrate my success with all your friends. Invite all of them to a feast, and then we can all rejoice in my accomplishment, in my success at the hunt! You are so blessed and lucky, O father, because I have done such an unbelievable thing.

CADMUS: [1244] Oh, this is a grief that is beyond endurance – I can't bear to look at it. You've committed such a horrible murder with your own hands. You made a sacrifice to the gods, striking down a noble victim. But this, this, this is what you bring back to Thebes and expect us all to be happy and give a feast in celebration?

[1248] O heavens – my first worry is for the evil that you have committed, then I worry about myself. The lord Thunderer – that Bromius – had every right to punish us, but he went too far with this, I think. After all, he was born from this family as well…

AGAVE: [1251] What's making you so cranky? Jeesh! I think the old age is starting to affect you and make you scowl and look at everything with a miserable eye.

[1252] I only wish that my son could become the kind of hunter that his mother has turned into. It would be wonderful if he could take after me whenever he heads out with the young men of Thebes on the hunt and after the prey.

[1255] But it seems that the only thing he knows how to do lately is to start fights with the gods. Father, he needs to be put in his place, he needs someone to talk some sense into him – and you're the one who should do that. Is there someone here who can go and bring Pentheus out here before me, so that he might see my good fortune?

CADMUS: [1259] Please – no more. When you realize what you've done, then you're going to experience such unbelievable pains, such unimaginable grief. But if you forever remain in the same maddened state that you're now in, then you'll think that you'll be the most blessed of creatures, even though you will be the most wretched woman alive.

AGAVE: Why are you so upset? This victory of mine isn't wonderful? It's painful? What? Why is that?

CADMUS: First, lift your eyes in the air toward the sky.

AGAVE: [1265] There – look, I've done it. But why did you tell me to do such a thing?

CADMUS: Do things still look the same as they did before? Or has there been a change?

AGAVE: It seems somewhat clearer than before – a bit brighter…

CADMUS: And does the same frenzy still drive you deep inside your soul?

AGAVE: [1269] I don't know what you mean by that. But somehow I feel like I am returning back to my old way of thinking, as if my mind is changing back to how it used to be.

CADMUS: Can you still hear me? And are you able to answer me clearly?

AGAVE: Father, I've forgotten the things that you were just talking about.

CADMUS: After you married, whose house did you go to? Who was your husband?

AGAVE: You gave me to Echion – the man, they say, who grew from the teeth of that dragon.

CADMUS: [1275] And what was the name of the son that you had with Echion?

AGAVE: His name was Pentheus – he came from our marriage.

CADMUS: And whose head are you holding in your hands?

AGAVE: It's the head of a lion – that's what the other hunters told me.

CADMUS: Look more closely at it. It won't take to long to notice.

AGAVE: [1280] O gods! What is this that I am looking at? What am I carrying in my hands?

CADMUS: Look carefully, and you'll be able to understand it all more clearly.

AGAVE: Ooh! I see such horrible pain and misery! What have I done!

CADMUS: Surely it doesn't look like a lion any more to you?

AGAVE: No – O gods, it looks like I am holding the head of my son Pentheus.

CADMUS: [1285] We were in mourning for him before you realized who he was.

AGAVE: But who killed him? And how did he get into my hands?

CADMUS: The truth can be a horrible thing – especially when it comes at the wrong time.

AGAVE: Please tell me. Please – my heart is pounding inside me with terror.

CADMUS: You are the one – you and your sisters. You killed him.

AGAVE: [1290] Where and how did he die? Was it at home? Or in what kind of place?

CADMUS: He was killed out there on Cithaeron – where once Actaeon was ripped apart by his dogs.

AGAVE: But why on earth did my poor son go up there to Cithaeron?

CADMUS: He went up there to both mock you Bacchantes and the god.

AGAVE: Us? But how did we get up there?

CADMUS: [1295] You were mad, possessed – and the whole city was driven into a frenzy.

AGAVE: Now I understand – Dionysus destroyed us.

CADMUS: He was insulted by your hubris – for you did not recognize him as a god.

AGAVE: But father, where is the body of my son, the son that I loved so much – where is his body right now?

CADMUS: It's right here with me. I managed to find all of the pieces, but it was very difficult.

AGAVE: [1300] Has everything been put back into its proper place?

CADMUS: Everything is there except for the head that you have there. But so much of it has been horribly mutilated.

AGAVE: But why did Pentheus have to suffer for my thoughtlessness – why was he punished for my hubris?

CADMUS: [1302] Just like you, he refused to worship the god, and for that reason the god brought us all one collective punishment – your sisters, you, and your son Pentheus. The god carried this out in order to completely destroy this house and, specifically, to destroy me. I have no more sons still alive, and now, my daughter, the god has forced me to witness this offshoot of your womb killed in a most horrible and shameful way.

[1306] O Pentheus, poor child! You held this house together. I looked upon you to keep this family intact, since you were the child of my daughter. And you kept the city in check, since Thebes was scared of you. Nobody would dare say anything insulting about me, even though I am now old, because they were afraid of you and the punishment you'd inflict upon them.

[1313] But now I'm going to have to leave, completely devoid of honour, forced out of my home and city. Me – Cadmus! I was once so great, having sowed the crop of soldiers who became Thebans. What a fantastic crop it was!

[1316] O Pentheus, dearest to me of all men – I still consider you the man I love the most even though you are no longer alive. I'll never again be able to feel you touch my beard, no longer will I get to feel you embrace me and say, "Grampa, has anyone been harming you or been treating you badly? Is there anyone who is causing you trouble or causing pain to your heart? Please, Grampa, just tell me who it is, so that I can punish this person who has wronged you."

[1323] But now, my poor young grandson, all that is left for me is misery – misery for me, for you, for your mother, and for her sisters. There's nothing but sorrow and grief for all of us.

[1325] If there's still any mortal man who thinks it's a good idea to despise the gods or to refuse to recognize them – well, let that man look at the death of poor Pentheus here, and then he can be sure to believe in the gods and worship them properly.

AGAVE: [1329] O father, you can see how my fortune has changed in so many ways. I am in so much pain, tortured, when just a few moments ago I was walking here in triumph, entering the city boasting with delight about my recent kill.

And that reward that I brought home from the hunt was hardly a reward – it turned out to be a curse. With my own hands I have placed the pollution on myself of having murdered my own son. How can I possibly think of placing my hands on his body now with my polluted and defiled hands? How could I even take his remains and clutch them to my breast, when I am the one who killed him? O gods, is there any type of funeral lament that I can sing? Can I sing a song for every part of his body, every part that we destroyed?

But still we must take care of you, my child. Is there a shroud somewhere that we can use to cover up his body? My son, my son – is there any hand more appropriate to care for you than my own? Is this the only way for me to lift the curse that sits upon me?

Father, come help me. We have to place the head back on the body of this poor boy. We have to make one piece again – as much as we can do so, at any rate.

Oh my dear child! O face that is so dear to me! Your mouth, still like that of a boy. Now I will cover your head with this blanket, placing together the poor abused pieces of your body, doing the best I can to bring them together. O just look at what's left of your body, the one that I gave birth to.

CHORUS: Let all of those who are prepared to learn take note of this – here is Dionysus, the son of Zeus.

Enter Dionysus, who appears in the air, high above the stage

DIONYSUS: I am Dionysus, the son of Zeus, and I have come back to Thebes, to show men that I am a god. But the men of Thebes did not treat me with due respect. In fact, they spread lies and slander about me, saying that my father was a mere mortal. And they didn't stop at blasphemy, for they even dared to threaten to harm me with violence. I once loved this people so strongly, yet they committed such evil crimes against a god who only held love for them.

Because of these blasphemies, these horrors against me, I'm now going to explain all of the pains and miseries that are bound to happen for the people of Thebes. Just as if they were enemies who were defeated in battle, the Thebans will be driven out of this city and they will have to settle in cities and lands that are far away from here. Wherever they end up, they'll all have to become slaves to their new masters, and then they'll live out the rest of their miserable lives in their new cities, as if they were prizes won in battle, passing the rest of their days in absolute humiliation.

This dead man here received the death that he so richly deserved, ripped to shreds and tossed around the sharp rocks in the mountains. All the rest of you here can be witnesses to this – for this man came toward me with anger. He tried to tie up my hands, insulted me, and he did all kinds of things that he had no right to do. And this is the reason that he has died in such a way – he has justly been killed by the hands of people who shouldn't have killed him. What happened to him was just and proper.

As for you, Agave, to both you and your sisters, I announce this misery: you will have to leave this city to atone for the murder you committed. You are all polluted, and it would be against divine laws for murderers to live in peace beside the tombs of those they have killed.

And now I'll speak of the horrors that are still in store for you, Cadmus. You are going to be turned into a serpent, and your wife Harmonia, the daughter of Ares, will share your fate, since she will also be turned into a serpent.

Along with your wife, the oracle of Zeus proclaims that you are going to drive a team of oxen, and that you will lead an army of foreigners, barbarians all. You're going to invade and destroy many cities with your army, but when your troops try to ravage the shrine and oracle of Apollo, then it will find its way back home to be full of miseries and horrors.

However, Ares will arrange it that both Harmonia and you will be redeemed in the end, and then he will secure for you an eternal place in the Land of the Blessed.

[1340] This is what I say, and this is my word. I am the god who wasn't born of a mortal father, but the god Dionysus – the child of his father Zeus. If you had only known and recognized how to behave properly, how to act appropriately – a thing that you were unwilling to do – then you would have been well off, since you then would have found an ally in the son of Zeus.

CADMUS: [1344] O Dionysus, we beg you – please hear our prayer. We wronged you so horribly.

DIONYSUS: You've come to this realization too late – when the time was right, you didn't acknowledge me.

CADMUS: Yes, you're right – but your punishment is too harsh.

DIONYSUS: I am a god who had been attacked and insulted by your hubris.

CADMUS: But it's better that gods aren't ruled by the same kind of angry passions that enslave humans.

DIONYSUS: [1349] Zeus, my father, agreed to all of these events a long time ago.

AGAVE: Oh gods! Then it's settled. O father – we're sent into miserable exile!

DIONYSUS: So then why are you still here and delaying the inevitable? You have to go.

CADMUS: ¹³⁵² O my daughter, what a horrible end we're arrived at – me, you, and your poor sisters! I'm an old man but I'm still going to have to go and live among barbarians in foreign lands. And the god has just prophesied that I am doomed to raise a foreign army and lead it against the peoples of Greece. I'll go with my wife Harmonia, the daughter of Ares, and we'll be turned into serpents – and then we'll lead a band of men holding spears as they wage war on the altars and shrines of Greece.

¹³⁶⁰ My miseries will never end – and I won't even find peace after I cross the waters of Acheron and into the realm of Hades.

AGAVE: O father, I am sent into exile and will be forced to flee and live without you!

CADMUS: O poor child, why are you wrapping your white arms around my neck like that, just like a swan might do to its old and useless parent?

AGAVE: ¹³⁶⁶ But where can I turn, now that I have been thrown out of my homeland?

CADMUS: I don't know, my child. Your father can no longer be of much help to you.

AGAVE: Farewell my home, farewell my home city – I am forced to leave you in my misery. I have to flee and become fugitive from the place where I had my marriage.

CADMUS: O child, maybe you should go now to the place of Aristaeus and seek refuge there.

AGAVE: I feel so horrible for you, father.

CADMUS: And I weep for my, my child – and I shed tears for your sisters as well.

AGAVE: ¹³⁷⁴ The lord Dionysus has brought terrible disaster to this house.

DIONYSUS: I did it because I was horribly dishonoured, and I suffered terrible things. Thebes didn't show me any respect.

AGAVE: ¹³⁷⁹ Goodbye, my father!

CADMUS: Goodbye to you, my poor daughter. I want you to fare well, even though I know your journey will be hard.

AGAVE: ¹³⁸¹ O friends and guides, please lead me to the place where I can find my sisters, so that we can all become exiles together.

¹³⁸³ I'd like to go far away from Cithaeron, where I may not see it and where that polluted mountain may never again see me, and where I may not have any reminders of the thyrsus. Let other Bacchae worry about such things – I want out.

CHORUS: ¹³⁸⁸ The gods take many shapes, and the gods perform many tasks that are unexpected. What was expected here did not happen, but the god instead found a way to bring about what was not expected. And this is how the play ends.

Exit all

Translated from the Greek by Stephen Russell, PhD